Best wishes
Joe Harrington

YANKEE SAMURAI

OTHER BOOKS BY THE AUTHOR

Kaiten (with Yutaka Yokota).
The story of Japan's human torpedoes. Packaged as one of Ballantine's "Best Books on World War II."

Rendezvous at Midway (with Pat Frank).
The story of *USS Yorktown* and the Japanese carrier fleet. (Hardcover and paper).

I-Boat Captain (with Zenjo Orita).
The story of Japan's submarines in World War II. Joint selection (June, 1977) by the Literary Guild of America for its Military Book Club.

YANKEE *SAMURAI* is the first work of a planned trilogy showing how the military service of Japanese-Americans knocked down all barriers and opened doors. A final work is to cover the Japanese-American experience in America right up to the time of printing, and will have the title *The War That Won Their Battle.*

YANKEE SAMURAI

(THE SECRET ROLE OF NISEI IN AMERICA'S PACIFIC VICTORY)

JOSEPH D. HARRINGTON

A PUBLICATION OF
PETTIGREW ENTERPRISES, INC.
50 VICTOR
DETROIT, MICHIGAN 48203

This, the first edition of this book, has been limited to 3000 copies.

This is book No. 1970

First printing, January, 1979

Library of Congress Catalog Card No. 79-83493
I.S.B.N. No. 0-93368-01-1

Printed in the United States by
Harlo Press
50 Victor, Detroit, Michigan 48203

Price: $11.95 Postpaid $12.95

for the *real* Carol Elizabeth Pettigrew

ACKNOWLEDGMENTS

Founding father for this book was Richard K. Hayashi, who never lost his determination to see that the widest possible audience became knowledgeable about what Japanese-Americans accomplished in the Pacific, an area from which 100 million fellow Americans were sure they'd been barred.

Counseling pediatrician was a driving personality called Shigeya Kihara, who coaxed, cajoled, harassed, nagged, persuaded and, for all I know, threatened aging graduates of the Military Intelligence Service Language School until these normally-reticent Nisei told me their stories.

Nursemaids to the infant were Kenji Goto, Dick Oguro, Key Kobayashi, Art Morimitsu, Dan Nakatsu, Soichi Fukui and Hayato Kihara. I hope none of these gentlemen ever again has to work as hard on any project as they did on this one.

About 1000 other Yankee *Samurai* wrote me letters, telephoned me, sent tapes, lent pictures, gave leads or tolerated lengthy interviews. They help tell their stories in the text.

To all I can only voice a heartfelt *"Dom 'arigato gozaimashita!"*

Thank you very much
for what you have done.

—*Joseph D. Harrington*
Sarnia, Canada 1979

INTRODUCTION

I was minding my own business, writing *It All Counts on Twenty* (a deathless Navy novel, yet unfinished), when queried about the *MISLS* story. Some investigation got me hooked, and I am at last glad the work is finished. A "true" Japanese does not boast, nor do his sons and grandsons. It took all the persuasion, pressure—and cunning— Shig Kihara and I could muster, before my subjects would talk. These pages do not, I am sure, contain all the story there is, and I hope that some Sansei or Yonsei will get the rest. This hole in American history needs to be filled. I've tried to fill it with what I've dug out. More needs to be done.

For nearly three decades it has been my wont to investigate men in conflict with each other on the broad Pacific. Along the way there has grown in me the hope that, as mankind advances in age and wisdom, what a child allegedly said will come true: "One day they'll give a war, and no one will come."

Lloyd George said all war is a relic of barbarism. I see it as an insane enterprise in which men dig up the earth's treasures and hurl them at each other. I hope this enterprise will become passé before all the men and/or treasures are gone forever, but a cursory glance at today's arrays of hates gives me little comfort. I was born in 1923, roughly about the same time as most of the Yankee *Samurai.* My parents, too, were immigrants. And from an area more desolate than Kumamoto—

Newfoundland. I have experienced discrimination, and prejudice. My mother was a scrubwoman, my father a longshoreman-turned-carpenter. I am not an intellectual, pompously scribbling about "our Japanese." I own no one; no one owns me. I differ from the Americans in these pages only in that my eyes are round and blue. We share a belief, I believe, that the American dream must be earned to be enjoyed.

This tale, long in the telling because little men hated a big one—Douglas A. MacArthur—and buried other stories along with his under a secrecy stamp, is as far as possible told in the words of the men who lived it. They displayed, in my judgement, *samurai* qualities—the virtues evinced by the nobler, worthier members of Japan's warrior class—and coupled these to the ingenuity, wit, drive and inventiveness that have won Americans the envied soubriquet "Yankee." I have not encountered, heard of, or read about any group that combined the finer facets of two conflicting cultures so well, wherefore the book's title.

These men feared war more than most, knowing they would suffer from a Pacific conflict more than any other people, but the Yankee *Samurai* seized upon the event to demonstrate that their loyalty matched any man's. Once having proved their worthiness, they then set about enjoying furiously the benefits and privileges of U. S. citizenship thitherto denied them because of race. *Yankee Samurai* is a success story, and I urge its reading on any minority group member who feels, in the words of my Canadian wife, "hard done by." Should it inspire one such person to achievement of even a minor dream, I will have given a contribution, left a legacy, made a dent.

I write for money, and judge anyone who says otherwise of himself either a liar or a poet. All I've done here is help tell the story of some men who really believed that America is what it says it is: a land where all men are created equal, and endowed by their Creator with certain unalienable rights; and among these are life, liberty and the pursuit of happiness.
Provided, like the Yankee *Samurai,* one is willing to get off his duff and go get them.

—*J.D.H.*

Chapter 1

When Cdr. Mitsuo Fuchida signaled his fellow fliers to roar down at Pearl Harbor on December 7, 1941, he triggered the Pacific war. It, in turn, precipitated the profoundest happening in human history. Within days, what until then had been merely more of Europe's and Asia's perennial grapplings, mushroomed into the first truly-worldwide war mankind experienced. It took less than a week for the struggle to become universal, eventually affecting every person then alive and all born since. No one's life is anything like it might have been, had that conflict not occurred.

Nowhere did vaster changes take place than in the massive melange of minorities making up the United States of America. Negroes, at last, became mobile, new national needs making it possible for them to escape the South's crushing heel. They swarmed northward to what they hoped was equal opportunity in defense plants. Mexican labor was imported. It became a fixture in U.S. economic life. Women timidly left home to take jobs, and remained to become vociferous demanders of equal everything. Their chirping chilled the fearful in legislative chambers three decades later. The military-industrial complex, that ever-hovering chimera in democracy's hall of horrors, was born.

Fuchida had no idea what his snapped command would generate. He would later become a Christian missionary and study war no more. Nor could 286,000 of his enemies see any further into the future than the Imperial Navy's flight commander. Yet, of all peoples touched by

John Aiso (r) escorts British G-2 boss, General Sinclair and Clayton Bissell (l) on tour of MISLS. Shig Yasutake, commissioned after Guadalcanal combat, brings up rear.

the awful conflagration that has been mis-named the *Second* World War, none saw their lives so radically altered as did Americans of Japanese ancestry. The only ethnic group in America, except for native Indians, to have unlitigated confinement used as a racial measure against them, Japanese-Americans won greater honor, glory and gain from the universal struggle than anyone, anywhere.

Many Americans know how valiantly Nisei (children of Issei, the Japanese immigrants) served the United States in Europe. The 100th Infantry Battalion and its successor, the 442nd Regimental Combat Team, were made up of Nisei soldiers (who refer to themselves as AJA's, Americans of Japanese ancestry). Both units fought with mind-boggling bravery. Once AJA's rescued a cut-off Texas unit at a cost of more casualties to themselves than the Caucasian lives saved. A motion picture, *Go For Broke*, was made of their exploits, and the empty sleeve of U.S. Senator Daniel K. Inouye kept America reminded of these. He left an arm in Europe.

Until now, less than half of the Japanese-American story has gotten told. A grudging Pentagon kept details of the rest secret for 30 years. But, across the world from Europe, nearly 5000 other Nisei served their country as translators, interpreters, interrogators and cave-flushers. Plus, when the occasion arose, combat infantrymen. To this date, hardly any Americans even know they were there. These "Yankee *Samurai*" displayed the bravery of Japan's ancient warriors, plus the ingenuity of America's pioneers, in getting their jobs done. Yet all had passed their 50th (some their 60th and 70th) birthdays, before government reluctantly let their story be told. Incredible, when the Pacific Nisei's contribution to actual victory was far greater than what their brothers and cousins gave in France and Italy via bloody sacrifice. Even more incredible has been the willingness of these Nisei military intelligence language specialists (or, as they call themselves "MIS'ers") to keep mum while others got lauded. The Yankee *Samurai* had been asked to keep quiet for security reasons, and they did. Until I could obtain and display copies of Pentagon documents, each marked with the date and authority for its declassification, these Nisei would not open up. They had given their word, and planned to keep it until death, even though the rules had been changed. What follows is the story of how an oppressed segment of America's citizenry quietly served the land they loved.

* * *

Ben Obata had no idea he was to be part of this story. On December 7, 1941, he got the news of the Pearl Harbor attack while watching a Sacramento basketball game. To Ben, an employee of the State of California's sales tax division, Australia was a faraway place with kangaroos. He would get a first-hand look at it, but first the State would fire him, John Arifuku, and other AJA's in a blatantly-racial action.

Don Oka was to see the Aleutians and Tinian. He was sacking groceries that Sunday in Los Angeles, wondering whether the part-time job would support his art studies until the draft caught up with him. Nor was Suyeki Okumura thinking much of war. He was resting from a job hunt in New York, hopeful his law degree counted for more in the East than in "No Japans Wanted" California.

Malaria, dysentery and mite typhus were still strangers to Henry Gosho as the son of a Seattle pharmacist arrived at church for choir practice. He would meet them later in Burma. In San Francisco, Kay Kitagawa's slight frame was flopped on a sofa, his radio tuned to hear New York's Philharmonic Orchestra. No daydream Kay had that Sunday could possibly have included his one day interpreting for Gen. Douglas A. MacArthur.

Frank Inami was making the weekly change of bedding at Jappa Sappa Chi, 1777 Euclid St., Berkeley. That was the name given a Nisei-founded clubhouse by whimsical students who knew their slanted eyes precluded admission to any fraternity at the University of California.

Nor did four Nisei soldiers have any idea of what the future held. Pvt. James Shohara was munching brunch at Ft. Warren, Wyoming, his mind on a dance scheduled for that night in Cheyenne. Rumor had it that some Nisei girls might show up, a rare treat. In South Carolina, two Nisei were getting off duty at Ft. Jackson's base hospital. Joe Akiyama headed for the movies, but all Akira Abe wanted was a hot shower. To the north of San Francisco, on Bodega Bay's beach, Ron Chagami whiled away the day with his fiance. He learned about the attack while stopped to buy gasoline on the way home.

The quartet, like 5000-plus other AJA's then wearing khaki (the Navy and Marines routinely told Nisei "We don't take Japs!") were short-timers, checking off on calendars their time left to serve. Caucasian buddies seemed to accept them all right. For some Nisei, life in the service was O.K. A goodly number had won fast promotions in the rapidly-expanding Army for the vigorous way they applied themselves to mastering military skills. More than one felt he had, like the semi-literate prewar Regulars who bossed him about, "found a home in the Army!" In 1941 a military career loomed brighter than a series of continuing turn-downs, once someone noticed your eyes were slanted, did. Meanwhile, life trudged along. No Nisei interviewed by the author remembered thinking that Japan and America might come to a sudden clash of arms. The majority expected one, but not for a while, and the rest hoped the flowering furor would die down.

* * *

There were two Nisei GI's who did expect war to break out at any time, but they weren't actually in uniform that day. Arthur Komori and Richard Sakakida weren't supposed to be in uniform. The two Army sergeants were spies!

The pair had been recruited on March 13, 1941, in Hawaii by an organization calling itself the Corps of Intelligence Police. Enlisted as sergeants without any training (Sakakida would retire a Colonel without ever being taught how to fire a gun), they were spirited out of Honolulu a month later in the Army transport Republic, posing as "workaways" enroute to Manila. There, while the ship's captain toasted in his cabin the health of a Filipino immigration agent, Komori and Sakakida were slipped over the side in darkness. Each was assigned a hotel where he was to stay, and each given 100 *pesos* ($50). Dick Sakakida was provided a cover job with Sears Roebuck. Komori, who had earned a degree in English at the University of Hawaii while getting a private pilot's license that let him indulge in his flying hobby, snared a spot with *Domei,* the Japanese news agency. Both passed themselves off as ship-jumping merchant seamen who were anti-American and wanted to dodge the draft. It helped that the liner *SS Cleveland* had recently been in port. The assignment of the two, if they could fool the proper principals, was to keep an eye on Japanese nationals in the Philippines capital.

Both men, who'd been selected after intensive investigation and rigid screening while at school in Honolulu, succeeded admirably. Komori ingratiated himself so well that, when Philippines Constabulary members smashed their way into *Domei's* offices on the day of the attack, bayonets at the ready, they found Komori sharing a toast with elated Japanese newsmen. Sakakida did at least as well. On July 26, all Japanese funds in the U.S. and its territories had been frozen by Pres. Franklin Roosevelt. The manager of Sakakida's hotel, knowing he was bilingual, asked him to help other tenants prepare financial statements and claims. Making these up got Sakakida a mass of inside information on dealings between Japanese nationals and certain Filipinos of questionable loyalty. All information gathered by the two Hawaii Japanese was passed via mail drop to intelligence officers working for Gen. Douglas MacArthur, then commanding all forces in the Philippines.

Once war broke out, the two Nisei climbed back into uniform. Both saw combat on Bataan and Corregidor.

Komori, although he didn't know of it for years, was subject of a rumor that flashed through Honolulu right after the Pearl Harbor attack. This was a false report, given much credence, that a Japanese pilot had been shot down, and found wearing a McKinley High School class ring. Komori was well-known for his sports prowess, having won a swimming letter at the Univ. of Hawaii. It was also known widely that Komori was a pilot. And, of course, he had disappeared mysteriously, eight months before.

* * *

Some other Japanese in uniform had an idea that war was imminent, but that was only because Lt. Col. John Weckerling and Capt. Kai Rasmussen kept saying so. The two intelligence officers commanded 60 Nisei GI's who were studying the Japanese language in San Francisco. Isao Kusuda was one of these. He lived and studied in an abandoned airplane hangar almost directly under the southern end of Golden Gate Bridge. Kusuda was one of 40 students to survive the rigorous course, and would sometimes wish he hadn't. Early 1943 was to find him on a stinking, disease-ridden island called Guadalcanal, not knowing which side was shooting at him. A 24-year-old from Anaheim, Kusuda became part of the vanguard of a Japanese-American group that got officially credited with shortening the Pacific war by at least two years, and in the process saving upwards of 1,000,000 lives. Unlike their relatives who served in Europe, the Yankee *Samurai* rarely fired a rifle, mortar or machine gun. They battled the land of their fathers with a weapon unique to warfare—*language!*

* * *

In 1942, LIFE magazine stated that, when war started, less than 100 persons in America had a real mastery of Japanese. Army intelligence officers agreed. They knew Japanese to be an extremely complicated language, perhaps the world's most difficult. They'd also heard officers of the Imperial Army boast in the Thirties that their native language provided a nearly-impenetrable code, in and of itself, for use in war. The brag had a basis in fact, each Japanese officer having himself had a minimum 16 years training in the puzzling tongue.

Sometime in the 6th century Japan, needing a language, adopted in its entirety the system of "picture words" used by the Chinese. Each ideograph, called *Kanji,* was given a new Japanese meaning, while its former Chinese one was also retained. So, from the start, nothing was simple. In another 1400 years, Chinese peasants were dumfounded to meet Americans, with Japanese faces, who could *write* the language of China, but could not speak it.

Throughout all those centuries, complications piled up. Three new sets of syllables were spliced into the original system, so that Japanese could have a syntax and grammar. Oriental nuances, subtleties, shadings and gradations were added, until each *Kanji* ideograph had as many as 25 different "readings." Still more variations were contrived, as the Japanese language got moulded to reflect who was communicating, with whom, about what, and their stations in life with respect to each other's. The ways to express one's self in Japanese became so myriad and mind-bending that even someone who knows the language very well cannot always be sure either of what he is saying, or that he is being understood. The author has had the experience of watching a Japanese "draw" the appropriate *Kanji* character in the air or on a palm while talking, to make sure both he and his listener could "see" what he meant to convey. If all gobbledygook-generating government drones joined with Madison Avenue flacks in "grammificating, wordwise" our native tongue for 1400 years, English might come close to being a counterpart of Japanese.

Because of the vast disparity between English and Japanese, hundreds of thousands may have needlessly died in the Pacific. Author John Toland provides a clue to this in *The Rising Sun.* With few peers as research-er-historian-writer, Toland spells out in pitiless clarity the difference between what Tokyo leaders wanted said and what U.S. Secretary of State Cordell Hull actually heard or read—and vice-versa—during the fearful fall of 1941. A reader must decide for himself whether translators on both sides truly were competent linguists—proficient in *both* languages—and whether any used his unique position to crank personal prejudices into the mass of exchanged communications. One fact, however, does emerge crystal-clear from Toland's meticulous work on the original instructions, their encoding, transmission, decoding, and the way they were interpreted by either side. When peace was at risk between Japan and America, neither Tokyo nor Washington actually knew what the hell the other was talking about!

* * *

Small wonder, then, that Japanese officers felt safe marking maps, battle orders, mine field charts and anything else in "plain" Japanese, not bothering to encode it, and that they continued this practice throughout the war. Or that Japanese pilots and radio operators made the bulk of their broadcasts "in the clear," confident no *gaijin* would know what they were sending. Few foreigners did, until language-trained Nisei began arriving on the scene.

It was no easy task to convince top military officials that the U.S. ought to have lots of Japanese-speaking specialists wearing khaki. All-too many seniors were men of small minds and large prejudices, who for years resented letting intelligence officers have cushy duty in foreign capitals to study foreign languages. One Navy officer, Ellis Zacharias, fought the good fight for years, but several items militated against his success. For one thing, the Navy routinely rotated all its officers, for "rounding off," language specialists included. They were not kept in shore billets where their value was greatest, but were sent to sea, where language skills meant nothing. I co-authored a work with Zacharias' cousin, and learned of several other strikes against the man. He was bright, aggressive, and a Jew. None of these endeared him to peacetime minds more bigoted than bold. Except for thrusting Reserve commissions on nearly everyone he met who had some knowledge of the Japanese language, and hijacking 50 sets of Naganuma Readers out of Japan against the wishes of a man who had the near-monopoly on teaching the language to foreigners, Zacharias accomplished little of what he hoped for, before war started.

U.S. Army officers had a little more luck, possibly because they had deeper insight into Nippon's war machine. They went on maneuvers with the Japanese army. Some even observed combat in China and Manchuria. As ground-pounders, infantry officers could more easily elude their "bear leaders," and catch sneak peeks at the forbidden. Bear Leader was the nickname Japanese officers gave any of their number whose job it was to escort visiting foreigners, knowing his job was to lead them around by the nose, showing them every courtesy but nothing of military value. John Weckerling and Kai Rasmussen did get a few furtive snapshots, but that was it except for what they could memorize. Few American naval officers got on board any Japanese ships for other than ritual ceremonies. The U.S. Navy remained blissfully unaware that Japan had the world's best torpedo, its largest and fastest destroyers, plus midget submarines, and that it was building super-battleships so large that a special ship had to be designed for ferrying their massive gun turrets down from Ominato, in northern Japan, to where the behemoths were being constructed.

Convinced that war was coming, Army intelligence pressed home forcefully the subject of language training expansion. Colonels Carlisle C. Dusenberry and Wallace Moore raised the subject frequently at the War Department, and were ably supported by Col. Moses W. Pettigrew, a man never publicly acknowledged for originating the idea of an all-Nisei combat unit. (Others claimed the honor, *after* Nisei covered themselves with glory in Europe.) Pettigrew cared for little other than studying the Japanese character. During 1937 he drafted an intelligence study of Japan's intentions, based on his appraisals of national character. When unearthed 10 years later, it read like a scenario for the Pacific war. This trio was encouraged by Col. Rufus S. Bratton, and finally achieved its objective.

Bratton was rated by his associates as tops in Army intelligence. It was Bratton who, on December 7, end-ran all Army channels early in the morning, trying to tell Chief of Staff Marshall personally that "the Japanese are going to attack us somewhere, around one o'clock Washington time." Bratton had earlier marked Pearl Harbor on one of his charts as a possibility.

Marshall could not be found. He had gone off on a business-as-usual, peacetime Sunday morning horseback ride, leaving no word as to his itinerary. What he did leave was a legacy of doubt for the "conspiracy" theorists, men who became convinced that Japan was somehow lured into attacking America by men close to Pres. Roosevelt, or by Roosevelt alone.

* * *

The War Department finally ordered a language school to be established. Location was in the Presidio of San Francisco, under the 4th Army, commanded by Lt. Gen. John L. DeWitt, a man whose name would become anathema to Japanese-Americans. This seemed an ideal location because the prime source of student input, Nisei already in the Army, were nearly all in West Coast camps.

Lt. Col. John Weckerling, then in Panama, was told to get the operation going. His search of the Presidio grounds turned up only one available facility—an abandoned airplane hangar. Crissey Field hadn't sheltered an aircraft for some time when Weckerling visited it in September, 1941. Although elated to have been pulled out of the Canal Zone, where a forthcoming war would surely have stranded him, the Louisiana native was getting frustrated. How in the hell was he to clean up this rundown shack, furnish it, pay staff, and train a bunch of soldiers in the world's toughest language, all on a piddling $2000? That's what the War Department had allowed him for the task.

Weckerling had one good thing going for him. That was his back-up man, Kai Rasmussen, only man in the U.S. Army to speak Japanese with a heavy Danish accent. A dauntless driver, possessed of boundless energy, Rasmussen considered the word "failure" his personal enemy. Unable to speak a word of English on arrival in the U.S. during 1922, Rasmussen won admission to West Point two years later. For him, problems were opportunities to surmount challenges.

The Dane, in turn, was fortunate in his own back-up man, an unflagging reflection of himself named John Fujio Aiso. The pair rapidly accumulated respect and admiration, then spent these like money in a juggernaut effort to keep Pacific field commanders supplied with linguists. Neither would end up loved, but both would live in contented self-respect, surfeited with evidence of accomplishment.

While Weckerling was still in Panama, Rasmussen had met with nearly every mainland Nisei on active duty during 1941. The Louisianan, helping out with recruiting, located John Aiso in a camp outside Los Angeles. The Burbank-born 31-year-old attorney was not exactly intrigued with Army life. A *cum laude* Brown graduate with a doctorate in jurisprudence from Harvard, who had taken special additional studies at Chuo University in Tokyo, the stocky Aiso had been greeted by an Army classification specialist with "Just what we need . . . another goddamned lawyer!" and assigned to the motor pool. He was issuing spare parts there and, by admission, "doing a lousy job of it." when Weckerling sought him out. An offer to make him chief instructor at the new school did not appeal to Aiso. He wanted to serve his remaining four months, get out, get married, and resume his law practice. "No, thank you, Sir," was his response.

The lean West Point grad laid a hand on the shorter

man's shoulder, looked deeply into his eyes, and said, "John, your country needs you!"

Tears glistened when Aiso recounted this to the author. "No one had ever called it *my* country before, Joe," he said. "The sonofagun had me hooked!"

Weckerling had luck with instructors, too. Right in the San Francisco area he found Akira Oshida and Shigeya Kihara. Eager as any other AJA's to show their patriotism, both immediately donated their personal libraries, free of charge, to the pitiful collection of texts on hand, and made copies of everything for everyone. Kihara and Oshida stayed on with the language effort long after America realized that arrogant spouting of English was not the best way to communicate with people of other tongues. They eventually retired from well-appointed offices at the Defense Language Institute in the Presidio of Monterey, but their first organizational meeting was held while seated on orange crates and discarded apple boxes in the basement of 4th Army headquarters.

When war broke out, Kihara had to make a dash for his brother Hayato's house, to scoop up the rest of his Japanese magazines and other useful material before the FBI confiscated them. Paradoxically, what the Army needed to help win the war was contraband if found in the hands of Issei or Nisei.

The fruits of Rasmussen's interviewing foray through Army camps were bitter. Fiercely-determined that their children get the educations denied themselves, Issei became America's only ethnic group that did not put their offspring to work. To these fugitives from the bitter farms of Hiroshima and Kumamoto, education was the golden key that opened all doors, and schooling stood paramount among a family's goals. No child left school, even in the hardest of times, without long adult discussion that included comment from neighbors and friends. In the case of one parent's death a child might be allowed to interrupt education temporarily, but as soon as the family's economic situation got better, back to school

Snelling looked like "another concentration camp" when Key Kobayashi reported there from one. Below, on pass in Brisbane are Yoshikazu Yamada (1) and Steve Yamamoto before Yamada did work with Kiyoshi Yamashiro on Z Plan.

he went. Many a Nisei graduated from school three to six years behind his peers, but graduate he did, with Issei urging him to be American as possible.

The Naganuma Readers are a Japanese near-counterpart of America's renowned McGuffey's set. Using these, Rasmussen tested the linguistic abilities of nearly 4000 Nisei in uniform. And found them, sadly, wanting. Less than 10% could read, write or speak more than a few words of their parents' mother tongue. Slightly more than 100 could be rated as "somewhat competent" in Japanese. Of the 60 finally selected for the Military Intelligence Specialist Language School's first class, Weckerling said that not more than 15 could be considered true linguists—proficient in *both* languages. The findings were an awful shock to the War Department. These Japanese, dammit, weren't Japanese! In fact, they were too damned *American!*

Nisei had become "too damned American" with a vengeance. Issei achieved that goal for their children despite prejudice, discrimination, burnings, beatings, laws that forbade their buying land, and more laws that prevented other Issei joining them where Liberty lifted her lamp beside the golden door. Everyone and everything, it seemed, conspired to thwart the efforts of these bandy-legged newcomers to equip their children for achieving the "American way of life," but against all odds the Issei succeeded. Nisei became the most educated ethnic group in the U.S.

Never before—or since—did the American public school system so measure up to its potential as it did with Nisei. America, not Japan, was their land, and is. English, not Japanese, was their mother tongue, and is. The Army's language school, as a result, was hard-pressed to find enough qualified people to fill its first rickety seats, but Nisei gave their very best effort. They had to, lest parents wail that "All Japan would be ashamed!" of Japanese whose sons failed them.

Sixty students sat down to studies at Crissey Field on November 1, 1941, at the MISLS (they and successors would call themselves "MIS'ers"). Iwao Kawashiri was there because he'd been promised a sergeant's three stripes if he completed the course successfully. Meanwhile, he was a lot closer to his San Francisco home than he had been at Ft. Lewis, Washington. Isao Kusuda had no idea at all what G-2 meant when he was recruited, but figured it might be interesting when a friend said it was "map reading, drafting, and stuff like that." For Gene Uratsu, schooled in Japan and therefore a Kibei ("returned American"), the whole thing was fascinating. "There I was," he said, "a farm boy turned soldier, studying a language I already knew, in the wonderful city of San Francisco. It was the happiest six months of my entire life!"

Some students thought the Army was starting an all-Asian unit. Others thought they'd be teaching English to Kibei soldiers, men who'd been sent to Japan by parents for part or all of their educations, and who usually came back bereft of English altogether. Most Kibei had to re-enter American schools, at lower levels, to catch up on the language.

Fred Hiroshi Nishitsuji was in the first class. His name gave evidence of the Japanese language's complexity—or richness. Issei took great pains selecting children's names. The "American" ones had to be as unlike Japanese ones as possible, but the Japanese names had to reflect qualities or virtues that parents hoped a child would exhibit throughout life. A minor industry, that of selecting names for a fee or as a favor, was extant in the Japanese culture. Help was often sought from long-time friends, better-educated associates, or councils of elders. Naming a child, like picking a bride, was a step not taken lightly.

Among other readings, Hiroshi can be seen as "wide, broad, or understanding." Fred Nishitsuji's mother and father chose the reading, according to him, for "doctor, or professor." They then prayed he would become one or the other. A later student at MISLS was Hiroshi Tanabe. His parents read the name differently. "They hoped I would grow up broad-minded, or intelligent."

he recalled. So—two boys, two sets of parents, two interpretations. Parents took whichever *Kanji* reading seemed apt, or suited perhaps a thought or sound, to give their child's name the meaning desired. A father might pick the reading of a character that pleased him most. Or a character that seemed to have great beauty. Or one that seemed most manly. Or, in some cases, was easier to read or write. The language offered broad latitude for this. Tomio Ichikawa's father was able to "read" his name as "Boy who climbs high, beautifully," but George Inagaki's father didn't take much trouble. Having chosen a sturdy Anglo-Saxon name for his son, the senior Inagaki then took the nearest Japanese phonetic equivalent, and made the boy's other name Joji.

Early-arriving language students pitched in to refurbish the old hangar. Wooden horses were obtained, and planks laid across these to form desks. Discarded theater seats were seized upon for chairs. Crude partitions were erected, to separate classrooms from office spaces, and bedding was lugged into adjacent sleeping quarters. Student life was extremely-spartan, except in one respect. Food was delicious! MIS'ers were fed at the 4th Army's school for cooks and bakers, where one could almost dine like a gourmet on the cooking samples. But a student had to run like hell, both ways, to eat and get back to class on time, because of the tight study schedule

Bunks were tiered three-high, and sometimes posed problems. Kazuo Kawaguchi was the largest man in the Presidio class. Tall for a Japanese, he towered over his buddies, who called him *"An-chan"* (Big Brother). "He was also our best *sake* drinker," one recalled. The first few weekends of school were peacetime ones, occasions for big busts in San Francisco's Chinatown. After some parties, short-legged friends of Kawaguchi's, trying to get him into his topmost bunk, often propelled him over the top of it.

At one point General DeWitt himself visited the school. He sat down behind Roy Kawashiri, and told him before leaving "Let me know if there's anything you need." Kawashiri was shocked, a year later, to read of DeWitt's telling a Congressional committee "A Jap's a Jap—you can't change him by giving him a piece of paper." DeWitt, who by that time had herded 110,000 Americans of Japanese ancestry into concentration camps, claimed that their citizenship made no difference.

Weckerling and Rasmussen got their project off the starting blocks on November 1, as directed. Five dozen men were five weeks into what was to be a rigorous one-year course when "air raid. Pearl Harbor. This is no drill," thundered at them.

* * *

That first Sunday of December was an unmitigated disaster. Despite frequent warnings, the Army and Navy in Hawaii were literally caught with their pants down. Except on board those ships with martinets for commanders, no reveille was held that day. Peacetime "late hammocks" prevailed, Navy men rising when they liked, and few crewmen were stirring about when Japanese planes attacked Battleship Row. Bombs and bullets came crashing through canvas awnings, a peacetime indulgence in warm climes. In ships truly cleared for action, these would have been earlier stowed, so that guns might elevate and traverse. No writer has earlier commented on this. Nor on the fact that, in those days, the Navy paid its people on the 5th and 20th. Adm. Chuichi Nagumo's carriers hit Pearl on payday weekend, the twice-monthly occasion for sailors' getting bent out of shape. Officers of all services had partied well the night before, and Iwilei District whorehouses did their usual bustling Saturday night business. So did the taverns on Waikiki Beach. The author, stationed at Pacific Fleet headquarters in 1956, was assigned to do an anniversary story on attack survivors then stationed at Pearl Harbor. He quickly learned that not all had been "just heading for church," or "coming out of the YMCA," as earlier versions have it.

Reaction against the 159,000 Japanese-Americans in Hawaii was a bit less paranoid than against 127,000 on the mainland. It had to be. Many Nisei had been working undercover for the FBI and military intelligence, for years. Cecil Coggins, a Navy doctor who was actually a counterespionage specialist, had more than 100 Nisei volunteers, unpaid, under him. Code-named Orange Group, they identified many dozens of potentially-dangerous aliens, who were scooped up within hours of the first bomb's falling. As it did for the European struggle, Hawaii supplied a host of anxiously-loyal Nisei to serve in the Pacific war. They recall December 7 vividly.

Warren Adachi lived a bit west of Pearl Harbor itself. Exploding bombs woke him. He responded with friends to emergency calls on the radio for help. But Adachi, friends, and the truck they took to evacuate Navy wounded, were turned away from the base at gunpoint.

It was drilled into Herbert Yanamura that a man mustn't marry until he could properly support a wife. He was therefore trained in domestic tasks in case he, like his father, might have to live any length of time brideless. Herb was ironing the family laundry at Kona, on Hawaii, while his Dad was out picking coffee for which that area is so famous. He heard "This is no maneuver. This is the real McCoy!" when radio announcer Webley Edwards screamed it into a microphone.

Explosions wrecked a store a few blocks from Sam Takamura's house in downtown Honolulu. Until the Navy admitted its own defective ammunition did the damage, Sam thought Japanese pilots had deliberately attacked unarmed civilians.

Up until the attack, Makoto Sakamoto's morning was cheerful. Sunday work, like Saturday work, meant overtime pay helping construct a new building for the Navy, alongside the drydocked battleship *Pennsylvania.* The steelworker dived for cover as bombs fell. When he came back to work the next day, Maxie was suddenly marched off the base at bayonet point with 31 other slant-eyed constructionmen.

Gulstan Enomoto, in Wailuku, Maui, had an appointment to sell a local policeman some insurance. When he arrived at the station, a radio was blaring "This is war! This is war!" Gulstan headed home, stopping enroute to share the news with his brother David. The elder Enomoto was nowhere around. Nor was his massive radio, and his wife wouldn't talk. It took time to unravel the puzzle, but on the panic-stricken mainland, Japanese-Americans known to own shortwave transmitters were getting jailed. At the same time, on Maui, one Japanese-Scottish-Hawaiian-American was being begged to enlist, so the Navy could have his radio set!

The Navy had a small airstrip at Puunene, and its equipment wouldn't transmit. The airfield commander wanted to enlist David Enomoto and his equipment, so Pearl Harbor could be raised. David pointed out that the Navy would never honor enlistment of someone with Japanese blood, but he did help Navy men load up his giant home-built radio set, and transport it to the field. For the rest of the war, while holding his job with the Maui Railroad, David secretly maintained his own and other equipment for the Navy, in his free time and without pay. It took the Navy Department 25 years to say thanks officially.

Fumio Kido heard explosions at nearby Hickam Field, then saw the *hino maru,* the red ball that identified planes overhead as Japanese. Kido joined other teenagers in a pidgin chant of "Oh, them dumb buggahs! Now they get it!"

Military police barreled into the middle of Tom Masui's baseball game to get help. Tom and 20 other kids hopped onto an Army truck, panicking their parents for three days. Tom then went home. He'd been riding back and forth between mid-island Schofield Barracks, and Kapa Hospital in downtown Honolulu, sleeping when and where he could. The kids had been taking cots, beds, blankets, mattresses and medical supplies to where they were needed.

Inside Pearl Harbor, on the shore of Aiea Bay, the family of Harold Onishi lived in a small fishing village. His parents, his brother Katsumi, and Katsumi's wife and son all saw the battleship *Arizona* blow up, a half mile from their front door. When steel rained down, the Onishis decided to give up their front row seat. All six piled into the 1937 Plymouth they jointly owned, and chug-chugged up the slope of Koolau Range, away from the water, amid a swarm of other refugees.

* * *

At Crissey Field, on the mainland, Isao Kusuda grew increasingly glum. This stupid war probably meant he wouldn't get the leave he'd been promised when school was over. And he'd be sure to get frozen in service, too. Rumors flew as fast inside the Presidio of San Francisco as elsewhere.

Weckerling tried to reassure his charges, telling them he'd had some trouble in an earlier war because of German ancestry, but that things would turn out as well for them as they had for him. Pvt. Kazuo Kozaki wasn't buying it. A Kibei, he got John Aiso outside the hangar, and addressed him with the formal title of respect Japanese gave all teachers. *"Sensei,"* Kozaki pleaded, "why don't we run away now, while we have a chance?" He was sure Kibei would be shot, in retaliation for the Pearl Harbor attack.

Aiso wasn't sure what to say. He'd just dashed downtown himself, to wire his fiance in Los Angeles he was O.K., but sweated his way back to the Presidio on a trolley car while a hysterical female passenger kept screaming "Kill him! He's a Jap! Kill him!" All Aiso could do was share his own anguished experiences, at Brown, Harvard, and elsewhere. "We'll have to be patient," he told Kozaki. "Up to now, there has always been some Caucasian around when I've had trouble, to step in and insist on fair play."

Kozaki subsided. Fear left him. He became first Nisei to win the Silver Star.

The rest of Weckerling's men also calmed down and returned to their studies, which were accelerated, while the colonel tried to maintain an island of calm in a hysterical military sea. It wasn't easy. General DeWitt, his fears fed by anti-Japanese elements in northern California, exhibited an increasing suspicion and fear of everything Oriental. Panic began to rule the day. Kai Rasmussen was suddenly yanked out of MIS and sent to a coastal artillery unit when rumors poured in of Japanese submarines and aircraft carriers offshore. The 4th Army automatically became Western Defense Command at war's outbreak, and DeWitt wanted the Japanese-speaking Weckerling as his staff intelligence officer. Some screaming telephone conversations took place, and Rasmussen's rapid return was arranged. The Danish immigrant directed the language training program thereafter. It earned him a Legion of Merit.

Anxiety bred problems, the War Department suddenly proclaiming no Nisei could be shipped overseas. There went the entire reason for language training. So—more angry telephone calls, more cursing, more sending of what the military calls "nastygrams." The order was rescinded.

Earl Warren, the attorney-general of California, planned to run for the governor's office. He fell into ranks on the side of the angels, if the State's white supremacists might be called that. Along with the Native Sons and Daughters of the Golden West, and the Hearst newspapers, Warren began urging that all persons of Japanese ancestry be ordered inland, away from the coast. Some Issei and Nisei could read the handwriting on the wall, and began a mass voluntary move eastward. This grew until General DeWitt, although he favored evacuation, had to order the activity stopped because of disruptions it was causing. Things weren't getting done the "Army way," and DeWitt couldn't handle that.

Language students at the Presidio, who still liked to enjoy delicious food at Chinatown restaurants when off-duty, began to feel conspicuous in a sea of white faces as other AJA's began staying in their homes for safety. They were cautioned to pair up, and stay in uniform, whenever leaving the Presidio. To sustain themselves,

Nisei language students drew upon the Japanese teachings that immigrant parents insisted they absorb. They knew that a man sometimes had to "sleep on firewood, and lick gall." Children of Nisei, the mod and hip Sansei, could read this a generation later as "Hang in, man. Cool it. Your turn's coming, sooner or later." In early 1942, the thought helped, but only a little.

Time passed. Not all students did, when the pace of the course was doubled. At April's end, 39 Nisei and 2 Caucasians celebrated their graduation with a festive dinner in Chinatown. A 40th Nisei did not graduate with them. Kei Kiyoshi Sakamoto was pulled out of school early, and sent away on a secret mission, first Nisei into the South Pacific from the mainland. Arthur Komori was already there, from Corregidor. And Yoshikazu Yamada, from Mindanao. The latter, a graduate student in chemistry at the Univ. of Michigan when drafted, had been evacuated from the Philippines on a stretcher after being snatched up for the language work.

Sgt. Yoshio Hotta led Sam Sugimoto, Masami Mayeda, Hideo Suyehiro and William Nishikawa north to the Aleutians and the lest-heralded theater of war, in May.

Sgt. Mac Nagata took Masaru Ariyasu, Iwao Kawashiri, Yoshio Noritake, Shigeru Yamashita and Isao Kusuda along with him to New Caledonia. There they would join the newly-forming Americal Division, which rushed to that island before the Japanese could take it and shut off Australia from America.

Two Caucasians who already knew some Japanese, and had taken the course mostly for brush-up purposes (and perhaps others described by Sheldon Covell later in this story), led teams out. John Burden, a doctor from the island of Maui, had the Kubo brothers, Tadao and Takashi, but he didn't know that until he met them on board ship. E. David Swift, an immigration official called to active duty from the Reserve, led eight men to Australia. They were William Hirashima, Gary Kadani, Steve Yamamoto, Kazuo Kawaguchi, Paul Kuyama, Fred Nishitsuji, Hiromi Oyama, and George Taketa.

The family of Taketa was gathered up, allowed to take only what they could carry in their arms, and shipped to a concentration camp not long after he reached the land Down Under.

Hideo Tsuyuki came down with jaundice, and was hospitalized. He later led a team to Australia, arriving in early 1943. James Fujimura, Kazuo Kozaki, Masanori Minamoto, Tateshi Miyasaki and David Kato would leave the mainland before him. Eleven other graduates, official plans for them changed, would remain in the States.

* * *

The war news continued bad throughout the course of study at the Presidio, America and her friends everywhere humiliated by Japan. In San Francisco, even Kai Rasmussen's proud grin faded. New and different problems cropped up. Like John Aiso's having to be discharged. Then he had to be re-hired as a civilian. It would have been easier to give John a commission commensurate with his post but, according to directives, he was too old to qualify for the rank considered meet. So, civilian it had to be. Many officers would be coming to study Japanese, and the pompous niceties of military tradition had to be observed. It wouldn't do to let them feel in any way inferior to a Private, even one with a Harvard education.

Nor could the job be done any longer at the Presidio. Earl Warren, the Hearst papers, and others urging Japanese-Americans evacuation from the West Coast, finally got their way. Pres. Roosevelt signed an order that let Gen. DeWitt round up and ship east anyone with Japanese blood—including *infants!* The blackest blot on America's escutcheon began to blossom. Student linguists later to face death on Guadalcanal and New Guinea were no longer safe on San Francisco's streets.

Chapter 2

Americans of Japanese ancestry evoked deep affection or deep mistrust in the first four decades of this century, dependent upon the life situation of any Caucasian encountering one. Whites of accomplishment—ministers, physicians, and men of other disciplines—took AJA's in stride. But persons still struggling for a place in the sun—notably politicians or business failures—looked askance at these striving, energetic people. Issei ("first generation of Japanese in America") and their children, the Nisei ("second generation of Japanese in America"), made unsure Caucasians feel more unsure.

True, AJA's did display several admirable qualities. Like love of children, respect for elders, capacity for uncomplaining hard work, reverence for scholarship, and a grim enthusiasm for anything red-white-and-blue. But, they did exhibit certain behavioral oddities. They ate lots of fish and rice, for instance. Sitting on the floor. With wooden sticks, yet. Many didn't celebrate Christmas, but went all-out for New Year's. Strange lot.

And how about those slanted eyes? A fellow never really could tell which way a Jap (they were rarely called Japanese) was looking. Better keep an eye on them, just in case. Thus did ignorance produce suspicion, which gave birth to fear. The fourth generation of these sick emotions—senseless hate—logically followed.

This confused the Issei. They worked hard, kept spotless homes, and sent well-scrubbed, properly-mannered children to school. Why, then, did the *hakujin* still treat

Marauder veterans (above) relax in India. Bill Wada at northern Honshu surrender interpreted Fletcher's terms.

them like foreigners? Whites were puzzling people. Had they no culture? All Japan knew that a *yoshi* let himself be adopted into a family that wanted its line carried on. He surrendered himself to his adoptive family, becoming a permanent member of its household. They, the Issei, had chosen to become *yoshi* to America. That meant automatically giving the new country their full love and loyalty. Forever. It was the Japanese way. Even *Tenno-san,* the Emperor, knew that. How could these "round-eyes" not understand?

The round-eyes didn't, and Nisei paid the price. Encouraged, even harassed, by immigrant parents to be good Americans, Nisei tried. In a continual outpouring of love, Issei compounded the problem. Scraping together pennies, then dollars, Issei established Japanese schools, making children attend these after coming home from public ones. They felt that two centuries of American culture were O.K., but adding 26 Japanese ones wouldn't hurt anything. From 9 a.m. to 2 p.m., Nisei learned in public schools that a group of portly gentlemen with be-ribboned hair were their "forefathers." From 3 p.m., and on Saturday mornings, they bowed to their *sensei,* who were quick to knuckle the knobs of those who forgot for a moment the glorious sacrifice of the 47 *ronin,* the "master-less *samurai*" who avenged their lord's treacherous death.

Japanese studies precluded other extracurricular activity. It was a rare Nisei who played high school sports, or debated, or had time for the dramatic society. In desperation, trying to get along, Nisei let things Japanese slide out of their lives whenever given a choice. It wasn't easy, trying to observe two sets of traditions, and live in two cultures. Guilt beset some Nisei. Inferiority complexes infected others. Psychologists, professional and amateur, later had a field day with this dichotomy.

What it meant to Kai Rasmussen was that damned few Nisei knew much Japanese!

Three problems pressed the Dane while Japanese troops were taking Hong Kong, Manila, Singapore and

Rangoon. His course was cut to six months, requiring instructors to cram craniums at a double clip. This reduced the time period available for identifying and bringing in new students for the next class. Too, he had to get his operation out of San Francisco, to some place where Nisei might apply themselves to arduous study without being distracted by sneers of "Dirty Jap!"

Rasmussen soon pinpointed Minnesota as the geographic area with the best record of racial amity. Though only 51 AJA's lived in Minnesota at the time of the 1940 census, he figured the Gopher State could absorb more without strain. After consultation with Gov. Harold E. Stassen, he obtained for Army use of 132 acres near Ft. Snelling, southwest of Minneapolis, called Camp Savage after the tiny contiguous town there.

Until Nisei made the place famous for patriotic effort, Savage had been noted as the home of Dan Patch, the internationally-famous trotting horse. Earlier, Camp Savage had been part of the Civilian Conservation Corps, and after that a shelter for indigent males. One of Rasmussen's first sights at Camp Savage was a flower bed. It moved him, deeply. He knew the families of many of his students, present and future, would spend the war in concentration camps. So it was especially ironic that the bed's flowers spelled out "Homeless Men's Camp." Nearly all mainland Nisei who studied at Savage knew no other home. Rasmussen had the flowers dug out.

Of the Presidio grads, Jack Ohashi and Yoshio Miyaoi were assigned to handle Savage's supply problems. Also kept back from overseas assignment, to teach, were Arthur Kaneko, James Matsumura, Gene Uratsu, Thomas Sakamoto, Joe Y. Masuda, Ichiro Nishida, Morio Nishita, Ryoichi Shinoda, and James Tanizawa.

* * *

On February 19, 1942, Franklin Roosevelt signed the infamous Executive Order 9066. Gen. DeWitt began herding AJA's into assembly centers, for allocating to concentration camps. Someone in Washington must have realized how stupid this looked, when DeWitt's own headquarters was training Japanese-Americans. Language training was then shifted to the direct purview of the War Department. Meanwhile, much had happened in the 15 weeks since war broke out.

Near panic reigned a while in coastal cities, east and west, once Americans realized how inadequate their armed forces really were, and became aware that they were *not* going to "lick those little yellow bastards in about three weeks!" The battleships *Arizona, Oklahoma, California* and *West Virginia* didn't look half so imposing in Pearl Harbor's mud as they had in Pathé newsreels. A host of senior officers were yanked out of commanding billets and stashed where, if they couldn't do good, they at least could do no harm.

Early panic became rage on December 8, after Roosevelt crossed out "history" to substitute "infamy" in a speech he prepared for Congress, a piece of purple prose that still helps hate well up. From sea to shinning sea, America was infuriated into unity, something it had not been able to achieve via peaceful means.

Nowhere were the Japanese stopped. They quickly took Wake, Guam, Makin, Hong Kong and Tarawa, and were soon ashore in the Philippines, Malaya, and Burma. British might was swiftly swept from the Far East, and American ships that didn't get sunk ran for their lives. All forces opposing Japan fell back before the onrushing yellow tide. The haughty *hakujin,* the Western Powers, were getting humbled for only the second time in history, and again it was a Japanese emperor's men who were doing the humbling.

Only a handful of AJA's are known to have hailed this succession of Japanese victories with *banzai's,* but if any other longtime victims of repression, prejudice and discrimination did, in their secret hearts, smile a bitter smile it would be understandable. It seemed, to some, the bully was getting what-for, and that made for a nice feeling.

As mentioned, Hawaii's AJA population suffered less right after December 7 than did AJA's along America's west coast. Climate may have been a factor, because warm sun and tinkling ukeleles do make for an easy-does-it atmosphere. Also, fewer island Japanese than mainland ones tended to complete. They seemed, at least, less serious than hard-driving mainland Nisei. Too, thanks to a tightly-controlled island economy, Hawaii's Japanese were more "manageable." Herb Miyasaki, later to serve in Burma with Merrill's Marauders, had a father who found this out. A store owner on the "Big Island," the elder Miyasaki once made the mistake of openly backing a political candidate the Theo H. Davies Co. opposed. His store was then forbidden, for a time, from selling to workers on a Davies plantation.

Pressure was usually more covert than overt. If a young firebrand made trouble, his father could be called in and reminded who had paid his way from Japan (even though the fare had long since been deducted from earnings). The Issei strong sense of *on,* the cultural obligation to show gratitude, was pointed up and played upon. Result—instant solution. Japanese sons obeyed their fathers. A somewhat similar system existed in the Southeast U.S., for keeping "uppity niggers" in line.

There were notable exceptions to the general trend. Y. Baron Goto, his cousin Kenji, Masaji Marumoto, and Ben Tashiro had strong professional and social ties with the *haole* ruling class.

Hawaii's Japanese could not be pushed very hard, as those on the mainland might. Locking up 159,534 men, women and children couldn't even be considered. Japanese were needed, for the labor force. Chinese preferred to work for themselves, and native Hawaiians didn't like working at all. This was why Japanese were brought to Hawaii in the first place.

Thousands of Japanese were already busy, strengthening Hawaii's defenses, and more were needed for construction yet to start. So, except for declaring martial law, setting a curfew, and restricting the movements of certain aliens it was not thought necessary to pick up, officials generally left Hawaii's Japanese civilians alone.

It was a different story for Japanese in the military. What would the uniformed AJA's do?

A lot of people wondered.

Pvt. Torao Migita might have told them, but he died for his country on December 7, trying to reach his duty station.

They could have asked Sgt. David Akui, one of the 298th Infantry Regiment. On December 8 he captured the first prisoner-of-war, when Ens. Kazuo Sakamaki swam ashore from a midget submarine he'd abandoned.

The Hawaii National Guard had been federalized 15 months earlier. Nisei volunteers and draftees then swelled its ranks, until 1300 or so were serving in the 298th and 299th Regiments. The latter was scattered through the outer islands. Had the Nagumo Force followed its air attack with an invasion of Maui, Kauai, or Hawaii, troops there to stop them were largely Nisei.

The 298th was at Schofield Barracks, later made familiar to the American public via the movie *From Here To Eternity.* In a Tent City there, 350 Nisei inductees were undergoing recruit training. None were wounded by strafing that took place, although the footlockers of many were holed. Most Nisei were, in fact, off-duty and away from the post on the morning of December 7, another clue to how lax things were on Oahu.

Among those free that weekend were Kazuo Yamane, Masami Tahira, Seian Hokama, Richard Omori, Kenneth Harano, and Goichi Shimanuki. So were Ben Yamamoto, Richard Ishimoto and Sadao Toyama, the last trying to recover from a whopping party he'd attended the night before. All obeyed promptly a radio command to return to their posts, but all had great difficulty getting back to Schofield. The road between Pearl Harbor and the mid-island Army post was jammed with vehicles of all kinds, rushing back and forth to help the Navy with its dead and wounded. When Richard Ishimoto's bus passed through the Hickam Field area, a hysterical MP kept jabbing a rifle toward him. The over-wrought soldier wanted to shoot Ishimoto because "the Japs blew up my buddy!"

Among the handful of men on duty at Schofield that morning were Hoichi Kubo and Edwin Kawahara. Kubo was a medical technician, made one because he took some college chemistry courses and had inoculated a few pigs on Maui. He was enroute to early chow, a privilege of dispensary staffers, when he saw planes coming through Kole Kole Pass from the island's north side, but he paid no attention.

Kubo then heard explosions from the direction of Pearl Harbor, but thought them "more blasts from that construction going on over there." He didn't know he was at war until haggard messengers rushed in and demanded "all the plasma you guys got!"

Kawahara was the "intelligence Corporal for the 1st Battalion headquarters of the 298th. I saw the planes on my way back across the road from the latrine, where I'd been brushing my teeth. I ran to sound the alarm, but someone beat me to it. Then I began calling up my superiors on the telephone," he said.

Not one could be found that dreadful morning. "No one answered his phone," said Kawahara.

"Not the CO, the exec, the S-1, S-2, S-3, or S-4. I tried all the company commanders. No luck there, either. Just then, in walked Lt. Robert Louis Stevenson, a deputy company commander."

Kawahara told the young man "You are senior officer present, Sir," and Stevenson went directly to the office safe. "He took out the M-94 cipher and the division field codes," Kawahara recalled, "and told me, 'Edwin, guard these with your life!'" Throughout his life to that point, the insurance salesman had felt the weight of Caucasian suspicion. Nearly four decades later he still regarded the incident as the most exhilarating experience of his life. "It was magnificent," he said, "to be the recipient of such total trust!"

Richard Moritsugu was one of Schofield's soldiers

who reacted. With another man he heaved a machine gun onto a truck and drove off, his assignment to defend Honolulu. "Pearl Harbor was a shambles when we passed it," he said.

Thomas "Kewpie" Tsubota was on duty at Bellows Field, detached from Schofield. "I thought the Rising Sun insignia was camouflage for war games," he said, "when the planes made a pass without firing. But when they came back, and opened up on us, I realized they were real Zeroes!"

The Nagumo Force was racing back toward Japan before Tsutomu Yamada, of the 299th, knew it had attacked Pearl Harbor. He was off-duty, fishing, on Maui. Herb Miyasaki was at home on the island of Hawaii. Reporting in, he was sent to Kohala airport to act as a weatherman. On the same island, Fusao Uchiyama came in from protecting Hilo's power station against sabotage. He'd been standing watches there for two weeks. Like Miyasaki, he was shocked. "What were those guys doing over there?" he demanded. The 299th had been fully alerted. Uchiyama couldn't understand why the 298th wasn't. He helped set up one of his unit's two 75 mm field pieces facing the entrance to Hilo's harbor, to stop the Japanese fleet if it came. He then went to beach defense with the crew of a 37mm anti-tank gun. "The only ammo we had for it was tracer," he said. Uchiyama's gun would have made a bright show, but it couldn't do any damage.

* * *

Navy Secretary Frank Knox, who flew out from Washington to see what had happened, must have been briefed by some pretty paranoid people. Eight days after the attack he was telling a press conference "I think the most effective fifth column work of the entire war was done in Hawaii, with the possible exception of Norway."

A "token" Republican member of the Democrat cabinet, Knox was a newspaperman who must have seen too many movies about newspapermen. All FBI checks were to show AJA's innocent of any sabotage in Hawaii. Clearly, Knox had let emotion override intellect. There was only one "legitimate" spy in Hawaii, Takeo Yoshikawa, who operated out of his country's consulate under a cover title, the same device Americans and others used worldwide. Two other spies arrived in November to collect Yoshikawa's information, and collect some themselves. They were Suguru Suzuki and Toshihide Maejima.

They posed as merchant seamen, the same thing Sgts. Richard Sakakida and Arthur Komori had been doing for eight months in Manila.

Men of the 298th, wondering what might happen next, started deploying to previously-assigned dispositions along Oahu's north, windward coast. Sadao Toyama might have had more to wonder about than some other Nisei. His father, Tetsuo, had for 30 years been publishing *Jitsugyo Hawaii* ("Industrial Hawaii"), a Japanese-language publication. FBI agents carried him off before noon of December 7. Sadao would not see his father again for 10 months, and then in a Louisiana prison camp.

* * *

Kai Rasmussen probably didn't even hear for some time about the December 10 incident, when rifles were taken from all Nisei soldiers at Schofield's tent city, and they awoke next morning to find themselves ringed by machine guns. The incident still had a bad taste in Nisei mouths 36 years later. So did the visits of Caucasian officers to the 27-mile defense line some 800 soldiers of the 298th hoped to hold on Oahu's north shore. The officers kept asking Col. Wilhelm Andersen, CO of the regiment, how he could sleep "where these Japs can slit your throat?" While the Japanese-fluent Rasmussen was urging some Nisei soldiers to give their all, other Caucasians were insulting the men he'd later need. The Dane had his hands full, getting one bunch trained and into the field, and getting ready to train another bunch at Camp Savage.

Kan Tagami was to be among the latter. On December

7, he was a member of the Presidio's garrison force, assigned from the 7th Infantry Division at Ft. Ord. Three nights after the attack, Tagami pulled sentry duty on Fisherman's Wharf, guarding a small motor pool the Army had there. During the wee hours he encountered and challenged a drunk, who streaked off into the night screaming "The Japs have landed! The Japs have landed!" Tagami's weapons were later confiscated and he was shipped inland, as were thousands of other Nisei. His family was rounded up, forced to live in Santa Anita racetrack's horse stalls for weeks, then shipped to a Poston, Arizona, concentration camp.

Terry Takahashi, also from Ft. Ord, was at another Presidio, the one in Monterey, "chasing prisoners. We'd run them over from Ord," he said, "to do landscape work." Off-post and off-duty when the attack began, Terry headed home. There he found his mother, brother and stepfather "destroying the Emperor's picture and everything else Japanese, for fear they'd be charged with disloyalty."

Mike Sakamoto, George Kayano, Ronald Chagami and Satsuke Tanakatsubo were among the many Nisei at Camp Roberts, California, whose weapons were taken away.

No one took guns away from Walter Tanaka, Roy Uyehata, George Ichikawa or Joe Yoshiwara at Ft. Ord. Joe helped guard the fort's water supply that night, and Walt developed a monstrous callus from hand-loading machine gun belts when the machine loader broke down. The four, with Shigeo Yasutake, Tetsuo Hayashida and a lot of other Nisei, were sent off to guard the shoreline north of Golden Gate Bridge, but that didn't last long. Nisei were pulled off it. Their faces terrified the civilians they had to challenge at night.

Dye Ogata, Calvin Morimatsu, Richard K. Hayashi and Shigeo Ito were at Ft. Lewis, Washington. There confusion ran rampant. Some Nisei had their guns confiscated, some didn't. Robert Yoshioka did. He was then sent to help guard the mouth of the Columbia River, but assured "You'll get your rifle back if there's an attack." Had Lord Cornwallis' redcoats marched through Ft. Lewis, playing "The World Turned Upside Down," no Nisei would have been surprised. Some were on one side of a road, confined to barracks, while others were on the other side, getting processed out of the Army and given the draft classification 4-F, for "undesirable." Nisei were being kicked out of the Army at other posts, too, in spite of having some records any Old Soldier would have been proud of. Most officers who tried to speak for Nisei soldiers were told to shut up.

Someone in Washington finally wielded a big broom, sweeping all Nisei GI's inland from the U.S. west coast. Many were put on a roster none had ever heard of before, something called the DEML ("Detached Enlisted Man's List.") This appeared to be some kind of military limbo in which soldiers were allowed to sweep streets, cut grass and haul garbage, but not get promotions for which they had been scheduled. Insult was added to injury when these menial tasks were performed under supervision of armed Caucasian soldiers.

* * *

Rasmussen's curriculum had been cut back from 12 to 6 months, and then still further for 14 selected Nisei entering the first class at Camp Savage. They got only 90 days of cramming, so they could get into the Pacific as quickly as possible. Leading their detachment out was Arthur Katsuyoshi Ushiro, who later legally changed his name to Castle. Art's father named him after two paternal uncles, reading the characters for his name as "winner of honors," a hope that became reality. Also with the class were three Caucasians, all officers; John Anderton, Barton Lloyd and Harold Moss.

Anderton was a noteworthy personage, the only prewar Caucasian graduate of *Kinmun Gakuen* (Golden Gate Institute) premier Japanese-language school of San Francisco. With a cover job on the *San Francisco Chronicle,* he'd been a Navy agent before taking service with the Army. Anderton decided to learn Japanese while a teenager, because he found calligraphy so pleasing to the eye. At first the director of *Kinmun Gakuen,* wanting no dilettante Caucasians, had turned him away. Anderton memorized several hundred *Kanji* characters, plus a complete syllabary, in just two weeks. He was admitted. He then completed Japanese language studies from basic primer through middle school (equivalent of U.S. High school) in 2½ years, while pursuing his regular studies at Lowell High. At Savage and elsewhere, Anderton's photographic memory for Japanese ideographs got him nicknamed "The *Kanji* Kid." He was forever tripping up instructor Paul Tekawa with remembrance of archaic ones Tekawa usually hadn't learned.

Leo Saito and Kazuhiko Yamada were the only Nisei in this class who had not received any education in Japan. Masaharu Takata had. He was, in fact, descended on his mother's side from the Go family of Hiroshima, famous as *samurai.* The warrior heritage was broad, and Takata had a number of senior military officers among his relatives. One uncle commanded Japan's equivalent of West Point, and once arranged acceptance of him at a special school that prepared youths to enter the Japanese Military Academy. Masaharu's father, who hated war, arranged his 11-year-old son's immediate return to America. Along with Arthur Castle, Hiroshi Tanabe, and Sunao Ishio, Takata received shabby treatment at Camp Roberts, but got Corporal's stripes after being shipped east to Arkansas. (He'd been on the ROTC drill team at UCLA). An excerpt from the illegal wartime diary Takata kept tells that, on May 27, 1942, he thought the rest of his class "a nice bunch of fellows."

Paul Tekawa, formerly a newsman for a Japanese-language publication, laid special emphasis on *heigo,* the Japanese lexicon of military terms, for this class. He helped select Chiuro Sakata and David Watanabe to be retained as instructors. Torao Neishi, Ken Omura, Albert Tamura and James Tsumura left with the rest for Australia on September 10.

Ben Hazard (mustache) and 306th Language Detachment, which helped to turn Okinawa battle tide. Translated artillery chart did the trick.

Only a handful of Nisei were actually working in military intelligence by this time, although the war was nine months old. Things were taking a lot of time to get squared around. Arthur Komori and Richard Sakakida had retreated from Bataan to Corregidor on orders, Richard interpreting for Gen. Jonathan Wainwright at the last. Japan was in control of the Philippines, Burma, Singapore, Malaya, Indonesia, and the Bismarcks (New Britain, New Ireland). Winston Churchill, elated that America was at last in the war, visited Roosevelt two weeks after it started. During that trip he told the President how England had been reading Germany's most secret communications for a long time, thanks to possession of a cipher machine stolen for it by a Pole. Japan had bought one of these *Enigma* devices from Germany, and Churchill may have given Roosevelt, at this time, the key to Japan's topmost secrets as well. One cannot be sure of that. What one can be sure of is that an American public not yet in possession of all the facts regarding the assassinations of Abraham Lincoln and John Kennedy is not likely to be made completely knowledgeable about the 1941-45 war, either.

On January 1, 1942, Roosevelt publicly deplored the treatment aliens and other foreign-born were receiving at the hands of Americans, but deplore was all he did about it. One week later Spady Koyama, a Nisei in Spokane, did something that would have surprised and pleased Hawaii's Nisei, who generally believed that mainland ones were too acquiescent. Koyama threatened to sue the U.S. Army if it didn't let him enlist. The Army enlisted Spady Koyama, and eventually paid him a Colonel's pension.

America, in early 1942, was desperate for heroes. And scapegoats. Top Army and Navy officers were dismissed for the debacle at Pearl Harbor before complete investigations could possibly be made. Leo Carrillo, a movie actor of no great talent but much popularity for playing a Mexican buffoon, urged his Congressman to move all Japanese-Americans from the west coast. America cheered when David F. Mason, a Navy pilot in the South Pacific, radioed "Sighted sub, sank same." He got a Silver Star. Postwar checks revealed he had hit nothing. Colin Kelly was hailed posthumously for having sunk the Japanese battleship *Haruna,* and Roosevelt made quite a public thing about asking "a future President" to appoint Kelly's baby son to West Point. *Haruna* survived the war, having gotten "sunk" as often as the American carrier *Saratoga,* which also survived.

Canada, on January 14, ordered all Canadians of Japanese ancestry away from its west coast. In a barbaric display of racism, Canada's national government later ordered all real property of these people sold, and used the proceeds to finance their imprisonment. Japanese-Canadians had no trouble identifying with Jewish-Germans.

Japanese submarines were off America's west coast. I-17 fired 13 shells at a Goleta, California, oil refinery on February 23, and William Randolph Hearst took to his heels from nearby San Simeon. The press baron thought the Japanese were after him for the campaign of vilification his newspapers waged against Issei and Nisei.

The Far East situation continued to go badly for the West. Torpedoes of American submarines didn't work for those commanders who had guts enough to close on the enemy. Imperial troops landed on New Guinea and made Australian ones do something against their grain—retreat. Singapore fell, 100,000 Allied troops surrendering to one-third that many Japanese. Australia lost an entire division at Singapore, its 8th, to the Japanese as prisoners-of-war. And, 49 days after allowing as how awful it was to treat foreign-born shabbily, Roosevelt signed Executive Order 9066. This authorized the War Department to establish military areas, and exclude anyone from them it chose. Ignoring due process guaranteed by the Constitution, this act made it "legal" to uproot and imprison 110,000 Americans of Japanese ancestry from California, Oregon and Washington. The order would remain on the books *for 34 years!*

At least two politicians may have been pleased about Executive Order 9066. Cong. Leland Ford had acted on Leo Carrillo's request, asking on the floor of The House of Representatives for removal of the Japanese. Earl Warren, on February 2, ordered special maps of northern California made, showing land owned, occupied or controlled "by Japs." He then presented this "evidence," which merely showed Issei and Nisei to be working land no one else wanted, to a Congressional committee that month, as "proof" of how they lived near dams, airports, power plants, and the like.

Writers were to opine that Warren later became so guilt-stricken about what he had done to Japanese-Americans that he swung well left to liberalism. This cannot be established beyond doubt. What is established beyond doubt is that Edison Uno, a Nisei, tried without success until his death in 1977 to get a public admission of error from Warren.

By March, the western Pacific was a Japanese lake. Her Navy had sunk or run off the combined sea might of Australia, England, America and The Netherlands. Japan changed her mind about an invasion of Australia, deciding instead to isolate her. Taking Port Moresby, on the south shore of New Guinea, a base that could cover northern Australia, was to be the first move. This, followed by capture of New Caledonia, Samoa and the Fijis, would isolate Australia from the east. On March 10, Gen. Douglas MacArthur was told to get out of the Philippines (the second time he was so ordered) and set up a new command in Australia, the only place from which a countermarch against Japan could commence. MacArthur obeyed, and left the next day, just as a newly-arriving American force landed in New Caledonia. Once that happened, Japan had second thoughts about the Fijis and Samoa. The very long, very thin, lifeline to Australia now had a chance of being maintained.

* * *

The first AJA's shoved off the west coast by DeWitt

arrived at Camp Manzanar on March 21, to prepare the area for others. The place was crawling with snakes. History was repeating itself, and would again at nine other concentration camps. Just as Issei and Nisei were allowed use only of land that no one else had a yen for, or had given up trying to make productive, so were they now being exiled again to the boondocks. The majority of all acreage used to execute the barbarous incarcerations resembled nothing so much as a lunar landscape. In the seven States, most concentration camps were well off the beaten track.

* * *

With Komori and Sakakida, on Bataan and Corregidor, was a helper they certainly never expected to have, in the person of Clarence Yamagata. He was a Nisei who had been working for the Japanese consulate in Manila. (Many Nisei, in the Thirties, were offered jobs with Japanese industry and government. All were college graduates who found that a sheepskin in the hands of a man with slanted eyes was practically worthless.) Yamagata was first imprisoned by U.S. Army authorities, then freed and pressed into service as an interpreter, working under the same man who controlled Komori and Sakakida. This was Maj. N. W. Raymond, a murky figure who was an American undercover man in the Far East for some 30 years before death came to him as a POW.

April found the two Hawaii sergeants ordered to leave Corregidor for Australia, where linguists were in extremely short supply. On the 13th, a patched-up trainer that had earlier crash-landed, lifted from Kindley Field, the Rock's tiny airstrip. On board were a pilot, Komori, Clarence Yamagata, and a Chinese officer who was Philippines representative for Chaing Kai Chek. Sakakida had given his place to the Nisei attorney.

"I was able to brush up on flying," said Komori, who took the controls while the route to Iloilo, Panay Island, was plotted. "Pappy" Gunn, a near-legend in the Army Air Corps, picked them up there in a B-25 bomber and flew to Del Monte, Mindanao, to top off his tanks. After taking aboard as many 55-gallon drums of aviation gas as he could stow, Gunn beat off officers trying to pull rank and retreat, taking only the four men from Corregidor when he flew away. Seventeen hours later the B-25 set down in Australia, completing the longest flight an aircraft of its type had made. In 1977, Komori was still convinced he'd been on the "test hop" that proved a B-25 could be flown great distances. He was certain his flight had been actual preparation for the raid B-25's made on Japan from the aircraft carrier *Hornet* a few days later, and that Gunn "proved" it could be done.

Sakakida, who'd insisted Yamagata be given his seat because he didn't feel very sure of someone who worked for the Japanese diplomatic service, someone whose Japanese-national wife had been shipped home to Japan just before war started, stayed behind on Corregidor to surrender and carry out secret specific orders he'd been given. He needn't have worried about Yamagata. Clarence was released from the U.S. Army in 1948 with the rank of Major, and had a Legion of Merit for work he'd done during the war. The author feels that Yamagata could have secretly been recruited before the war. Many men were, whose roles still have not been revealed. As for Sakakida himself, he would survive torture and confound his Japanese captors. His story appears later in these pages. Sakakida put his life on the line daily throughout the war, and many have made a greater single contribution to the Pacific victory than any man, of any race.

* * *

All told, 137 AJA's, 23 Caucasians, and 1 Chinese-American completed successfully the course that began at Camp Savage on May 28, 1942. The Japanese-fluent Chinese-American was Won Loy Chan, who could not possibly avoid the nickname Charlie.

The Japanese made a thrust at Port Moresby in May, from the sea, but Adm. Chester Nimitz knew their intentions on April 17, perhaps because of what Churchill might have given or told Roosevelt four months earlier. An American task force was able to decimate Japanese carrier air strength in a Coral Sea battle, marking the first time a Japanese thrust was turned back, and winning the hearts of Australians forever. The "Diggers" annually celebrate Coral Sea Week.

Chester Nimitz then set about to do another number on the Japanese. By May 24 he knew in minute detail their plans for another thrust, this time in the mid-Pacific. They intended to take Midway Island, which the U.S. could not allow, and thus draw out the remains of the U.S. Fleet for a showdown fight. Nimitz had to set up an ambush, the only way he could defeat Admiral Isoroku Yamamoto's vast armada.

At Pearl Harbor, in the headquarters of the Army and Navy, heads got worriedly scratched. A major conflict was pending, less than 2000 miles away. What about Hawaii's Japanese? How would they react? What would they do? On January 17, without explanation or warning, 317 Nisei had been discharged from the Hawaii National Guard. For months thereafter, they and others had clamored for a chance to serve, to prove their loyalty, but how were they feeling now? As late as March 11, the Chiefs of Staff had seriously recommended to Roosevelt the removal of 100,000 Japanese-Americans from the islands, and the idea was rejected only because not enough ships were available. A week later, the War Relocation Authority had been created. It would have been the "legal custodian" of 200,000 AJA's if the Chiefs of Staff had gotten their way. Had word of this secret planning leaked out? If so, anything could happen.

In the end, only one evacuation idea concerning Hawaii's AJA's got approved.

The battle of Midway opened on June 4, 1942. Before then all Nisei GI's had been pulled back into Schofield Barracks from the outer islands and from Oahu's beach defenses. Yukitaka Mizutari, Yoshio Morita, Roy Nakada, Harold Nishimura and many others who would later become MIS'ers had their arms taken away from them. They were told they were being reorganized into a "special Battalion," a lie that fooled no one because their numbers far exceeded a battalion's strength. On June 5, while the Battle of Midway still raged, 1404 Nisei soldiers, stripped of weapons, were spirited off Oahu in the Army transport *Maui.* George Fujikawa, Howard Hiroki, Bob Honda and Eddie Mitsukado were just a few of those filled with apprehension when not naked fear. Just what the hell was going on?

The American public was given a number of versions of this event. All were lies. When the 100th Infantry Battalion covered itself with glory in Europe, America was told that Nisei had left Hawaii expressly to train for Europe. Not true. No official plan existed, in June of 1942, for forming an all-Nisei outfit for Europe. Every American hope of victory at Midway hung upon catching the Japanese carrier task force by surprise, upon bushwhacking it from the flank at its most exposed moment. If that could be swung, victory was possible. If it couldn't, defeat was certain. There'd be no way of preventing Adm. Yamamoto's steaming his ships right into Pearl Harbor's entrance. So long as nervous admirals and generals considered that a possibility, no matter how remote, it was inconceivable that 1400 armed and trained "Japs" be allowed free run of Oahu.

The Hawaiian Provisional Battalion, later designated the 100th Infantry Battalion, then nicknamed "One Puka Puka," and finally hailed as "The Purple Heart Battalion" for earning in combat 1703 of the medals with George Washington's profile on them was, purely and simply, shanghai'd.

Chapter 3

Until an arrogant Matthew C. Perry, USN, tore open its doors on July 8, 1853, Japan was a nation entire of itself. By the time the first Japanese diplomatic delegation arrived in Washington seven years later, astute American financiers had already raped the native Oriental country of its gold. This helped Japan catch on more quickly to the wily Occidentals than other nations that had been "helped" by the West. Although it previously had no direct contact with the U.S., Japan's scholars were extremely-knowledgeable about this young country. They knew well what Perry's anchoring his ships in Tokyo (then Edo) Bay augured.

The shogunate, a system under which a "barbarian-conquering chieftain" who was charged with defending against invasion actually did all the ruling while a succession of Japanese emperors lived in stately seclusion, was overthrown in 1868. The young emperor Mutsuhito, known to all Japanese by the name of his reign, Meiji, took the throne. Japan's best and brightest men were then identified, and dispatched to all corners of the world. Their mission—bring back as quickly as possible everything of use to Japan, so it could be put to use before "concerned" foreigners took over Japan's sovereignty as they had China's.

The exporting of brains to import ideas was a smash success. In one generation, Japan vaulted out of the Middle Ages into modern times. Within 20 years she had an iron-clad Navy, and 10 years later she handed the white race its first defeat at the hands of a colored one, in the Russo-Japanese war. Peasants had been allowed to serve in her army, which was no longer limited to traditional warriors *(samurai),* and divisions provided by each prefecture vied for praise and reputation. Japan established May 5 as her Navy Day, commemorating Adm. Heihachiro Togo's crushing of the Russian fleet at Tsushima Strait in 1905. Pres. Theodore Roosevelt, whose own birthday would become Navy Day in America, rushed to help make peace. The little Oriental country was exhausting her meager resources and, should the conflict continue, Russia would end up dominating the Far East. The U.S. could not allow that. Roosevelt spoke softly and carried a big stick. He got the Nobel Prize for arranging peace. To that time, America and Japan had little contact with each other.

* * *

There is evidence that Japanese seamen may have washed up in Hawaii as much as 700 years ago, but the first "official" immigrants didn't arrive until June 19, 1868. These 163 souls were rushed out of Yokohama in the British ship *Scioto* when the Tokyo government revoked their passports. White sugar planters in Hawaii couldn't keep native Hawaiians working, and tried other races without success. They had turned to the Japanese as possibly more pliable.

Those first 163 became known as *gannen-mono* (1868-'ers). To be related to one ranks, in Hawaii, with being a DAR member elsewhere. They settled quickly in the Kingdom of Hawaii to work out their three-year labor contracts and return to Japan. With what they hoped to save, they planned to live in comfort.

That dream died a'borning. Japanese laborers got treated in Hawaii as Negro slaves did in the South. They got whipped, driven and beaten, their rights as human beings totally ignored. What whites didn't know, however, was that they were dealing with a different breed of cat here. These were not humble Chinese. These were the

Minoru Hara and George Hayashida (left, above) enroute to Leyte invasion. Tunejiro Tanaka's wedding picture. Bride processed through Angel Island, as did Nisei enroute to war. Aleutians campaign veterans (l-r) George Tsukichi, Mitsuo Shibata (KIA, Ie Shima), and Yoshio Morita. Below right John Burden (r) gives intelligence info to combat commander during battle for Guadalcanal.

proud sons of Nippon, whose leader was directly descended from the sun-goddess Amaterasu. They had *Yamato damashii* ("Japanese spirit"). Although they knew that at times a man must endure the unendurable until things could be changed, they also knew their own race. Word of their protests got back to the Meiji government. Immigration was halted, the supply of sugar cane workers cut off. This brought Hawaii to heel. After much diplomatic discussion, 40 of the *gannen-mono* opted for return to Japan. They then told their joint horror story, and no more official migrations were made until February 8, 1885. A new treaty had by then been negotiated, and on that date 859 new immigrants disembarked at Honolulu. Immigration then continued steadily for the next 40 years. Few voices were raised, as compared with a great many in California, against it.

Reflecting the curiosity that might be more peculiar to Japanese than other peoples, some immigrants began to by-pass Hawaii, heading straight for the U.S. They'd heard tales of Chinese making fortunes helping to build a railroad. In 1898, America won what has been written of as "Mr. Hearst's War," with Spain. It picked up Guam, and annexed Hawaii, thrusting itself into the Pacific, a move that made a lot more countries than Japan nervous. One result of the annexation was that many Japanese automatically became U.S. citizens. They'd had the foresight to become citizens of the Hawaiian kingdom, and were able to transfer this status with annexation.

Japanese soon began making their mark among mainlanders, who didn't like it. Kinji Ushijima drained land no one wanted, hand-tended it, and started on his way to become "The Potato King" of California. Japanese took opportunities to serve their new land, as well. Among men who went down in 1898 on the battleship *Maine* in Havana, precipitating the Spanish-American war, were seven Issei. (The U.S. Navy in those days had to fill its ranks mostly with foreigners, native-borns getting a special bonus to serve in it.) George Kakuji Hayashi in 1914 spent the enormous sum of $2000 to become a pilot.

Though not a citizen, he later flew combat missions in France, wearing America's uniform. With others, Hayashi founded an American Legion Post later, in Los Angeles.

Issei had a tradition for observing the law, but also of knowing both sides of it. While learning what was expected of them, they made a practice of learning as well what they might expect. So it was they found out about the Constitution's conferring automatic citizenship on every person born in the U.S. or its territories. They also learned that color bars had been removed from the 14th Amendment. Ignoring the jeers of fellow immigrants, a goodly number enlisted in the 1914-18 war, to show their loyalty. A 1935 law would give them citizenship for having done this.

Nothing other than envy, hate and greed emerge as grounds for the widespread antipathy shown toward Japanese in California and nearby States. During the first year of the 20th century the Japanese population in California more than doubled, moving past 20,000, and alarm spread. Before long the *San Francisco Chronicle* ran a year-long series on inflammatory articles about the "Japanese invasion." It did not improve feelings any when Adm. Togo's ships shattered a Russian fleet in 45 minutes. This Japanese success militated against Japanese-Americans. The stoic Issei tried to remain stoic. When an earthquake shattered San Francisco, 30,000 persons formally applied for aid. Not one was Japanese. AJA's remained self-reliant.

But Japanese knew how to petition, when aroused. When San Francisco's school board ordered that 93 Japanese kids (out of a 25,000 school population) be isolated in one school, the shock waves reached Tokyo, then Washington. An infuriated Teddy Roosevelt raised hell about Californians troubling the international waters. The school order was withdrawn.

Prejudice became more subtle after that, with great energy going into American efforts to "make it legal." In 1908 the State Department, pressured, got the Japanese government to make a "gentleman's agreement" under which no more passports would be given to laborers wishing to migrate to the U.S. About this time the first "picture brides" began arriving. They were spouses selected from photographs exchanged, after go-betweens in Japan acted for Issei in America.

* * *

Hawaii tolerated better the Japanese, most of whom seemed content to settle on the plantations, work hard, and raise a crop of shiny-faced kids in the sunshine. Mainland Japanese were another matter. No labor contracts for them. By 1910, because they were willing to do "stoop labor" Caucasians disdained, and because they tended all land as lovingly as they had Japan's hardy soil, Japanese were producing 70% of California's strawberries, and making inroads on other crops. So, Californians came up with their Alien Land Act in 1913. It forbade Issei buying any land. Five other States, equally jealous, were to follow suit.

The Orientals proved to be wily. They read the law carefully, then proceeded to purchase land *in the names of their children.* Born on U.S. soil, the Nisei were *not* aliens.

The battle raged on, sometimes openly, sometimes secretly. Pres. Woodrow Wilson vetoed in 1915 a bigot-inspired immigration law that would have required a literacy test. Wilson knew the South had been using that device for decades, to bar Negroes from voting. America went to war in 1916, and the raucous rabble had to shut up. Japan had joined the Allies. It wouldn't look good, to be rude to an ally. Another "gentleman's agreement" was worked out in 1917, but this one favored Japan for a change. The U.S. recognized her "rights to hegemony" in China. (Translation—"Feel free to push your neighbor around, without us interfering.")

Once the war was over, and Japan's friendship no longer needed, old attitudes were re-adopted. Japan, in 1920, was pressured into stopping the migration of picture brides. In 1921, U.S. immigration quotas were set to 3% of each nationality as reported in the 1910 census. This radically reduced Japan's quota, while it bothered European nations' hardly at all. So many draft-dodgers had fled Europe early in the century that their countries' counts were well up. Most doors to America were now slammed shut against Japanese. No one anywhere could doubt that a campaign against them alone had been, and was continuing to be, waged.

A code-cracker, Herbert O. Yardley, made it possible for America to eavesdrop on Japan's most secret transmitted instructions to her delegation in Washington during negotiations for a naval disarmament treaty, and thus learn of Tokyo's diplomatic anxieties. Result—another put-down for the yellow race. Japan was coerced into accepting secondary naval status in the Far East, after two decades of supremacy there. She signed the "5-5-3" treaty, which limited her battleship tonnage to 60% of that Great Britain and the U.S. were each allowed. During that same year, 1922, the U.S. Supreme Court denied naturalization to Takeo Ozawa, claiming he was "neither black nor white," and so not qualified. Thus was an 1870 law subverted, to keep California Caucasian.

There was one warm-hearted surge of goodwill. On September 1, 1923, a great earthquake shook the Kanto Plain, devastating Tokyo and Yokohama. An outpouring of goods, money and medical assistance gushed out of West Coast ports toward Tokyo Bay. A relic of that wonderful episode is still visible. American medics, in 1923, wore gauze face masks as a defense against disease. Japanese adopted the idea. Millions can be seen wearing them in Tokyo all winter, hoping to ward off the flu and pneumonia.

Tokyo hardly stopped vibrating before Japanophobes struck their final bitter blow. On March 15, 1924, all further immigration from Japan to the U.S. was stopped by law. No Issei could sponsor a relative for entry, although aliens of other nationalities might. Had Japan any huddled masses, yearning to breathe free, Miss Liberty's torch did not shine for them. With this one final coffin nail, any possibility of improving relations between Japan and America was entombed. As if that weren't enough, the corpse was given a kick. From 1924 on, all American-Japanese traveling between Hawaii and the mainland had to carry a card proving they were natives of Hawaii. Harold Hanaumi went to get such a card in 1940, and found that his and many other births were not registered. Fees entrusted to a messenger in the outer islands by midwives who birthed many children had been pocketed by an emissary instead of paid over to Honolulu. Harold's brothers and sisters, whose births *had* been registered, were required to provide affidavits "swearing that I was born in Hawaii, too." Civil servants, as arrogant in the Forties as they still are, dragged their feet issuing Hanaumi's card, but finally did on learning his parents hadn't gone anywhere since getting off the sixth ship bringing contract laborers from Japan. On what the couple were paid, they couldn't have.

In 200 years, America has not inflicted such an indignity on any of its citizens except those of Japanese ancestry. Other than during wartime emergency, all other races have been free to exercise their Constitutional right to move about their land without hindrance.

The two decades prior to the Pearl Harbor attack were the most painful ones for Issei. America had truly dashed their hopes. What would it do to their children's? Issei who'd achieved some material success returned to Japan, but few met happiness there. They themselves were aliens in their own homeland. Other Issei, despairing of ever achieving retirement to Japan, scraped together money and sent children there for education, and rearing by relatives. They thought this would give Nisei an option—choice of either culture.

That didn't work, either. A rejected, resentful Japan had become imbued with an expansionist and martial spirit, which certain leaders were able to whip up by distorting the meaning of two respected Japanese phrases

—*bushi do* ("the warrior's way"), and *Yamato damashii* ("the spirit of Japan"). The citizenry was adeptly manipulated and maneuvered, with Nisei suffering as a result. Native Japanese considered them Americans, and enemies. Nisei were given a hard time at school by other kids, and often made the butt of *sensei* jokes. Few could adjust to this. Most watched for their chance to escape back to America. The result was some weird educational and maturation patterns.

Hiroshi Tanabe completed a business high school course in Kobe. When he was able to get back to the U.S., he had to re-commence his education at Grade 9 level. Jim Matsumura, another Kibei, was 24 by the time he finished public high school. Henry Gosho suffered less than most "because my brother and I tried to act as 'Japanese' as possible in school. That spared us a lot."

Joe Akiyama, Ben Kawahata, Frank Hachiya, Harry Kubo, Hughes Tsuneishi, Grant Hirabayashi and Kazuo Yamane also survived a varied gamut of emotions and experiences as Kibei. Some knew what it was to become a "schoolboy," a special employment in California under which a returning youngster hired out just for room and board. He performed every task a Caucasian family asked of him, while he completed his American education. In 1942, these men and many others began applying their Japan-acquired educations against the land where they'd obtained them.

* * *

Despite the tons of glowing prose written about Japanese-Americans and their 1941-45 experiences, not all were reverent, thrifty, clean and obedient. Nor were all chafing at the bit, just raring to get at America's enemies. Most had to operate under a cloud of suspicion even when their intentions were totally open, obvious and honest. This cloud did not dissipate until long after victory was won. Many Nisei resented it. Some still do.

Among Caucasians who started in the first Camp Savage class was Sheldon Covell. "We were told," he said, "that our principal mission was to learn sufficient Japanese so that we could be sure the Nisei were translating, interrogating and reporting accurately, and not deceiving our intelligence people with false information." Covell hastened to add that he noticed no such activity on the part of Nisei during his service, "but that is what we were trained to detect." Lachlan Sinclair, a classmate of Covell's, suggested to the author that he *not* tell readers that all Nisei were loyal. He pointed out that, just as Americans served on both sides in our Civil War, there were Nisei on both sides in the 1941-45 war. "To gloss over this fact," wrote Sinclair, "is unfair to the 'Yankee *Samurai*' in your story who chose loyalty to America in the face of ridicule, scorn and hatred from those who picked Japan as the winner." Sinclair was privy to top secrets, and should know what he was talking about. So should John Anderton, who "encountered but one suspicious instance while working with 700-800 Nisei in Australia." Anderton handled the situation by ordering the man to a forward unit, along with secret instructions to "have him die in combat if anything suspicious happened." Nothing did. The man survived the war. Anderton decided that he might have been wrong, and kept the man's name secret to his grave.

Nor did every Nisei step smartly from the front rank, salute, and offer to lay down his life. Tetsuo Hayashida refused selection to the original, Presidio, class, being quite content in a medical battalion. Menial work at Camp Walters, Texas, where he and hundreds of other Nisei had been shanghai'd from their regular units, he found humiliating. Hayashida was ordered, not asked, to take language training at Savage. So was Kazuhiko Yamada, known better as "Rocky." He'd been ordered in from Ft. Custer, Michigan. Hiroshi Tanabe got orders, too, from Ft. Reilly, Kansas, where he'd been cleaning latrines. Tanabe scrubbed human excrement from Camp Savage floors, too, the derelicts who were the previous residents having declined to use the toilet bowls.

George Hayashida's family voluntarily moved from

Los Angeles to Colorado. He found Camp Savage depressing. So did Arthur Castle, who slept in a warehouse on arrival, then stuffed mattresses so he and others would have something to sleep on. Terry Takahashi felt he'd been conned into Savage by Joseph K. Dickey, an officer assistant of Rasmussen's. Terry's stepfather died while living in a horse stall at Tanforan racetrack. "Dickey painted a rosy picture," he said, "saying it would be like going to West Point. I got the impression I'd be part of an elite program, and that all graduates would get commissions."

Takahashi had to be persuaded to accept language school, but he knew he wasn't really qualified. "My Japanese," he said, was *awful!* Only George Tsukichi spoke worse Japanese than I did!" Tsukichi came from Cheyenne, and there were few Japanese to converse with in Wyoming, while Terry had grown up in a "non-Japanese" section of San Francisco. He'd seen little of Japan Town in that city until his father died, and in fact through high school and college had pronounced his name with every "a" harshly-flat. They usually get a soft voicing by AJA's.

Dye Ogata probably had less reason than anyone for coming to Savage. His father, Rinzo Ogata, had served the Northern Pacific Railroad faithfully, without promotion, for 20 years. Then, 11 days after war began, Rinzo was handed a terse note that read "Your services will be dispensed with until further notice. You are also advised to stay in your quarters." Dye had an idea how desperate the Japanese in Japan were. While he was studying there, he'd seen concrete manhole covers take the place of iron ones, so the latter could be melted down for the metal after the U.S. cut off ore exports.

Mike Sakamoto was open about his sentiments. An anti-Japanese sergeant, who'd served in prewar Hawaii, confiscated Mike's rifle at Camp Roberts right after war broke out. Reliving his hurt 36 years later, Mike said, "If it had any bullets in it, I'd have shot him!" Mike turned down Capt. Dickey at Ft. Sill, his third refusal in a year. "Screw 'em!" Mike thought, "Why should I volunteer, after the way I've been treated?" He got orders anyway, and retaliated the only way he could, by scoring dismally on the preliminary test. "I was able to get into Class 18, of 22 classes!" he said exultantly. "It was a country club!" Class 1 was tops, and Class 18 was designed for people with little knowledge of Japanese. Sakamoto was not popular with John Aiso or Kai Rasmussen, but that suited him just fine.

Joe Yoshiwara adjusted, but it wasn't easy. While at Camp Walters, he saw Caucasian girls who talked to him to get arrested as "vagrants" by deputy sheriffs. Things only got better when a representative of the Inspector-General, the Army's "ombudsman," came out from Washington to look into things. At Savage, Joe scrubbed floors and whitewashed walls, all the while listening to threats of what might happen to his family if he did not apply himself to his studies.

* * *

Across the Pacific, the two "spies" from Hawaii were not faring too well. Arthur Komori reached Australia, and there wrote an excellent report on how to deal with Japanese POW's. He was, at the moment, the only Nisei in use with any experience at it. The "kindness and understanding" approach was used on Japanese POW's, as Komori recommended, and it reaped vast intelligence dividends in the war. A bandage, some medicine, a drink of water and a cigarette was all it usually took to get one of Hirohito's subjects talking.

Charles Willoughby, chief of intelligence for MacArthur, had no spot for Komori when he reached Australia. In spite of war, things were still being run "Old Army." There was no provision in the headquarters structure for a sergeant who spoke Japanese. Komori was made a driver.

Komori shrugged, muttered *"Shikata ga nai"* (It can't be helped), as Japanese do when facing the inevitable, and adjusted to idle living. Duties were light, and he got per diem, an extra $120 per month, over and above his NCO pay. It was heaven. Komori began enjoying it, and in fact soon fell in love.

For Richard Sakakida it was a slightly different story. Named Motoso, a contraction of his father's and grandfather's names, Dick needed all the "strength of faith" that could inspire in him. On Corregidor, his first translation job was interrupted by an air attack, and he thought "My ancestors must be damned mad at me, for translating their language!" Sakakida alternated with Komori on Bataan's front lines, usually in 3-day stints. "Cherry blossom time is approaching in Japan," he broadcast via loudspeaker to enemy infantrymen. "Why are you here fighting, when only warlords profit from this useless struggle?" Dick also wrote propaganda bulletins that were reproduced in quantity, then stuffed into pieces of pipe and hurled from giant slingshots into Japanese lines. Asked what kind of response he got, Sakakida grinned and said "More shells!"

About 300 Japanese prisoners were taken on Bataan. Sakakida, wearing his uniform and chevrons, helped interrogate them, and became first Nisei in the war to have a direct effect on the fighting because of his language ability. When he translated a captured set of Japanese plans for a landing, American tanks moved up and ambushed the attackers when they arrived.

Sakakida knew it was a disgrace for a Japanese soldier to be captured, and became aware that many gave false names for fear their real ones would get back to Japan. But he did have captured personnel rosters, and also collected "dogtags" that were sewn into enlisted men's belts. During the first day of interrogation Sakakida'd pretend to accept whatever was told him, and that night he'd check everything against gathered proven knowledge. Next day he'd go back, confront POW's with their lies, and charge them with having no honor, no *Yamato damashii.* This usually broke down all resistance. "After that," Sakakida said, "they'd spill their guts." This surprised Caucasian Americans, but not Nisei who knew Japan. "Japanese soldiers were indoctrinated to fight to the death," MIS'ers told the author, "so when they were captured alive they didn't know what to do about living. And, because they were expected to fight until death, they'd had no security training. Hardly any were security-conscious at all. To them it was O.K. to talk, because one life had ended and they'd started a new one. It just never occurred to them, at least early in the war, that they might someday return to Japan after being captured."

At command posts, Sakakida watched the number of red pins that denoted enemy lines increase, while blue ones denoting his own decreased. In March he was ordered to Corregidor for the last time, and given a code-breaking assignment, work he'd never done before. Still, working with a colonel and a U.S. embassy employee who was a Reservist, Sakakida had some success with the Japanese 4-digit code. He was starting to put it into book form for others to use, when orders came to get off The Rock and head for Australia.

Sakakida insisted on giving his seat to Clarence Yamagata, and himself stayed behind to surrender with Gen. Jonathan Wainwright. He accompanied the general's chief of staff to Bataan when time came to discuss surrender terms, and was beaten by a Japanese NCO, eye glasses cutting his face in the melee. Sakakida played no further role, the Japanese insisting that their own man interpret for the proceedings. He returned to Corregidor, got rid of his uniform, and pretended to surrender as a civilian, like he'd been told to do.

In Bilibid Prison, where the 21-year-old Hawaii Japanese got taken, an officer shouted "You are Sergeant Richard Sakakida, of the United States Army! Two of our men have identified you. You interrogated them, and you were wearing a U.S. Army uniform at the time!"

Sakakida denied that status, insisting he was a civilian. He repeated the cover story he'd been using for more than a year—that he was a draft-dodging merchant seaman who jumped ship in Manila. "I had no other

John Weckerling started it all, with only six weeks for getting staff, space, students and supplies together. He went on to top job in Washington intelligence, a station from which he could learn how his men were performing.

clothing," he told captors, explaining away the uniform. "I was not allowed to return to my hotel, once the war started." He further insisted that the U.S. Army forced him to work as an interpreter against his will, lending him clothing needed.

Captors bought Sakakida's story, but not for long at a time. They tied his arms behind him and strung him up, a rope over a rafter hauled on until his shoulders gave off loud cracking noises as they were dislocated. Sakakida held on, repeating and repeating his story, while at the same time hoping people on Corregidor had burned his Reserve commission recommendation. It was locked in an intelligence office safe on The Rock.

Because Gen. Masaharu Homma, against the wishes of other senior Japanese officers, wanted to keep the Philippines peaceful as possible, Sakakida was not shot. He was kept imprisoned for nine months, several times being charged with new offenses, with the charges always laid aside. On one occasion Sakakida sat three days before a military tribunal without any trial going on, while they discussed whether or not to just shoot him as a traitor under a law that held all people of Japanese blood to be Japanese citizens, no matter where and when born. Until February 11, 1943, when he was conditionally released (probably because it was a Japanese holiday, the 2603rd anniversary of ascension to the throne by Jimmu, Japan's first emperor), Sakakida did not know from one second to another whether he was going to live or die.

* * *

Yoshikazu Yamada, although not a MIS'er, was doing language work in Australia before any MIS'ers got to do any. An Army medic at Del Monte, a secret air base on a pineapple plantation in the Philippines that B-17's used until the Japanese discovered it, he'd been evacuated to Australia on a stretcher, and put to work after hospitalization when it was learned he knew Japanese. Yamada went into the Allied air forces intelligence section, where for a good while he was the only American. All other members were Australian.

Nisei who arrived in Australia with David Swift kind of milled around. They got to Brisbane on June 20, and left two days later to join MacArthur's staff at Melbourne. They were there when Chiefs of Staff, informed of Japan's intent to isolate Australia, decided to take an island called Guadalcanal, where the enemy had been spotted building an airfield.

The U.S. Navy stayed bitter for many years about how it had been so decisively humbled by the Japanese Navy. It is therefore understandable that Army people in Australia had no idea what to do with the 8 Nisei who reported to Melbourne. How could Australians who fled Malaya before the Japanese, or Americans who fled the Philippines before them, trust anyone with slanted eyes? So, for a while, their leader having gotten ill, the Presidio Nisei were idle.

Then someone came up with an idea. The Indies, Malaya and Burma had fallen. Why not train these Orientals from America in Dutch-Malayan, then parachute them behind Japanese lines? Zany as it was, the idea got official approval. And, willing enough to try anything that would demonstrate their loyalty, the 8 Nisei went along. The idea of getting $4 per diem, like Arthur Komori, might also have been some inspiration.

Two other Nisei might have been working at what they'd been trained for, but the Army had goofed. Masanori Minamoto, who'd been sent out early, ended up at Tonga Tabu, where there wasn't any activity at all except for the aircraft carrier *Yorktown's* pulling in there to lick her wounds after the Coral Sea battle. Minamoto was put to work driving a truck. As for Kei Kiyoshi Sakamoto, another Presidio grad sent out alone, he rode a Navy transport to—of all places—Bora Bora. An islet in French Oceania, not far from Tahiti, so breathtakingly beautiful that it still fulfills the fantasies of anyone dreaming of balmy breezes and lissome lasses, Bora Bora was far from any battle scene. Sakamoto joined up with Task

Force Bobcat, the 102nd Infantry Regiment of the Connecticut National Guard and a coastal artillery unit. They protected beautiful Tahitian girls from potential invaders.

* * *

It took a while for Allies in the Pacific to steady up, they reeled so from Japan's onslaught. On March 7 Alexander Patch arrived in New Caledonia, there to await what would later become—via a name-selection contest among its troops—the Americal Division. Until then the men from Massachusetts, Illinois and North Dakota were Task Force 6814, dispatched to protect the island from invasion.

Australia was in a state of near-panic when MacArthur arrived. It had only one division, its 1st Armored, plus some militia to protect it. The 8th was lost in the fall of Singapore. The 6th, 7th and 9th were fighting in Africa. Troops in the homeland had been drawn in to defend the industrial centers and food supplies around Brisbane, Melbourne and Sydney. Darwin, her northernmost city, was evacuated on February 20 after an attack by Japanese carrier planes on February 19. Australia was preparing to yield the northern third of her total area to the Japanese, before stiffening in defense along a line that ran east-to-west from Townsville. The 6th and 7th, due home soon, would be deployed in a defensive posture, too.

MacArthur changed all that. On St. Patrick's Day, from Alice Springs in the middle of Australia's great desert, he made his famous "I shall return" statement. Shortly thereafter, he was shocked to learn that he had nothing in Australia to return *with.* But MacArthur had guts, and a flair for the dramatic. The Japanese after the war came to believe he had a common ancestry with them. He did not, but he certainly was full of the *bushido* spirit, having an instinctive feel for "the way of the warrior." With a few words MacArthur eliminated the Townsville Line, and ordered every square foot of Australia to be defended. Soon after that, troops began arriving from the Middle East, and America. The first needed rest, the second training, before MacArthur could use any of them. Meanwhile, the 1st Armored was sent to the Northern Territory, with orders to hold it. A member later told the author that his unit got the nickname Koala because (like the "Teddy Bear") "we were protected against export and no one was allowed to shoot us." As a force-in-being, the armored division did not have to fight but they kept the enemy away. Australia was not invaded.

Language-trained Nisei were to become MacArthur's second secret weapon. He already had one—a code-breaking crew like the Navy one at Pearl Harbor. He, like Nimitz, was "reading Tojo's mail," and learned in advance of Japan's plan to take Port Moresby. It didn't take much figuring to recognize that other logical targets were New Caledonia, Samoa and the Fijis, if Australia was to be isolated.

May was a momentous month. Mandalay fell. The British fled Burma for India. The Japanese took Tulagi, a small island near the south end of the Solomons chain, northeast of Australia, and began establishing a seaplane base there. American carrier pilots took a toll of Japanese ones in the Battle of the Coral Sea. More than 16,000 shells rained down on Corregidor in one day, and 48 hours later it fell. The final combat of the Philippines took place, and the Japanese had 83,000 more prisoners-of-war. The first evacuees from the U.S. west coast reached the Gila River, Arizona, concentration camp, and a short while later learned what the U.S. government planned to pay them—$19 per month, tops—for any work done while imprisoned. The 32nd Division, with which many Nisei would serve gallantly, arrived in Australia to join the 41st, and de-ciphering experts at Pearl Harbor broke the Imperial Navy's code. (At least, this month is given officially as the period during which it was broken, a statement the author finds hard to accept.) Initial evacuees also reached Tule Lake, a California concentration camp that was to spell trouble for the War Relocation Authority. Roy Kawashiri and other members of

Mac Nagata's team reached New Caledonia. They joined what had now become the Americal Division.

* * *

The Battle of Midway came and went. Chiefs of staff heaved joint sighs of relief. America now had elbow room, and MacArthur had three divisions. He wanted to attack and seize Rabaul, a move he recommended to Washington, along with the wry offer to use 40,000 troops the War Department had told him were available on the U.S. west coast.

The Japanese took Kiska and Attu in the Aleutians, perhaps as consolation for not having taken Midway. The first V-mail, letters reproduced in miniature after being microfilmed to save weight, went overseas from New York to Europe. Pilot Officer Tadayoshi Koga, flying a Zero in the Aleutians from an aircraft carrier, crash-landed on Akutan Island, broke his neck and died. Koga's plane was spotted a month later, taken back to the U.S., and studied. From this, the Grumman "Hellcat" was designed to be a superior aircraft, and would take its toll of other Zero's before the war ended.

While George Taketa and Gary Kadani studied Dutch-Malayan in Melbourne, their families went to concentration camps. On July 2, the Chiefs of Staff decided the Navy and Marine Corps would invade the Solomons and take Guadalcanal, while MacArthur was given orders to take the remainder of the chain, plus the northeast coast of New Guinea. Tojo's mail had been read again. MacArthur and Nimitz knew that the Japanese planned to take Port Moresby via land, since they had failed to take it by sea. A reconnaissance force was to land at Buna, on the northeast coast, and go over the Owen Stanley Mountains to Moresby. The 37th Division arrived in the Fiji Islands, so Japanese general headquarters gave up on plans to take them, or New Caledonia. Australia's lifeline was secure, but it could still be threatened from the Solomons.

Despite the setback at Midway, things still really didn't look too bad for Japan. A dent had been made in the defensive arc she had set up from the Aleutians to New Guinea, but behind it was a great network of anchorages and bases, all being strengthened. On the north shore of New Guinea she held Lae and Salamaua, barriers athwart the northwest road MacArthur would have to take back to the Philippines. Taking Moresby via transmontane attack would strengthen these holdings.

All areas between New Guinea and the China Coast were under firm Japanese control. They included the Philippines, Indonesia, Malaya, Burma, Formosa and Hong Kong, plus a host of small islands. The Indian Ocean was a Japanese fish pond, the British having been driven as far back as Madagascar.

In the central Pacific, Japan held the Marshalls, Gilberts and Carolines, and spots seized from the British like the Solomons and Bismarcks. Japan also held Wake, the Marianas, and several island outposts that served the homeland as sentries. Nearer home she held Iwo Jima and Okinawa, two bastions no invader could ignore enroute to the beating heart, Tokyo, of the Japanese empire.

So, in spite of losing four carriers and hundreds of pilots, Japan could feel relatively secure. Backed by her still-mighty Imperial Fleet, the island defense network could entrench and replenish. Top Tokyo strategists knew for sure that, once America's industry got geared up, there was no way she could be defeated. American forces could still be stymied, though, while Japan drew what strategic materials she needed from conquered areas to sustain herself, and her navy watched for a chance to defeat the American one in the "decisive battle" both countries had long planned for. Crippling America's sea arm would give U.S. citizens pause. Japan might be able to obtain a negotiated peace, one that could leave her dominant in the western Pacific, all she had really hoped to achieve by war. It was never any part of

Japan's strategy to achieve victory in the sense—subjugation of one's enemy—that most men think of it.

* * *

Both sides knew what had to be done. The Allies had to use Australia as a staging area, sending men and equipment there. The Japanese had to prevent that. So, for a while, all activity focused itself on the southwest Pacific. Japan needed to spread an air umbrella over the eastern approaches to Australia, then control these with surface and submarine forces. The Allies, on the other hand, had to prevent that, and keep supply lanes open. For either to win, air supremacy had to be obtained and kept. This issue was to be decided at an island dim, except for Australians and British, to anyone in the world but an order of Catholic missionaries—the Marists. Even their motto matched the island where they served. *Ignoti et quasi occulti* means "hidden and unknown."

The island was Guadalcanal.

Chapter 4

To the northeast of Australia lie the Bismarcks and Solomons, forming a long string of mountainous islands running northwest to southeast. At the string's upper end is New Britain. Rabaul, its capital, was seized by the Japanese in January, 1942, and rapidly developed into a key link of their defense chain. From Rabaul's excellent anchorage, warships and transports could sortie down to support any site along the 600 miles to Guadalcanal. Planes from its cluster of airfields could command the air over New Guinea, and eastern approaches to Australia. Also, troops could be staged through Rabaul to wherever they were needed, southwest to New Guinea, or southeast throughout the two island chains. Nisei linguists came to know New Georgia, Vella Lavella, Guadalcanal, and other islands in the string, although decades would pass before other Americans knew they'd known them.

Rabaul's reach was extended in May with the seizure of Tulagi, 600 miles away, and establishment of a seaplane base there. Plans then moved forward for building an airstrip on Guadalcanal, just a few miles to the south of Tulagi Island. When eavesdropping and decoding let the U.S. Chiefs of Staff know what the Japanese were up to, they at once ordered Guadalcanal to be taken, quickly, before the enemy could develop it. Thus was kicked off what the official U.S. Navy historian, perhaps in an effort to make the successful struggle more deserving of glory, labelled "Operation Shoestring." In actual fact, American forces at the outset were far more than necessary to overwhelm and eliminate the tiny Japanese garrison on Guadalcanal. Only fear of the unknown kept the campaign from ending in just a few days.

A U.S. Navy task force rounded the western end of Guadalcanal on August 7, 1942, and unloaded troops at Lunga Point. Marine Corps cymbal-clashers at once got busy, blaring the praises of leathernecks. The landing did not at all go well. Some marines claimed they were combat troops, although they hadn't done any fighting to that date, so objected to helping unload their own supplies. By evening, 11,000 of them were ashore and milling around, wondering where the enemy was. They outnumbered him 20-1, but he could not be seen to be shot at. The 500 Japanese soldiers on the island melted into the jungle once they saw the size of the American invasion force. The 1700 airstrip laborers took off with them. It would be more than six months before the island could be declared secured and free of Japanese, and at one point things would get so fouled-up for the vastly-superior American force that Pres. Roosevelt seriously considered taking his marines home.

* * *

Seventeen days before the Guadalcanal landing, Japanese forces beat Americans and Australians to the punch with a landing near Buna, on New Guinea's northeast coast. Next day they landed more troops at nearby Gona, and now had possession of flat land that could become airstrips. A counterattack by 100 Allied planes did not daunt the Emperor's men. They dug in. Buna was starting point of the Kokoda Track, which led over the mountains to Port Moresby, only 120 air miles away. An attack was planned for August 7 on a New Guinea settlement held by the Australians, but got postponed when air support for it was diverted to Guadalcanal. Reinforcements were also turned back, until the picture at Guadalcanal became clear to Rabaul authorities, but on August 7 more than 7000 Imperial Army men were ashore near Buna. It was MacArthur's job to drive them out or kill them.

The general, firing up the Australian people by personal example, moved his headquarters north to Brisbane on July 20, very near the area Australia earlier planned to let the Japanese have. Australian general Thomas Blamey was left in command of ground forces in the interests of Allied unity, but MacArthur axed his own staff unmercifully, to develop a winning team. A new air chief, George C. Kenney, was brought in. He wrote a page in Air Corps history it could be proud of. Kenney believed in fighting. His men soon did.

Herbert Leary, the admiral in charge of American naval forces in Australia, disappeared into oblivion, but this may not have been necessarily for ineptitude or lack of daring, neither of which MacArthur could tolerate. Of all that has been written about MacArthur, and his protective staff, perhaps the most pungent comment has been made by crusty Elliott Thorpe, his counterintelligence chief in Australia, the Philippines later, and Japan. "General MacArthur was a delightful man to work for." Thorpe told the author, "He never raised his voice, he never interfered, and he gave you total support. But if you blew it, you found yourself out on the street, a medal pinned on your chest, your throat cut from ear to ear, and on your way back to the States."

When MacArthur was ordered out of the Philippines, the U.S. air chief in Australia asked Admiral Leary for loan of some of the twelve B-17 Flying Fortresses that, somehow or other, had come under Navy command. Leary refused. All the air chief could send to Mindanao, the rendezvous point, were three battered B-17's that had fled the northern fighting when grossly outnumbered. They were hardly able to fly. One crashed in the sea, one had to turn back, and one landed at Del Monte in such bad shape that it couldn't be used. It was sent back, empty.

The dilatory Leary caused MacArthur to be held up for days at Mindanao. What the general said to Washington or Leary has not been released to the public, but in short order four of Leary's B-17's were at Del Monte. Not long after fighting started again, Leary left Australia as well.

In his function as top censor, Thorpe got to read the spate of hate mail "including outrageous lies!" that senior American naval officers wrote home about MacArthur. The hate might have been prompted by a combination of their being clobbered by the Japanese, whom they considered in every way inferior, plus MacArthur's frequently asking in the beleaguered Philippines when the Navy was coming to his rescue, as prewar strategy dictated. One of the more blatant canards about MacArthur that infuriated Thorpe was the claim that the general had taken loads of furniture "including a piano, for God's sake!" with him to Australia. In point of fact, the general and his family each took no more with them from Corregidor in a PT-Boat than the average passenger takes on board an airliner, about 40 pounds apiece.

While Marines landed on Guadalcanal, 464 men of Australia's militia tried to block the Japanese advance over the Owen Stanley Range to Port Moresby, by setting up defenses at the small village of Kokoda, along the mountain trail. Japanese attacked next day, and the Aussies had to retreat. By August 13, Japan had as many men in the Buna-Gona area as America did on Guadalcanal. They were set to cross the mountains and take Moresby. The Imperial Army also had orders to recapture the half-completed Guadalcanal airfield from the U.S. marines, and seize Tulagi back from them, too.

Japanese naval strength focused on Guadalcanal, sinking four Allied cruisers on the night of August 9. MacArthur sent the rested Australian 7th Division into battle, two of its brigades starting up the Kokoda Track to meet the oncoming Japanese. A third landed at Milne Bay, at the western part of a long inlet at New Guinea's east end. Milne Bay offered excellent airfield sites for whoever snatched it first, and this time the Aussies had been "fustest with the mostest." Enemies beat one

Nisei could look back from invasion front row seats on other landing craft (above). At Camp Blanding for jungle training before Pacific combat are (l-r) James Taga, Ted Nishiyama, Hiroshi Nakamura and their pal, Ralph Saito.

another, into Buna and Milne Bay respectively, by about a week. Now Australians, helped by Americans, set about conquering the northeast coast of New Guinea.

* * *

Meanwhile, a shameful folio was inserted into USMC chronicles by a unit called Carlson's Raiders, which hit a Japanese outpost on Makin Island, in the Gilberts. Disembarking from two giant mine-laying submarines, marines overwhelmed and slaughtered the small Japanese garrison, capturing books that showed Japanese were unsuspectingly still using codes that had been broken for Midway. In his retirement, a USMC general described the Makin raid as a "piece of folly" that only encouraged Japan to stiffen her defenses in that area, an action that cost the Corps a high price in dead marines at Tarawa later, but Holland M. Smith might not have known the true reason for the fierce fighting Americans encountered in the Pacific after Makin. Marines paid in blood during 1943 at Tarawa, during 1944 at Peleliu and Saipan, and in 1945 at Iwo Jima and Okinawa for what marines in 1942 had done at Makin. Carlson's Raiders, a force that included the President's son, butchered Japanese corpses, stuffing penises and testicles into mouths of the dead. Sherman Grinberg, as avid a student of that war as the author, and producer of the TV series "Battleline," got the details two decades later from a Raider who photographed his comrades' grisly work. Small wonder Japanese fought so fiercely thereafter. No man looks forward to desecration of his manhood symbol.

The Japanese still wanted Milne Bay, and put an invasion force ashore. On August 26 the Australians met it in battle. The Diggers covered themselves with glory, sharing it with a small number of Americans at their sides. The Aussies chopped the Japanese force to bits, killing one man in every three. The rest, badly battered, were pulled out by order of the Japanese 8th Fleet's commander, marking the very first time a Japanese invasion landing had been turned back by anyone.

On Guadalcanal, the fight teeter-tottered. The Ichiki Detachment, a force earlier slated for Midway, was fed onto the island from Truk in chunks, and quickly wiped out. Next came the Kawaguchi Detachment, diverted from its original New Guinea mission. Rear Adm. Raizo Tanaka, later to win fame as "engineer" of the Tokyo Express, running reinforcements down The Slot to what soon was getting called "Death Island" *(Ga Jima)* by the Japanese, advocated writing off Guadalcanal, pulling halfway back to Rabaul, and digging in at the Shortland Islands. Tanaka's opinions got him booted to a rear echelon job. The Japanese top command was determined to keep Guadalcanal, and committed itself to that. Fighter aircraft and naval support were withdrawn from New Guinea. MacArthur's airmen now controlled skies over the island, which resembles a fat lizard, tail and all, with a bird-like cranium. The northwesternmost end of New Guinea, in fact, is called Vogelkopf ("Bird's Head").

* * *

September found the Aussie attack around Buna-Gona bogged down in mud, and soaked by rain. Japanese, struggling up the Stanleys, entered Isuruva, losing to disease and starvation enroute most of their officers and senior NCO's. Fighting was tough, and carving 20,000 individual steps into the steep trail had been necessary.

That month the War Department was asked to release some Nisei temporarily from prison camps to work on farms needing harvest help, and permanently if they enrolled in schools well away from the West Coast. A national convention of the American Legion protested this. Selective Service was not far out of phase with what an Alabama governor was to call "the heroes union." It changed the draft classification of Nisei from 4-F (undesirable to 4-C (ineligible because of nationality). No more Nisei could be drafted. While this was happening, Kai Rasmussen's staff frantically beat the bushes for more language students.

The first week of that month featured one bright spot—the Japanese withdrawal by sea of its Milne assault force. This tiny victory had a significance all out of proportion to its tactical value. It gave heart to the Australians. To Americans it meant that Japanese were *not* invincible, that they could be met and defeated by men of stout heart with good weapons. Nowhere, until that time, had there been a clear-cut victory over Tojo's troops. Japanese troops were dying by the hundreds on Guadalcanal, but the issue was not at all clear there. Milne Bay, on the other hand, was an actual Japanese *retreat!* It shocked both sides.

* * *

On September 7 the special class of 12 men finished their course at Camp Savage. Graduation was held next day in front of the messhall. Chiuro Sakata and David Watanabe were held back to be instructors, their places filled by David Kato and Jim Fujimura of the original Presidio group. Four days later, Japanese coming from Buna reached Iroibaiwa Ridge, 32 miles from Port Moresby. Gen. Kenney's planes had pounded every effort to resupply them, and they were on the verge of starvation-exhaustion when the 21st and 25th Australian Brigades got into position to challenge their final effort. The Aussies went all-out, and won. On September 16, 1942, the Japanese began retreating back up over the mountains toward Buna. Nippon's troops were never to advance again in the Pacific war, from that day forward. For Hirohito's soldiers after that it was retreat, dig in, fight, and perish. Nearly every Japanese soldier to face an American gun would die under it.

American news media men seized on any morsel of good news that developed or could be created. They needed all they could gather. On September 9, 1942, a submarine-launched aircraft piloted by Nobuo Fujita flew over Oregon's forest and dropped fire bombs. The West Coast again panicked. Writers did what they could to puff up heroism stories from Guadalcanal, but the facts were that fighting there was not heroic. It was dirty, rotten, and sickening for men of both sides, few of whom ever got a clear look at their enemy. Cong. Homer D. Angell helped feed the California panic with a House floor prediction of an all-out Japanese attack on America's west coast. As Angell spoke, 19,000 marines faced 5000 Japanese on Guadalcanal who were mostly sick and starving. A week later, Fujita again firebombed Oregon.

On September 19, a novel unit of MacArthur's command was inaugurated. This was the Allied Translator and Interpreter Service (ATIS) which had nearly as many words in its title as it had staff members. Eight graduates of the Presidio, plus Arthur Komori and Yoshikazu Yamada, joined the group under a recovering David Swift, who had been ill. One of the first documents translated by them was a diary taken from a dead Japanese officer on New Guinea. It told a tale of malaria, diarrhea, and lack of medical supplies, plus having to fight for 16 days on 8 days of rations. When the Aussies took Iroibaiwa, furthest point of the Japanese advance, with bayonets and hand grenades they were puzzled to find many dead bodies without any indication of wounds. Autopsies were performed. Starving, the Japanese had eaten poison fruits and roots. New Guinea was not a convenient place to fight a war.

In Brisbane, Arthur Komori became first Nisei to be done out of a deserved commendation. He'd been recommended for the Purple Heart, a medal inaugurated during America's early days, for gallantry. The recommendation came back down, denied. Komori was told Washington had changed its policy on the Purple Heart Medal. It was to be given only to men who got wounded.

* * *

Besides the special, hurry-up class of 12 linguists from Savage, another 6 were snatched out in mid-course and led to New Caledonia by Frederick P. Munson, arriving on Christmas Eve. They were Tetsuo Hayashida, Hiroshi Matsuda, Makoto Sakamoto, Terno Odow, Joe Yoshiwara and Roy Uyehata. Hayashida, because he'd been a medical technician earlier, was made a "doctor" enroute. The rest alternated with a 6-man Navy gun crew on watches. Sam Fujimura might have been with the sextet, but he'd been yanked from school because his father had chosen repatriation to Japan on the Swedish liner *Gripsholm,* the ship that brought Munson and others back from Japan. They'd been trapped there at war's outbreak, before Munson completed his language studies.

Fujimura was only one Nisei under suspicion. Many months after arriving in New Caledonia, after having worked on hundreds of high-security documents, Tetsuo Hayashida was walked out into the boondocks by Munson and grilled about a remark he'd made *while taking a shower back at Camp Savage!* The author has difficulty understanding how so many Nisei did so much good work under such clouds.

* * *

The 37th Division, from Ohio, arrived during June in the Fijis to defend them from invasion. John Burden and the Kubo brothers joined it there, but found no language work to be done at Suva. Burden was given charge of 10 counterintelligence specialists who until then had no officer.

The Maui medic was quite a character. He was an *Edoko,* "a child of Edo," the Japanese expression for anyone born in Tokyo. Burden grew up in the Shinjuku and Yoyogi areas, and could send Tokyoites into gales of laughter by telling how those were "out in the country" when he was a boy. His printer-publisher father gave John a steamship ticket to the U.S. and a $50 goldpiece when he was 16, saying "Go get yourself an education." Burden did, washing dishes, operating elevators, and working as an X-ray technician with a medical unit in Colorado while Boulder Dam was being built. He was 36 before he became a doctor, "but had a lot of fun along the way." Burden, married by then, joined the Army Reserve when a friend mentioned there were two weeks' summer training and

$125 in the deal. His intern's pay was then $9.13 a month, and he was really too old to qualify for a commission, but when Burden mentioned his language ability all barriers were dropped. The Army got another indifferent Reservist.

Burden liked being where the action was, and staying busy. He nailed a couple of enemy agents in Suva, one an Englishwoman working for the Nazis. The other was an American male. Burden never was totally convinced the man was guilty, but shipped him off the island anyhow. It was quite a switch, from plantation doctor on Maui to counterspy in the Fijis. Burden loved it. He would not practice medicine again for another five years, but would cross the Pacific four times and see China.

Commanding the 37th was Robert S. Beightler, the only National Guard general to lead his division into combat, and a stickler for reports. When Burden, volunteering to inspect camouflaged gun positions from the air, signed a report, Beightler read it and made him camouflage officer. This gave John use of a Piper Cub and the general's aviation aide. The pilot was totally bored by his assignment, and whiled away time by teaching Burden to fly. His name was Thomas Lanphier. He was not to stay bored for long.

* * *

David Swift had lived in China and Japan. His spoken Japanese was excellent, his written less than fair. He and Burden had expected extra training, especially in *heigo* (military Japanese) when they finished at the Presidio, but this was not to be. They shipped out in the *SS Uruguay,* Swift continuing on to Australia when Burden turned at Auckland to head for the Fijis. Underway from San Francisco, the two got yellow fever shots. Swift, just ahead of Burden in line, reacted to his. On arrival in Australia he was hospitalized for weeks, leaving eight enlisted men adrift and leaderless, hence their being assigned to study Dutch-Malayan. The Japanese-Dutch Malayan dictionaries they were starting were scrapped when they left to form ATIS, except for a souvenir copy Gary Kadani filched.

Linguists continued to flow into the Pacific. Some even got to put their skills to work. Shigeo Ito went to Alaska. So did Mas Imon, Ben Moriwaki and Roy Ashizawa. All worked with Bill Nishikawa there, translating a batch of mail received from Japan by a Japanese family with extensive real estate holdings in Seward (Alaska, unlike California, didn't forbid Issei owning land). Ito and his buddies also tested sleeping bags and other arctic equipment. The 7th Division had been training vigorously in the California desert to meet Rommel's legions on the Sahara, but instead got slated for the Aleutians. Gear they would use had to be proved out.

Other Nisei also went to the Aleutians, an area that worried both Tokyo and Washington. It was the shortest route between the two antagonists, but nearly-impossible to defend. They were Roy "Snuffy" Miyata, Howard Nakamura, George Tsukichi, Satsuke Tanakatsubo, Mitsuo Shibata, Frank Imon, Frank Otsuka, Sam Umetani, George Kobata and Mickey Kuroiwa. John White, who'd studied some Japanese years before, at the University of Washington, and who'd been on active duty in Alaska on December 7, was ordered north to head the growing group.

* * *

On Oct. 23 the 43rd Infantry arrived in New Zealand, and moved up to Noumea the following month. Attorney Eugene Wright and former Osaka newsman Mike Mitchell led a language team out to join it.* Their team consisted

---

*Nisei got an unfair deal regarding advancement during the war, although 100 or so were commissioned in 1945 as a public relations ploy. Very few got commissions before then, and the author has made no special attempt to write in their NCO ratings. Despite their colossal combined accomplishments, few Nisei ended the war higher than Staff Sergeant, and most finished at a lower grade.

of more volunteers who'd been asked to ship out before the course was completed. Shigeo Yasutake ended up team leader after a while.* Kiyoshi Nishimoto, Richard Matsumoto and Mamoru Noji were quiet, scholarly types. Yasutake described Haruo "Slim" Tanaka as "go-go-go," and Wright called him "the finest soldier I ever met." The Seattle lawyer said Tanaka constantly itched and volunteered for front-line action, and got it. Charlie Hamasaki, roly-poly and always cheerful, was the elder of the group and constantly talking about the baby girl who was born just after he left the U.S. The other four slots on the 10-man team (things were starting to get organized, now) were filled by Lloyd Sato, Charles N. Nakagawa, Ted Kihara and James Sato (no relation to Lloyd). All but Kihara and Noji were Californians. Kihara was from Winnemucca, Nevada, a town of which a night club comic might say "It was so small it didn't have a town drunk. They had to take turns!" Ted's Japanese was scanty, and Yasutake said "he worked like hell to do his fair share." Mamoru Noji was an Oregonian from Hood River, a town that would so cover itself with disgrace that a search of the local library's newspaper files in 1978 failed to turn up a photograph that won Hood River dishonor. The incident would occur in the war's final year.

* * *

It was almost 1943 before the brainchildren of prewar Army language officers got anywhere near organized, although they were scattered up and down the Pacific's seascape. Robert Lury, a motion picture executive, and Charles Fogg, a Caucasian NCO commissioned upon graduation (which did not make Nisei college grad NCO's too happy), wandered from the Fijis to New Caledonia trying to report to the Americal Division. It was the end of

---

*Except where necessary for clarity, military ranks are not used, especially since Caucasian officers rose an average of three grades working side-by-side with Nisei who rose hardly at all.

January, 1943, before they got transportation to Guadalcanal, and joined the division's headquarters.

Kei Sakamoto had to be brought up from Bora Bora, and Mas Minamoto from Tonga. John Burden, monitoring broadcasts relayed via Suva to Hawaii, Australia and the U.S., noticed that Guadalcanal kept screaming for a language officer. Demands got so vehement that he packed, sure someone would order him there. Nothing happened. He unpacked. He packed again. And again unpacked. When Adm. Nimitz was in Suva, passing through, the 37th's intelligence officer asked how he was making out with assigning a language officer to Guadalcanal. "They're hounding the hell out of me!" complained Nimitz, whereupon the G-2 dropped Burden's name. Nimitz directly ordered the Maui medic to Guadalcanal, where he arrived in October, 1942. He then heard of another "lost" Nisei on Tonga Tabu, so he flew down and got him. This was Tateshi Miyasaki, a Kibei from the Presidio class, who stayed on Guadalcanal with Burden for nearly a year. Miyasaki had been driving a general's jeep, no one on Tonga having an idea of what to do with him.

Gilbert Ayres and Jerome Davis led out a team, headed for the 37th Division. Kazuo Komoto was its leader. With him were Dye Ogata, William Ishida, Frank Sanwo, George Tokunaga, Taro Asai, Haruo Ota, Kiyoto Shintaku, Tomoyoshi Uyeda, and Seichi Okazaki.

* * *

Kai Rasmussen's people were working like hell, turning out linguists, and a lot of the students were working like hell, too, staying up so late trying to study that special officer watches had to be posted, to turn off latrine lights and make men at Savage to to bed. The Army, however, was having difficulty getting commands to accept the services of these men, and was trying to decide how best they might be exploited. Still, suggestions for their use poured in. Two teams were made up and sent through an air intelligence school, for the express purpose of training them to work with crash teams overseas. America had toppled, rather than climbed down, from its tower of superciliousness. Although the Zero fighter had already claimed over 200 air victims before it appeared over Pearl Harbor, and despite a full report on it having been sent from Col. Claire Chennault in China two years before, there were those who refused to believe in 1942 that Japan had any decent aircraft. Minds finally changed, and the two teams were set up for assignment overseas. The idea was that crash teams would recover shot-down Japanese aircraft, and the Nisei linguists would swiftly identify all parts and instruments. George Goda led an air technical intelligence team to Australia. It consisted of judo expert George Marumoto, plus Eichi Nakazono, Albert Fujikawa, Kaoru Tanita, Haruo Ashida, Yutaka Hasegawa, George Hikida, and Walter Tanaka. Not one ever examined an enemy aircraft. Shunji Hamano led another such team, to New Caledonia. Richard K. Hayashi, Kenji Kato, Joe Shiraishi and Ray Nakabayashi were on it. They didn't examine any enemy aircraft, either. All did translating or interrogating.

Paul and George Aurell were in the first Camp Savage class, the sons of a businessman who'd had them living with him in Osaka. Paul led a team out from Savage with Faubian Bowers, a man destined to step onto Japanese soil at the side of Douglas MacArthur. George Ichikawa was enlisted team leader for these two officers. He had Kazuo Kozaki along. A large team accompanied them. Roy Fugami, Chikateru Inouye, Hiroshi Kubota, Wataru Shintaku and Harumi Kawaye were the team's guts. Like Kozaki, they were Kibei. Their first-hand knowledge of Japan, joined with that of the two officers, was vital to the whole team's success. George Kayano, Ernest Hirai, Robert T. Kimura, William Kodama, Paul T. Tamaki, William S. Yamaki, Mitsuo Ichisaka, Tatsumi Kawamoto, Jack K. Nagano, Toshito Nakatsuru, Harry S. Okubo, Takeo T. Sekiya and Narihiko Yamanaka were also in the crew. Adding color to it with their personalities were a judo expert named Masao Matsumoto, and a chicken-sexer from Fresno named Tadashi Mori. Plus the lad from the "non-Japanese" part of San Francisco, Terry Takahashi, and Case A. "Casey" Kawamoto. Rounding off the team was a lad with the unlikely name of Elbridge K. Okazaki. (Issei had quite a predilection for giving their offspring first names that were definitely *un*-Japanese. Later in the war, out of Hawaii would come two language students with even more improbable names—Gulstan Enomoto and Meyer Ueoka.) This group would win a helmetful of medals. Some would stay on, and make a career of the Army.

Five graduates were kept on instructors. They were George Matsui, Ronald Chagami, Toshiyuki Sakai, John Kawachi, and Kan Tagami, the guy whose Oriental face had so terrified the drunk on Fisherman's Wharf. The quintet joined Noboru Tanimoto, who was Mike Sakamoto's cousin, on the Savage staff, which had begun to expand and deepen. The Navy, late, was fighting its own prejudice against Japanese, and seeking teachers. Rasmussen's men had to move fast. They got Shoji Takimoto, George Yamamoto, Shizuo Hamamura, Tetsuo Imagawa, Masato Morikawa, and Yutaka Munakata to join them, some being recruited out of concentration camps.

* * *

As stated earlier, not every Nisei was a hero, nor have all claimed to be. Nor were all unrestrainedly eager to prove their patriotism via arduous, unstinting service. Many felt that government treated them and theirs viciously. After all, Joe Dimaggio's father was an enemy alien, the U. S. being at war with Italy, but there was no talk of locking *him* up. Or putting Joe's baseball-playing brothers, Vincent and Dominick, into concentration camps. Or Joe himself, for that matter, although his status was exactly the same as that of every locked-up Nisei. The Yankee Clipper was the native-born, citizen son of a resident immigrant alien from a country with whom the United States was then at war. That the Dimaggio

Japanese officer explains minefield layout as Tamotsu Koyanagi (right) interprets at Yap surrender. Cooling it at Savage are (in doorway) Ben Yamamoto and Russell Kono. Loafers below are (l-r) Bill Fujii, Eddie Mitsukado, Dick Oguro, Henry Kimura—December, 1942, class.

brothers walked free while George Taketa's brother Tom (who later volunteered, and won a Bronze Star in India) was imprisoned without charges, representation, or trial states the case succinctly. Clearly put, the Dimaggio boys did not have slanted eyes. Tom Taketa did.

By the end of 1942, more than 100 Nisei had been dispatched to the Pacific. Some were on New Guinea and Guadalcanal at the moment their relatives were getting herded into concentration camps. Some already knew what it was to sell family possessions for a pittance, so confined parents would have some money in the camps.

Walter Tanaka felt family suffering more keenly than other Nisei might have. His father, Tunejiro, had migrated from Kumamoto Prefecture, where he'd been the playmate of a *samurai's* son. When California schools refused him admittance, Tunejiro learned English from Caucasians while topping sugar beets, chopping wood, and working for the railroad. In 1905 he helped clear a mountainside to build the beautiful city of Carmel, and with his own hands planted some of the stately pines that still graced its main street in 1978.

Through correspondence generated via membership in an *uta,* a prose society, Tunejiro met and married a loving lady, but they did not fare well in America. Fog and damp weather destroyed his bean crop in Castroville one year. In Watsonville he lost a sugar beet crop when the tractor used to pump its water broke down and was out of service a month. In Gilroy he took a partner, who held back from selling so long, hoping for top price, that disaster struck. The U. S. government dumped surplus supplies of canned tomatoes on the market.

Tunejiro did poorly as a potato farmer in Salinas, and even worse raising produce for sale off a family-operated roadside stand in San Luis Obispo. The Depression busted him, but no *samurai*-inspired man could take refuge in bankruptcy. Creditors got his horses, tractor and farm tools, but not Tunejiro's honor. The entire Tanaka family then forgot about school for a while. All worked as sharecroppers. Walter Tanaka left school at the 8th grade, entering the 9th for finishing high school four years later. "There is strength in unity." said Tunejiro, and his family believed him. They once picked 800 crates of lettuce for a total return of $20, and massaged their father's muscles at night so he could lead them back to the fields in the morning. A strong believer in religion, Tunejiro easily explained his switch from Presbyterianism to Buddhism when the family who transported the Tanakas to the former church moved away. "There are many trails to the top of a mountain from which one can see the moon," he said.

Just when things began to look bright for the Tanakas, just when hope began to appear again, the sun of Dec. 7 rose over the horizon. Tunejiro had started a Japanese language and history school in San Luis Obispo, and was president of the Japanese Association there. For these horrendous offenses he was seized and locked up at Sharp's Park, Calif. Walter was in the Army, so the rest of the Tanaka family quickly turned in a .22 rifle and a shotgun to the local sheriff, then burned Walt's *kendo* suit and mask lest his interest in the Japanese martial art of stick-dueling get him labelled disloyal. Tunejiro was later permitted to join his imprisoned family in Poston, Arizona, but he felt strongly that America, the bright shining land to which he'd come in 1900, had let him down. The final, crushing blow was struck at him while he was in a concentration camp and his son was in a New Guinea foxhole. Thieves stole the last of the Tanakas' few possessions from the farm they'd been working when war came. It was all just too much.

The Tanaka family's story merely mirrors those of other mainland Japanese. A lot of pap has been fed the American public over the years about how "stoic, uncomplaining, persevering, dedicated and patriotic 'our' Japanese" were. It is all just so much bushwah! Japanese were, it has slowly been brought out, as infuriated and enraged as American citizens of right ought to be.

* * *

When viewed from Australia, the picture looked less

bleak, even to George Taketa, whose family lived in one of the rows and rows of tarpaper shacks that made up the Tule Lake concentration camp. David Swift's men set up shop for ATIS in a place called Indooroopilly, just a few miles outside Brisbane. All were housed, not in tents or barracks, but in a sprawling mansion. Other than having outside toilets, it was luxurious. Men bunked two to a room, except for Corporals and Sergeants, each of whom had a room to himself. To top things off, a civilian couple worked in the mansion as cook and houseboy. Set in the southern hemisphere at about the same latitude Hawaii occupies in the northern one, Indooroopilly was blessed with balmy breezes and a sub-tropical climate. ATIS was not quite accepted yet. It was feeling its way along. The pace of work was not frenetic. Swift and his men walked over a little bridge to work. During the free hours, the Nisei used some of their per diem to feast in Brisbane on Chinese food.

* * *

If the 10 Nisei in Australia found life pleasant, there were 10 in the U. S. who did not. It all came about because of one of those incredibly-stupid errors the mindless Washington bureaucracy regularly makes so that people like the author may continue to call it a mindless Washington bureaucracy.

Not long after 110,000 Japanese-Americans were locked up, some bright mind realized that this had been a pretty stupid thing to do. So had been the discharging of Nisei from the Army. The Navy simply refused to take in AJA's, the Army stalled them off, and Selective Service wouldn't draft them.

Meanwhile, crops were in danger. A suggestion was made that Mexican labor be imported for the harvest. Even Californians preferred Japanese to "those stinking greasers," so some inmates went out to work the harvest. They liked the idea of making more than $19 per month. When they returned peaceably, it occurred to someone that an awful lot of troops were tied up, watching people who made no trouble, so it was decided to let younger ones out to attend college, plus others who could get employment away from the West Coast area. Talk had started about making an all-Nisei fighting team out of the unit at Camp McCoy, too. Men would be needed for that.

Some kind of filter system needed to be set up, to determine who it was safe to let out of the camps. So, bureaucrats devised a form which they felt, if completed, would do the job. It was a double-barreled, gold-plated disaster! Labelled "Application for Leave Clearance," it was distributed indiscriminately to all confinees. Rage, rebellion, rack and ruin resulted.

* * *

Questions 27 and 28 on the list were, are, and probably always will be referred to by Japanese-Americans as the "Yes-Yes, No-No" questions.

No. 27 asked "Are you willing to serve in the armed forces of the United States on combat duty, wherever ordered?" This query absolutely bowled over Issei men, nearly all of whom were past the mid-century mark. As for women, both Issei and Nisei, they could either wag puzzled heads or grin at it. Teenage girls just giggled.

Nisei men of draft age, some of them recent dischargees from the Army, some recently turned down by recruiters, and all rejected by their draft boards, wrote qualified answers like "It depends on whether you are going to keep violating my Constitutional rights by keeping me locked up here" instead of yes or no. Lots, feeling they'd been harassed, herded, and humiliated enough, scornfully refused to answer the question at all. On paper, at least. Many did answer it verbally, their responses sometimes centering on insertion of the questionnaire into a bodily orifice the U.S. government did not possess.

No. 28 was truly a marvel. It asked "Will you swear unqualified allegiance to the United States of America and faithfully defend the United States from any or all attack by foreign or domestic sources, and foreswear any form of allegiance or obedience to the Japanese emperor, or any other foreign government, power, or organization?"

One can imagine Tunejiro Tanaka, who'd left Japan 42 years earlier, trying to fathom this question. The United States had rejected him. Its citizens had discriminated against him. Its school system had refused to educate him. Its police had allowed his last few possessions to be stolen. He had nothing to show for four decades of work. Nothing except his *jus sanguinis*, his right of blood, to be a citizen of Japan, the only land that wanted him. Walter Tanaka's father had not read Edward Everett Hale's *Man Without a Country,* but he had no intention of being such a man. No Issei wanted to be such a man. Nearly all either refused to answer Question No. 28 or answered in the negative.

* * *

At Camp Savage, Kazunobu Tamura was given a set of orders for himself and nine other linguists. Paragraph 2 of a commendation all 10 later received, read in part "Your assignment, no doubt, at times was very difficult and trying and required you to exercise the utmost of your ability in understanding and judgement in working towards the objective of your team's mission."

This piece of gobbledygook went into Tamura's service record, plus those of Edward H. Aburamen, Isamu Adachi, William T. Ishida, Akira Kato, Hisato Kinoshita, Fred H. Odanaka, Kenneth M. Uni, Kazu Yoshihata and Taro Tsukahara. Of all the rotten jobs the Army has ever come up with, this assignment certainly rated some special award for lowness. The 10 Nisei were assigned to do *loyalty checks*, associated with the infamous questionnaire, in concentration camps! They were to do this while wearing the uniform of a country that oppressed themselves, their relatives and their friends.

One can but attempt to fathom the feelings of Fred Odanaka. He worked it out so he could be sent to the camp at Granada, Colorado. That would give him a chance to visit his imprisoned parents there, before asking for an overseas assignment.

Odanaka might have asked for the Wyoming concentration camp, too, but he knew he could only get one. His wife, Fuki, was locked up at Heart Mountain.

Chapter 5

Unless an American ferrets out the truth, he's likely to accept that the Pacific war went something like this:

Pearl Harbor gets attacked;
Japanese Navy suffers a defeat at Midway;
Marines take Guadalcanal, Tarawa, Saipan, Guam, Iwo Jima, and Okinawa;
Two atomic bombs get dropped;
Japan surrenders.

As Australians with whom Nisei served might say, "Not bloody *likely!*" Just as in Europe, the bulk of fighting in the Pacific was done by GI Joe, the dogface infantry soldier, who fought on after marines withdrew. Two reasons explain why recognition has not been fairly focused on this fact.

First, the words of Elliott Thorpe seem fit. He told the author "The Marines never lost a headline!"

The second reason is that nearly all Army historians are incredibly-dull writers, averaging one inch of footnotes per page of print. Because of their penchant for listing every numbered unit, right down to the last platoon, they tend to lose a reader's interest. He ends up with little idea of what they are trying to tell him.

This combination of bad writing and Marine Corps cymbal-clashing has obscured the fact that the U. S. Army did the bulk of our Pacific fighting. One Army division, the 32nd Infantry, spent more of the war's 1348 days in a combat situation than did most of the entire Marine Corps. Moreover, the attention span of war correspondents was as scant as their accuracy. Few journalists, once a beachhead was established, stuck around. Like smash-and-grab thieves, they seized the more sparkling baubles of news while public attention was at its peak, then adjourned in a body to the nearest Navy flagship. There they enjoyed hot showers, steaks, and ice cream while awaiting the next landing.

* * *

The 1942 winter could have become one of discontent. Although the war's tide was turned at Midway, a mighty Japanese effort had nearly turned it back. By fall two more American aircraft carriers, *Hornet* and *Wasp,* were on the bottom, and Roosevelt was sounding public sentiment. Off-year elections were coming up. The President needed to know how much strength his party would lose if he pulled the stymied marines off Guadalcanal.

Arthur Castle and 13 other linguists sailed under Golden Gate Bridge just as Australians began pushing Gen. Tomotaro Horii's troops back over the Stanley range. To lend a hand, MacArthur's air chief laid on America's first mass airlift. Cramming most of the 32nd Division into bombers, transports and whatever commercial craft he could get his hands on, George Kenney had them flown from Australian bases to Port Moresby. By Sept. 25 part of the division was protecting the Aussie left flank, and soon another part struck off over the Stanleys at an angle to the Kokoda Track, keeping the enemy off-balance by constantly threatening his flank and rear. On Guadalcanal, meanwhile, marines were doing no better than holding. They were chopping up the Japanese there, a job made easy because the enemy believed in charging.

October found Horii's troops doing a *tenshin,* making what Japanese preferred to call a strategic "turned advance" rather than a retreat, falling back on Buna. The airstrip there had been mauled by Kenney's bombers. It was the job of Allied infantry to keep pressure on so it couldn't be repaired, and try to take it for their own planes' use. On Oct. 6 a remarkable man named Sidney

Mashbir arrived to take over ATIS, and a week after that 2852 soldiers of the Americal Division joined the marines on Guadalcanal. Now 23,058 Americans were on the island, facing 5000 sick and starving Japanese. Nimitz thought the enemy forces triple their actual number, and figured he needed a total of 35-40,000 troops to defeat them.

Nimitz emulated MacArthur on Oct. 18, replacing a flag officer with one more aggressive. William Halsey took over the South Pacific naval forces. MacArthur ordered another airlift, now that his men knew how to manage one, and put more troops on the north side of New Guinea. Fred Nishitsuji and Bill Hirashima were with one pincer trying to take Gona and Buna, while James Tsumura was working his way over the mountains with part of the 32nd making up another pincer. The three quickly learned about being wet round-the-clock, rattling with malaria, feeling clothing grow moldy, and having shoes rot off in a week. What they endured caused design of better equipment for later Pacific foot soldiers. Meanwhile, they subsisted on bully beef and hardtack, with occasional rice.

The U. S. attorney-general picked Columbus Day to free alien Italians of restrictions, an action that didn't sit well either with Nisei or the inmates of 10 concentration camps. The struggle for Guadalcanal hung in the balance, and Rabaul scheduled a three-pronged attack for re-taking Henderson Field, the name given Guadalcanal's airstrip by marines. Carrier-type aircraft would bomb it first, then surface ships would shell it. While it was immobilized, Imperial ground troops would seize it in one glorious rush.

Japanese air and sea efforts accomplished their ends, although at a price, but Americans won the ground struggle. This makes an interesting story because wartime writers did not get the full truth of it. As a result, neither did the American public. Marines got all the Guadalcanal headlines, documenting a Thorpe-ism that "History is a collection of lies agreed upon." USMC accounts of the Battle of Bloody Ridge, which saved Henderson Field, credit its own members for doing the job, under a pigeon-breasted colonel named Puller. Truth to tell, Army men saved the marines' necks. Specifically, Army men of the Americal Division. More specifically, its 164th Regiment. Or, right to the point, that regiment's 2nd and 3rd Battalions.

When the Japanese threatened in October, marines to the east of Henderson Field were exhausted, and their ranks thin, so the 2nd Battalion was given a flank to hold. It did. Puller's lines were broken by charging Japanese on the night of Oct. 24. The 3rd Battalion was fed in, amid pounding rain, to stiffen them. It did. Next night another Japanese attack came, but the Kawaguchi Detachment was stopped in its tracks, 1000 members killed. That was it. Henderson Field was never threatened again. Overwhelming numbers of American troops began to pour ashore under the protection of its planes. They drove the enemy toward the island's western end.

Correspondents wrote what USMC public relations officers told them, so history books don't tell that the slaughter of the enemy was largely done by Americal soldiers. Marines are believed to have blunted the *banzai* attacks. It was soldiers who did the job, with the new Garand rifle and its rapid-fire 8-round clip, while marines re-cocked their obsolescent Springfield Model 1903 rifles after each shot. Soldiers saved Henderson Field, but USMC cymbal-clashers drowned out the rattle of Army musketry for nearly 40 years.

Strategically, the battle was over, although fighting on the island continued for another 14 weeks. Guadalcanal was American, and both sides knew it. The invasion of North Africa could go forth in full strength on Nov. 8, 1942, none of it needing to be diverted to beef up the Pacific. Nor did Atlantic warship numbers need to be reduced. Antisubmarine efforts could be intensified. More bombers could be flown to England, for assaulting German industry. The Pacific could wait a while for some. Churchill could relax with a cigar, Stalin with a pipe, knowing that forces for the "second front" both wanted were building up. Roosevelt's cigarette holder could resume its jaunty angle, and a few reflective puffs could be taken on MacArthur's corncob pipe. The Southwest Pacific's commander saw that the enemy could be kept reeling, if he delivered left hooks to alternate with Nimitz's right crosses. Taking a hold on the north coast of New Guinea, for an advance along it to the Philippines, would be just such a punch.

* * *

The last batch of Japanese-American evacuees to reach their destinations were locked up* in Jerome, Arkansas, during the first week of November, completing the transfer of 110,000 internees from the Army to the War Relocation Authority. At Camp McCoy, Wisconsin, which they'd reached during June in three shuttered trains taking widely-divergent routes, the 100th Infantry Division (as the men from the Hawaii National Guard regiments were now called) shivered and wondered. They took infantry training—*for the second time*—while the U. S. government tried to figure out what to do with them. They were kept busy, which let lies be told later about their "training intensively for European combat" in Wisconsin. The truth was that the 100th was being kept in

---

*The author insists on terms like "concentration camps, prisoners, locked up," etc. instead of euphemisms, when telling of Americans who were not charged with any crime, who were refused due process, whose Constitutional rights were violated, and who were imprisoned simply because their eyes were slanted. This type of "they're different" thinking, when accepted by another nation's people, led to the slaughter of 6,000,000 Jews. Qualifying, or differentiating, merely begs the question. No American, unto the furtherest generation, should be allowed to forget how this country went insane at the time Hitler did, lest she be allowed to go insane again, which can happen at any time, so long as certain lock-up laws remain in effect. In 1979, they were still on the books.

Early 1942 made San Francisco a lonely place after AJAs were evacuated, and YMCA (above) became Presidio MIS'er hangout. On Eniwetok (below) are George Matsui, Minoru Nakanishi and Jesse Miyao, where translation of enemy chart helped Navy clear mines, establish new anchorage.

mothballs until some way could be found to explain their panicked expulsion from Oahu. To dump them into civilian life, as had been done with other Nisei soldiers, might cause riot, even revolution, in the Islands.

Men of the 100th were mystified that same week, when 2 officers and 25 men were spirited out of McCoy on a classified mission. When they returned, the entire battalion erupted in laughter over the "secret." Apparently someone in Washington had decided that Japanese "smelled different," and that war dogs could be trained to sniff them out. Amid profane pidgin mirth, the 25 regaled their pals with descriptions of their ludicrous struggles with heavy masks and padded clothing. Dogs in the Pacific did bite some Japanese later. And Americans, too, if they got close enough.

During November's second week, the Americal Division killed another 300 of the enemy on Guadalcanal. Paul Sakai, of Seattle, landed in North Africa with the 9th Infantry Division as sergeant-major of one of its battalions. Sakai almost was suspended from active duty when a dispatch from Washington ordered reassignment of men with German, Italian and Japanese surnames. "They missed names like Ohara," recalled Sakai, "thinking the guys were Irish." Maj. Gen. Manton S. Eddy told Washington what it could do with its message, and took his division overseas intact. Sakai may have been first Nisei in combat on that side of the world.

Japanese on New Guinea lost their leader that week. Rushing down-mountain to take charge of his forces at Buna, General Horii was swept from a raft in the Kumusi River, and drowned.

During the third week of November, an interesting group of 14 Nisei from Camp Manzanar, California, volunteered for MIS school. One of them, Koji Ariyoshi, would later be accused of being a Communist. Another, Karl Yoneda, had been one for 15 years, and in fact ran for Assemblyman in San Francisco on the Party ticket. Yoneda told the author he didn't challenge the concentration camps because "the immediate objective was to destroy Fascism, and thus there was no choice for us but to 'accept' the U.S. racist dictum at that time over Hitler's ovens and Japan's military rapists of Nanking."

Ariyhoshi and Yoneda were kicked off San Francisco's docks, where both were longshoremen, after Dec. 7. They did not fight evacuation, their rationale being that *all* human rights, not just their own Constitutional ones, would be lost if the Axis powers were victorious. Yoneda, a Kibei, was actually a deserter from the Imperial Army, having gone over the hill and back to the States when drafted in 1926.

Many Nisei volunteered from concentration camps, tough as the decision was. Pro-Japan factions made pro-American individuals the targets of their contempt or worse. Yoshiaki Hirabayashi, fearful of this life after volunteering, got himself locked up overnight in Manzanar's MP office for safety. Families of some Nisei were ostracized when their sons answered the call for MIS school. The situation was puzzling. Volunteers were wanted for that assignment, but no other. How was anyone, willing to serve America, to understand what was going on?

* * *

While troops on Guadalcanal developed a giant offensive against Japanese on the island, those on New Guinea worked to defeat the enemy in the Buna-Gona-Sanananda area. It was needed, for airstrips from which to launch further Allied advances. Things hadn't been going too well on New Guinea, and MacArthur decided to have a firsthand look. The war showed his use of airpower to be more knowledgeable than an other U. S. officer's. He insisted on control of the skies before each forward thrust. On the day after Thanksgiving, MacArthur was on New Guinea, staff officers worried about his being so close to the enemy. He saw for himself that his men were sick, hungry, and tired, but he still had to defeat the Japanese. He took the 32nd Division out from under Australian control and told Gen. Eichelberger "Go out there, Bob, and take Buna, or don't come back alive!" Soon after that American troops got their hands on flamethrowers. They could now do something about Japanese bunkers.

* * *

Early in December, after desperate fighting, Aussies flashed "Gona gone!" to MacArthur. The general was elated. The Diggers took 40% casualties, but they had a victory. Using delayed-action fuses that let their artillery shells burrow into the ground before exploding, they stunned their enemy, then finished him off with grenades and an archaic tactic called the bayonet charge. Gary Kadani, Paul Kuyama and others at Indooroopilly translated diaries that praised the fighting of Australian soldiers, saying they "fought like Japanese!" American soldiers would have to wait a while for similar praise.

Arthur Castle (translating his name from Ushiro via a Chinese-Japanese combination made it come out "Right castle"), Phil Ishio and Kazuhiko Yamada moved up front in Buna, to be closer for interrogation of prisoners and translation of documents the 32nd captured. It had been recognized that the quicker these could be exploited the better. The three Nisei were ordered to stay very near the command post, a policy in effect since Fred Nishitsuji had nearly been mistakenly shot weeks before.

As the 32nd started its drive to control the Buna area the Japanese seized Wewak, Finschhafen and Madang, further up the coast, in case they were needed for other strategic retreats. The Japanese cleared out of Buna Station, one of two local strong points, before month's end, the 32nd too exhausted to prevent this. The real enemies in New Guinea—malaria, dysentery and hunger—were taking a toll of both sides.

On Jan. 4, 1943, the Japanese high command ordered Guadalcanal evacuated as impossible to regain. Forces in Buna were told to move back to Lae and Salamaua. The tide of war was turning again, nevermore to be reversed. Whether she accepted it or not, Japan was on the run.

America's forces in the Pacific were building. Three

American divisions were under Alexander Patch in the XIV Corps; the Americal, the 25th, and the 2nd Marines. Eichelberger had three others in I Corps; the 32nd, the 41st, and the Australian 7th. Backing these up were the 37th in the Fijis and the 43rd on New Caledonia. Nisei linguists *sometimes* worked with all six divisions and the two Corps headquarters, but pretty much on a catch-as-catch-can basis, in spite of the war being a year old. This was because of something the Army calls a "Table of Organization." No linguists listed on your TO? Then you couldn't have any. If you did have any, you couldn't promote them, because they weren't on your TO. This failure of the Army to get organized would cause a lot of resentment, because only people like Sidney Mashbir had enough imagination and guts to get their men promoted for work done, without waiting for approval to come in triplicate from a faraway uniformed bureaucrat.

Until the end of 1943 (half of the war), Nisei linguists were generally free-lancers, provided they could get someone to trust them. This wasn't easy, because officers instructed to watch them were pretty busy working, too. Nisei volunteered to go here, or were suddenly ordered to go there. All they could do was what they were told. Nisei on Guadalcanal went there because of panicked appeals. They worked for whoever yelled loudest, and sweated out the day when every headquarters would *insist* on having its language team, just as it insisted on having a special jeep for the general. Nisei on New Caledonia worked for Admiral Halsey, although the Navy officially didn't want them. Nisei in Australia and New Guinea were under Gen. MacArthur, whose chief of intelligence recognized their potential. Willoughby personally shook hands with Steve Yamamoto and the first group on Independence Day, 1942, and welcomed them in his high-pitched, Prussian-accented voice. Otherwise, the Nisei language effort was an administrative mess. Except in the Americal Division. Perhaps that was because it was the first U. S. division to be activated overseas. Far from paper-shufflers, Alexander Patch's G-2 officer knew the value of

Nisei linguists. He exploited Mac Nagata and his team, a faith that in a short while would pay off handsomely.

At Indooroopilly, Sidney Mashbir made it clear that he was in charge. He said hello to David Swift, whose missionary parents he'd known in Japan years earlier, and gave all hands the word. ATIS, a joint Allied operation, would be *joint!* Let no one be mistaken on that score. All hands would pull together, and all information received would be pooled. Rank would be ignored for the moment, so that a job could get done! With those few words, Mashbir laid the foundation for the Nisei's remarkable military intelligence success in the Pacific. Since he had Gen. Willoughby's ear, and Willoughby had MacArthur's, no one could say Mashbir nay.

Mashbir took a liking to Gary Kadani. He had him interview the first POW brought to Indooroopilly, giving the ex-salesman a list of questions to ask. Kadani felt "like I was in a mystery movie, with a microphone hidden in the inkwell, and all." The prisoner, at once recognizing from Kadani's accent that he was not a native Japanese, was more relaxed than the Californian. Nothing of value was obtained from the POW.

A pattern, however, had been established. Arthur Komori's earlier recommendations were applied. Thenceforth a prisoner's wounds were tended. He was given a cigarette perhaps, and spoken to in calm tones. Kibei linguists, who had lived in Japan, knew that country's military customs from experience. On reaching draft age, each man had to register in his home prefecture. Each prefecture, vying with others since the 1870's, when peasants were first allowed to serve in the Army, produced its own proud divisions. Thus, if a man turned out to be born in Kumamoto, Nisei knew at once he was with the 6th Division, Japan's best, which was made up from the hardy people living in that southern area.

While Castle, Ishio and Yamada were working in the Buna-Gona-Sananda area, Tom Masaharu Takata and Howard Ogawa went up to Port Moresby, and there worked for Aussie forces under Gen. Sir Thomas Blamey. They grilled POWs brought in from the other side of the mountains, and Takata was appalled at conditions they described. Port Moresby was getting bombed daily by planes from Rabaul, but Takata still felt bad about being "in the rear." To salve his conscience he sent a dozen peaches over the mountains, via a messenger heading that way, for Phil Ishio.

George Aurell led the three Nisei to Buna. John Anderton ended up in the same area, through some kind of a mixup. Although supposed to be working in intelligence, the lanky lawyer found himself leading soldiers in combat for the 41st Division in the Durapan Valley. When someone learned what he'd been trained for, Anderton was ordered back to Indooroopilly. There he became Mashbir's second-in-command. Arthur Komori got assigned to General Elliott Thorpe for counterintelligence, and other Nisei were divided into translation and interrogation sections. About this time, captured diaries began to arrive in quantity, taken off dead Japanese.

There were usually more diaries than POWs. Far more. The Aussies, having learned what happened to some of their own after capture, were reluctant to take the enemy alive. Soda pop helped change the attitude of a few jungle fighters. Three bottles of Coca Cola were awarded any infantryman credited with a prisoner. Pretty soon business got brisk.

There appeared to be no restriction in the Imperial army, as in the American one, against keeping private diaries. These proved revealing, it being the habit of Japanese to inscribe their deepest feelings in these books, which became part of "remains" (along with hair cuttings and fingernail parings) shipped home if they got killed. Diaries often revealed where a man had been, with whom, his unit's name, his officers' names, his home prefecture, and the state of morale, equipment and supplies, as well as his movements since leaving the homeland. Clues to Japan's "order of battle" (what troops she had, and where) could be ascertained.

Some diary writings were most intimate. Several Nisei

told the author "Those Japanese had to be the sexiest guys on earth!" when referring to what they wrote wives and sweethearts in clinical detail. Too, pornography was as popular with Japanese soldiers as Allied ones. Gary Kadani still laughed nervously, 35 years later, telling how a document given him in haste to translate turned out to be a lurid composition titled "One Night in a Hotel."

* * *

On Guadalcanal, things were as fouled up as anywhere. Despite being ordered there personally by Nimitz, John Burden got little work to do. He'd be told that a POW was on the way in, then later told the man died enroute. When this kept happening, Burden got suspicious. Taking Tateshi Miyasaki along, he went to where the prisoners were supposed to be. Things improved. When one group of Japanese got surrounded, Burden was called by Maj. Gen J. Lawton Collins, commander of the 25th Division. "You said these Japanese would surrender," the general told the tall doctor. "O.K., you've got 48 hours to bring some in!"

It took Burden most of that day to get the necessary equipment together. That night he made his first loudspeaker broadcast to the enemy. No results. He made two more broadcasts next day, and a single Japanese soldier finally began working his way out of the surrounded gully. When the man kept sliding back down the wet slope, Burden clambered down and gave him a hand. The grateful POW offered to cooperate with him. Another dozen gave up that day. "I might have gotten more," Burden said, "but the time allowed me ran out."

The doctor, Miyasaki, and the Kubo brothers then pooled their efforts with 10 enlisted marines who'd supposedly been given a cram course in Japanese. "They jabbered pretty well to one another," Burden said, "but when I gave them a prisoner to work on, all they got out of him for a full day's effort was his name, rank and birthplace. I knew then why Admiral Nimitz had been so urgent."

Shigeo Yasutake was asked to take over a platoon when he landed on Guadalcanal, officers being in short supply. Yasutake led his men inland from the beach, but was pulled out of the jungle later and, with his language detachment, sent to the 43rd. A wholesale produce worker from Gardena, he preferred combat to language work, even though parents and three brothers were in an Arkansas prison camp. "Hell, I was young and full of beans in those days." Yasutake said, "As long as I was in, I wanted to fight!"

It was in the Solomons that Nisei linguists brought off their first grand coup. It made officers all the way to the top realize how important were the Nisei's services. Mac Nagata had gone up to Guadalcanal with Isao Kusuda and Shigeru Yamashita from Nouma. They were joined by Kei Sakamoto, who arrived in *USS Ward* when the destroyer escorted a half-dozen landing craft needed for putting assault forces ashore behind enemy lines. Then a thick document turned up. One version is that it came off the Japanese submarine I-1, which ran aground on Guadalcanal after being rammed by the Australian corvettes *Kiwi* and *Moa.* Another is that it was picked up on Tulagi. A third is that it came from Makin. None matters. The document was photographed, the original sent to Washington, and copies given Yamashita, Sakamoto and Kusuda to translate. When the three Nisei finished, they had provided for Nimitz, Halsey and MacArthur a full list of Imperial Navy ships, plus their call signs and code names, and the same for the Japanese Navy's air squadrons and bases.

Japan's naval "order of battle" was now known to the Allies. It contained some surprises; the names of ships America didn't even know existed, and a couple of ship *types* that were new, as well. The translation provided a solid base upon which to base the necessary composition of American task forces thereafter and, until the Japanese code was changed, a convenient means of identifying where various units of the Imperial Navy were. Only one's imagination limits one's recognition of how vital to the U.

S. Navy's efforts was this one piece of work by three Nisei enlisted men of the Army.

* * *

At Camp Savage, the grind continued. Word was filtering back from the Pacific, and pressure built on Kai Rasmussen to keep linguists coming. But, he wondered, where was he to get them? Hundreds of Nisei had been summarily kicked out of the Army, almost all the kind he needed—Kibei with a command of Japanese—discharged simply because they'd been schooled in Japan. Hundreds more were still in uniform, but scattered to hell and gone, thanks to panicky West Coast citizens. Nearly all other able-bodied Nisei were heading for concentration camps. What to do?

The only thing *to* do, Rasmussen decided. Simply ask each one if he wanted to serve, and take a chance he'd say yes.

The Dane was sure that a lot would seize upon a chance to demonstrate loyalty, and he was right. More than 30 responded from the Tule Lake concentration camp, including Satoshi Nishijima and his kid brother, Victor. "Suts," the elder, had gotten married in April. He and his sweetheart didn't want to be separated while locked up. He'd see Tokyo before they could settle down. The Nishijima's had been allowed to take into confinement only what they could carry, so they sold their $1500 Buick for less than $500, while realizing about 10% of value on other possessions. All told, confinees would lose an estimated $400,000,000 in property and possessions, a figure that translated into $1 billion of 1945 dollars, if wartime inflation is taken into account.

S. Bill Doi went with the Nishijima brothers, along with his brother-in-law Noboru Yamada, who helped a Kibei girl named Mariko Horike drill Bill in Japanese long enough for him to pass a screening test. With them was Harry Iida, who'd been helping in the camp with the Boy Scouts effort.

Masao B. Ishikawa left a mother, two brothers and

sister behind in Tule Lake when volunteering, despite his being "asked to resign" from a State job when war broke out. His mother approved. She said "I do not know Japan. This is my country. Kibei tell me the treatment of Nisei in Japan is not good. Our future is with America." Charles Nagano was with the group. He and his fiance had married at an assembly center, and honeymooned in Tule Lake. Tom Taketa, whose brother George was already in Australia, sending his total pay home, signed up. His father, who encouraged Tom in the martial arts of judo and *kendo* fencing, while also making sure he joined Boy Scouts, told the boy with tears in his eyes "This is your country. Go fight for it, even if it means fighting against your mother and father's native country, Japan." Eddie Fukui and George Nakamura came out of Tule Lake, too, to die in the Pacific. Among others who signed up were Tom Osasa, Aki Hayashi, Salem Yagawa, Jim Sugimura, Paul Hayashi, Gus Hikawa, Fumio Yokobe, Frank Oikawa, and John Tanikawa.

The last man was really something. Tanikawa was 41 years old at the time, holding the Purple Heart and Croix de Guerre for valorous actions in an earlier war, which he got into by lying about his age. Fired from an ice plant laborer's job when Pearl Harbor was attacked, Tanikawa worked on farms around Sacramento until a curfew prevented his travel after dark. Fellow members of the American Legion and Disabled American Veterans brought food to his home after dark, to feed his four children, but John turned down their offer to petition against his evacuation. He felt his family would be *safe,* imprisoned, from burnings and bombings that had begun to occur.

Another prison camp that provided language students was Poston, Arizona. Roy Takai told how he, James Sasano, Yumiji Higashi, Juichi Nishi, Tom Tsuyuki, Sam Rokutani, Minoru Hara and Pat Nagano had to be smuggled out of Poston after dark, because a big strike was taking place against the camp rule. Pat's brother William was already in the Army, and his father objected to Pat's leaving, but relented after 24 hours of reconsidering. The Nagano's were prominent and prosperous in Morro Bay, California, which may have been why the FBI picked up the father. The Kumamoto native had bought a lot of land in the names of his three sons.

Out of Gila River camp in Arizona came some more volunteers, including "bad boys" Ben Sugeta and Hiroshi "Bud" Mukaye. Ben got into trouble for punching a messhall attendant who'd been rude to a sick lady, and Mukaye had a streak of rebelliousness that observant military seniors later converted into leadership. Sugeta loved to entertain friends by singing Japanese songs, and did so throughout the war, even while surrounded on a Burma hill. Harry Fukuhara, John "Nana" Fujimoto, and Frank Mori also came out of Gila River. Except for his sister Marion, all of Fukuhara's family was in Japan, where his widowed mother had earlier taken them. One brother, drafted into the Imperial Army, was fighting in China. Two younger ones would enter the Imperial Navy. Shoso Nomura, along with Shizue Kunihiro, Sam Takahara, Hilo Fuchiwaki and George Itsuo Nakamura was also in the Gila River contingent. Nomura and Nakamura would see China, where Mao Tse Tung would attend the latter's 21st birthday party.

Harry Akune signed for his brother Kenjiro, a minor, when they volunteered from the Amache, Colorado, camp. His brothers Saburo and Shiro were living in Japan. They would wear the Imperial uniform.

* * *

MIS candidates were gotten from at least a dozen Army camps. Lots had been interviewed and tested before the war. Rasmussen had to order out as scouts every officer and NCO he could spare, then go out himself to help with the recruiting. Although the Dane believed in the essential loyalty of Japanese-Americans, all his Caucasians associates didn't. Rasmussen made it clear he wanted only volunteers, but his example was not always followed. Most Nisei who showed up at Camp Savage were

Walt Minaii and Harry Oka (above, left), visiting Corregidor. On Iwo Jima (right, above), George Kawamoto digs in deep. Presidio pioneers Bill Hirashima, David Kato, (below, left) were vanguard of eventual 75,000 students. Cruising Manila harbor amid Japanese wrecks are (l-r) Conway Yamamoto, Sam Osato, Mas Doue, and Walt Minaii.

volunteers, but even the bitterest Minnesota winter in years was better than conditions nearly all had been enduring at other Army camps. There are other ways to chill a man than low temperatures.

From Camp Robinson, Arkansas, came Harold Hanaumi, Noboru Nishimori, Nobuo Furuiye, Frank Hachiya and Ken Uyesugi. Ken's fiance was locked up at Gila River, and he hoped to marry her if he got any leave later. Hachiya, of Hood River, Oregon, was a studious, reflective Kibei who kept saying "Nisei are going to play a vital part in this war!" Hanaumi was probably the shortest of all MIS'ers. Born in Hawaii, he demanded that a Los Angeles recruiter enlist him. Gazing down his nose at the sawed-off Oriental, the NCO asked "How the hell tall are you?"

"Five feet and one-half!" shouted Hanaumi.

"What? Wait a minute!" The NCO made Hanaumi stand still for measuring, and the "one-half" turned to be a half-inch. He was about to throw Hanaumi out, but asked him what he did. "I'm a bacteriologist," said the Hawaii Nisei, and got sworn in, but he was ordered to school against his wishes. "I have trained to save lives, not take them!" the ebullient lab tech told an interviewing major.

Tatsuo Matsuda got to Savage from Ft. Leonard Wood, Missouri, where he and five other Nisei were marooned when the 6th Division shipped west without them. His family had voluntarily moved from California to Nebraska, escaping confinement.

From Camp Grant, Illinois, came Shigeto Mazawa, a photography student from Chicago who got so scared after his Dec. 7 going-away party that he hid in a friend's house for three days before undergoing his Dec. 10 induction. Taro Tsukahara came in from Ft. Leavenworth, Kansas. His nearest relatives were in Texas. They never faced evacuation. From another Kansas camp, Fort Riley, came Moffet Ishikawa, Spady Koyama and Taro Yoshihashi. Taro's father had been locked up because he'd been a member of the Japanese War Veterans

Association, although he, as many Americans do, long since dropped out of his military organization because of boredom. Koyama's real name was Ayato. He inherited the nickname "Spady" from his pick-and-shovel wielding father, a longtime laborer for Great Northern Railway. The spoil-sport Army made Koyama legalize his name to keep it. Ishikawa had shivered his way into the Army the day after Pearl Harbor, scared spitless of several hundred Caucasians who were taking physicals in the same San Jose civic auditorium.

Seishin Kondo and Larry Saito arrived from Ft. Harrison, Indiana. Kondo, a Kibei, said he "sacrificed myself, so Sansei and Yonsei (third and fourth generations of Japanese in American) might have a better life." Those were his sentiments at the time. A declining Nisei soldier called him stupid, saying "You're going against your own mother and father!" Kondo got ready to attack his attacker, shouting "I'm an American! In an American uniform. If you don't agree, take yours off!" The jeerer subsided.

Up from Ft. Bliss, Texas came Shigeru Iba and Ben Honda. Iba was to find himself in New Guinea with the 41st Division, from which he'd gotten booted with other Nisei at the war's start. Honda had been refused emergency leave to attend the funeral of his brother, who died as the family was assembling for prison camp. No Nisei, in uniform or out, could return to the West Coast once he'd left it.

Don Oka reported from Camp Carson, Colorado. His brothers Isao and Masao followed him into MIS later, but his brothers Takeo and Keiji would fight for Japan. Shigeo Tanaka came up from Ft. Jackson, South Carolina, after marrying Bernice Matsumoto in the Arkansas camp at Rohwer. She, her parents and six brothers were there, along with Shig's parents and brother. Victor Abe and Calvin Morimatsu came from Ft. Warren, Wyoming. Abe's father, in the 1920's was California's first Nash automobile dealer. Morimatsu had bucked Dave Beck's prejudices in Seattle, and won grudging permission to start a Teamsters Union local for Japanese produce salesmen and drivers. Despite preconceived opinions of Nisei from Hawaii about those on the mainland, lots of Californians, Washingtonians and Oregonians of Japanese ancestry were plenty gutsy. Many had to be, because there was no way they could melt into a background of other Japanese faces.

Hiroki Takahashi, Susumu Toyoda and Frank Tokubo came north from Camp Walters, still described decades later by Nisei as a "Texas hell-hole." Tokubo and Takahashi were Kibei, while Toyoda had done years of "stoop labor" with his father growing fruit and vegetables for sale. He had "fooled around in Japanese school, though, dipping girls' pigtails in the *sumi* ink we used for brush writing. It was a wonder I learned any Japanese at all," he said. Toyoda's brother Robert was the Whittier High School classmate of a driving, determined boy named Richard Nixon.

From Ft. Sheridan, Illinois came Nobu Tanabe, who'd been orphaned at age 19. Never possessing robust health, Tanabe spent a bunch of months in Army hospitals, but held up well enough to serve overseas with OSS cloak-and-dagger types.

* * *

All this dashing about the landscape, doing what had already been done the year before, didn't net Rasmussen and his men anywhere near the number of students he needed. Men who showed interest in 1941 had become completely turned off, thanks to the William Hearsts, Earl Warrens and others whose sentiments gave the families of Nisei grief. Hardly any of the new crop of students could really be called "volunteers," although their records indicated they were. Their main motivating factor had been getting away from lousy concentration camp environments, or even worse Army camp ones. Even then, bad as Army conditions elsewhere were for Nisei GI's, a batch had to be ordered to Savage against their will. Kai Rasmussen and John Aiso had headaches.

They would get bigger. Over in Wisconsin, at Camp McCoy, were nearly 1500 brawling, boiling Hawaiians, who'd had it up to here. All had now *twice* completed basic training, and a man gets awfully tired of the manual-of-arms and military drill, especially at zero temperatures. On arrival in their shuttered trains during June, the Hawaiians headed for the Post Exchange and bought out its entire beer supply in minutes. They'd been repeating the process nearly nightly since. To the fun-loving, free-wheeling men of Hawaii there was only one thing to do with money—spend it. "Keep the change!" was as common an expression with them as "Aloha."

It's not clear to the author why Rasmussen and Weckerling hadn't approached Nisei soldiers in Hawaii before the war. Perhaps fearful on-the-scene seniors in Hawaii wouldn't permit it. One can't tell. Evidence is available in enough quantity to establish that senior officers in Hawaii *feared* the Nisei. If they didn't want them in military intelligence, a military bureaucracy provided sufficient means for thwarting realization of a good idea. In late 1942, Rasmussen was getting desperate.

A decision was finally made. "Use the Hawaiians!"

It would prove a wise decision. Far more Hawaiians than mainlanders were Kibei. The islands were closer to Japan. It cost less to send a son to the home country from them. Too, Japanese communities in Hawaii were more cohesive and comfortable. They weren't scattered up and down a 1500-mile shoreline, and they didn't dot the landscape like earth-bound islands. Issei could speak their native tongue all day to nearly everyone they met. As a result, their children spoke it well also. Hawaii Nisei went mostly to McKinley High School (called "Tokyo Tech" by local Caucasian kids), and usually to the University of Hawaii campus if college was possible. They rarely strayed far from touch with parents. They were more "Japanese" than the mainland Japanese-Americans.

Rasmussen had to get his hands on some of them.

Chapter 6

Late 1942 found nearly all AJA influentials, the people who theretofore affected the thinking and activities of others having Japanese ancestry, behind bars or barbed wire. It did not matter that the sole justification for putting them there had disappeared, that Roosevelt's chiefs of staff had assured him the U.S. west coast was safe, or that the Battle of Midway had precluded all possibility of a Japanese thrust toward America.

History, at moments, is people's insanity put in print. Locking up Issei was such insanity. They had provided the means for shortening the war and, as events proved, saving a million or more lives. No Issei knew this at the time, of course. Damned few learned of it later, the Pentagon keeping facts classified for three decades. Thousands and thousands of Issei died without knowing how much they had done to help win the Pacific war. The Japanese schools they established with hoarded pennies had provided the bulk of input to Rasmussen's school. The only other Japanese-Americans* who qualified were Kibei.

---

*A very nice Nisei lady asked the author not to use the expression "Japanese-Americans," saying "We don't want to be hyphenated, just American." With all due respect, my responsibility is to the widest possible readership, and *hakujin* readers are more familiar and comfortable with the hyphenation. The lady and I will simply have to hope that future generations of our countrymen will become civilized enough to use only the term "American" when referring to each other.

They'd gotten their Japanese in Japan, and the Army got rid of them in 1942 as fast as each could be identified.

Japanese schools got started in Hawaii, the first one opening in 1893 with 30 pupils. By 1940 the islands had 200 such institutions, with more than 40,000 enrollees. To keep these schools, Hawaii Japanese fought one battle right up to the Supreme Court. It ruled in 1927 that the schools provided children "instruction deemed valuable by their parents," and that such instruction was not in conflict with the public interest. The Court's decision was unanimous, which was probably why 21 other States attempting to control foreign language schools ceased their legislative efforts.

One man who taught Japanese to Army students has depicted the language as reflecting the Japanese character and culture. He used comparatives like "difficult, and complex; emotional, not logical; vague and imprecise; intellectually inaccessible." Perhaps Japanese is these things. Who knows? Learning Japanese can occupy a lifetime, as many a scholar can attest. Readers need know little about the language itself, except that study of it at Camp Savage gave Minneapolis opticians and optometrists a windfall as Nisei students taxed eyeballs to the limit and beyond.

Numerous unqualified Caucasians took a shot at trying for the school, but got quickly shot down. No doubt a desk in what the Army calls its Zone of The Interior had more appeal than a foxhole, but MISLS staff screened the opportunists out. One officer told the author, "There are some people who think you speak Italian by adding an 'o' onto everything, and Japanese by adding a 'u,' like in 'bread-u.' We got rid of them fast."

At the Military Intelligence Service Language School, instructors had to strain mightly, to qualify those who did pass the screening tests. Following is a brief that gives some idea of written Japanese they had to teach.

Kaisho. The printed version of *Kanji.* In various forms, it is used for most publications, which can only be read by someone who has memorized a great number of ideographs. For Americans, a formidable barrier.

Gyosho. Hand-written Japanese. Comparable, although not precisely, to the Palmer Method of Penmanship the author and his peers had to master in prewar grammar school. Very difficult for Americans.

Sosho. More or less a shorthand rendering of *Kanji,* called "grass writing." Highly individualized. Almost impossible for an American to master. Most Japanese Army field orders were taken down over a telephone in *sosho.* The ability to translate rapidly this personalized "scribbling" from documents siezed near the front was the most potent weapon in the arsenal of a linguist.

It was usually Kibei who proved best at deciphering *sosho.* Those who'd been kicked out of the Army had to be found, approached, solicited, and persuaded to give the Army a second chance. Most were behind barbed wire when approached. A ridiculous situation, true, but when mankind indulges in the insanity called war, nuttiness becomes the norm.

* * *

Rasmussen's recruiters did what they could in late 1942. It was not enough. Morio Nishita got concentration camp inmates to join the effort, even though his own relatives were being locked up, the sight of his uniform enough to persuade some he was sincere. Other MISLS staffers worked hard, too, but an early head count showed that the quota was not being met. So, 67 Nisei from Camp McCoy were identified and ordered to Savage, and more ordered later as needed. Dick Oguro got passed over in the first selection, because he excelled in the martial arts. A qualified judo instructor was automatically suspect.

Oguro felt he got shanghai'd with the second batch, because of a letter he'd written a Minneapolis newspaper, wondering when trained Nisei soldiers would be put to use instead of just being kept languishing in a camp.

Not all the Hawaii men were sold on language school, but the inside of a classroom had a lot more appeal than drilling—and drilling—and drilling in the snow, at sub-zero temperatures. Besides, McCoy was not really a happy place. Not so long as civilian AJA's were locked up, right next door.

The Hawaiians did eventually accept their situation with resignation, working off anger against "those god-damned Japs!" If it hadn't been for the attack on Pearl Harbor, they reasoned, they wouldn't be in the fix they were in, 4000 miles from home and shivering. It seemed logical to blame everything on the guys who executed the December 7 attack.

Linguists from the 100th began calling themselves *Sempai Gumi* ("The Yellow Band"), taking some pride in the fact they would be first Hawaiians into the Pacific. Few realized it at the time, but what made them adjust quickly was—schmalzy as it may sound—what they'd learned at mother's knee. Caucasians find it difficult to comprehend that Issei believed their children would be better Americans if they were also good Japanese, but it was true. And, in Hawaii, it was *easier* to be Japanese than on the mainland, and therefore more American.

In the Nisei home, father ruled supreme, usually as benevolent despot although not always, able to restore peace and quiet with "That's annoying!" in grated Japanese. Mother was his silent partner, a lady with the longest working day of any American. First up and last to bed, an Issei mother saw more sunrises than a milkman, because she caught the two he missed on his days off. In addition to handling all household tasks and responsibilities, she softly supported and encouraged her children's aspirations, while buttressing father's orders and wishes with her own more palatable version of them.

A good Nisei obeyed father, while hoping with all his heart never to disappoint mother.

Behavior expectations were based on Confucian morality. Loyalty to country, respect for parents, and maintenance of harmony in family and other personal relationships were paramount. These topped all considerations a Nisei might entertain. Issei fathers could never digest so radical a concept as human rights. These had no place in the scheme of things. The race, the group, the family came first. The individual came last, if indeed he got any consideration at all, which was not likely. Living consisted of observing one's obligations, not dreaming of entitlements. A well-reared Nisei's life was guided by the principles of *on, gimu* and *giri. On* was a moral debt one owed nation, parents and teachers, from whom all blessings were known to flow. The nature of *on* was such that the debt could never be fully repaid, and was therefore lifelong. *Gimu* covered moral and legal duties. It required that every Nisei be a good American, a good student, a good worker; that he honor and obey his parents; and that he meet all responsibilities. *Giri* worked in the social area, with moral overtones. A Nisei had to be meticulous about repaying all favors, gifts, and help provided by anyone. He dared not bring *haji* (shame) on his race, family, or even neighborhood by breaking the law or committing other unworthy acts. Failing in school was unforgivable. Also, a Nisei had to neglect or overlook no opportunity for bringing honor on his family, so that it might have pride.

Everything was based on self-abnegation. Teachings, sayings and stories from an age-old culture illustrated each major and minor point.

Loyalty? "A *samurai* can serve but one lord."

Young Nisei learned that such loyalty was lifelong. They repeatedly read and heard of the 47 *ronin,* whose *daimyo* (master) had been foully tricked into unworthy behavior, which required his killing himself. The "masterless *samurai*" deliberately spent years debasing themselves to the level where fellow Japanese considered them un-

Kai Rasmussen had this ironic flower bed removed before the first set of students arrived at Camp Savage. Parents of many were imprisoned.

worthy of notice. The *ronin* then assembled, broke into the stronghold of their lord's enemy, and slew him. They then repaired to their dead master's grave and committed mass *seppuku,* disemboweling themselves. Moral? No insult must be left unavenged. Honor counted for more than anything.

Stoicism? "A true *samurai* picks his teeth when his stomach is empty." Nisei were conditioned not to show pain, sorrow, disappointment, hunger or anything that indicated weakness. The restriction extended to boasting and undue hilarity. Small wonder that Caucasian neighbors considered them inscrutable.

Beneath the mask, however, emotions burned fiercely. Nisei kids early learned the dying words of Masashige Kusunoki, who perished at Minatogawa fighting for his Emperor. *"Shichisei hokoku!"* he cried, wishing he had another seven lives to give for his ruler.

Behavior codes, to the Western eye, were complicated, but in Japan they made for a well-behaved citizenry. They did the same in America for AJA's, too, but in both lands they suffered for this predilection to behave well. Militarists twisted Emperor Meiji's rescript on education, before and after his death, to convince citizens they owed everything to the Throne, including their lives, which they must be willing to sacrifice along with any other possessions for the eternal glorification and preservation of Japan.

In America, this generated an attitude of "To get along, go along" among Issei and Nisei, who paid awful penalties for their forbearance.

To illustrate how militarists whipped up the populace into expansionist tendencies, making them ever more manageable in spite of hardships they had to endure, one need only consider two expressions—*Yamato damashii* (Japanese spirit), and *Bushido* (the way of the warrior). For the first 25 centuries of Japan's existence, the two sayings were rarely written or voiced. Rather, an individual Japanese took a quiet pride in being a member of the nation that was his, and he tried to observe a code of civilized behavior. Nowadays, *Bushido* actually leaves a bad taste in the mouths of some educated Japanese. As for *Yamato damashii,* one is about as likely to hear it voiced as often as one hears a shouted "God Bless America!" and is as likely to feel uncomfortable in one instance as the other. One concerned MIS'er, a Kibei and a scholar, still disturbed about how 70,000,000 people of his blood were manipulated into nearly committing national suicide via a war that brought so much needless death, told the author that "Japanese—and Americans—and we who are called Japanese-Americans, would all be one hell of a lot better off if none of us had ever heard the expressions *Yamato damashii* and *bushido*!" The author, all too aware how these same expressions were twisted into hateful propaganda for use *against* the Japanese enemy in the war, had to agree.

Still Issei, and the *sensei* they hired, had to work with the tools at hand. They did what they knew how to do. In the process, they gave Nisei a feeling for their native land, American, few other ethnic groups have exhibited. Nearly every Nisei qualified to serve, and allowed to serve, *did* serve the United States in that war. It's a statement that cannot be made of any other nationality. No Nisei, certainly, stayed home to make a buck off the bloodshed.

* * *

Home and school teachings shaped the Nisei. So, sadly, did prejudice. Most teenage Nisei had fathers in their 50's or older. This came about because it took an Issei so long to earn enough money to marry or send for a bride that a gap nearly two generations wide yawned between him and his offspring. Many cultural advantages were lost by falling into this chasm, which was a barrier to effective communications. One can certainly obey, but how can one respect the opinions of, a parent who speaks chiefly in another tongue. What one learned in the *hakujin* school militated against it.

Conformance was an aid, here. Nisei were taught that one must observe filial piety. It was the Japanese way. It strengthened one's resolve. It made one able to bear a little bit easier what it took to be a good American when you were "different." Although many Nisei found themselves troubled, nearly all had one stout anchor to windward. All could find a modicum of comfort in the homilies of their immigrant parents. The Issei even had one for when all else failed, when nothing but disaster loomed or occurred. It served them well when, on short notice, they were allowed only an armful of possessions to take along to imprisonment.

Shikata ga nai ("It cannot be helped.").

* * *

Although they didn't have to clean up their sleeping areas, as preceding class members did, December arrivals at Camp Savage didn't find the atmosphere inviting. The coldest winter Minnesota had in decades was on. Three old-fashioned pot-bellied stoves heated each barracks, and one man was given the "coal detail" in each building. He had to shiver himself awake in plenty of time to stoke up the fires. Woe betide him if at night he didn't bank the fires just right, and they went out. John Aiso used the circumstance to get more effort out of his charges, letting it be known that men who flunked the course got assigned to the coal gang until orders came through for duty elsewhere.

A lot of missionaries' sons, and formerly Japan-based businessmen, entered the second Savage class, many having been repatriated on the Swedish liner *Gripsholm* when the U.S. and Japan exchanged nationals. William Laffin, who was half-Caucasian, half-Japanese, was one of these. He was fortunate. James Hamasaki, a diplomatic service employee, was one of the only two Nisei who sailed home from Japan on the repatriation ship. A 1942 message to Yokohama from the State Department *specifically directed* that no Nisei be listed for boarding the *Gripsholm*. A friend of the author's, Masaru Fujimoto, was one of those who had to spend the war in Japan. I've met others still bitter decades later at how their nation had abandoned them.

Laffin was to lead 14 Nisei who would help write some history in Burma, but the Pentagon would keep blotting the page. Howard Furumoto was one of those Nisei, and anxious to serve. A veterinary student at Kansas State University when war broke out, Howard was run off by one Col. Campbell, professor of military science and tactics there, when he sought advanced ROTC and a commission. "Your kind is really not welcome!" Furumoto was told, "Now get the hell out of my office!"

"We got the usual promises of promotions and stuff!" one MIS'er said of the second Savage class. Dozens of 100th members put in to transfer back to their old outfit, however, when word came that it was going to go overseas. Every such request was turned down. Rasmussen often resorted to telling a petitioner "See John Aiso about it," then telephoning Aiso and ordering him to deny the man's request when he showed up there. Demands from the Pacific were building. No potential linguist could be allowed to get away.

Instructor staff lived a few miles down the road from Savage, while students lived on what they quickly dubbed "the pig farm." For some reason no one ever ascertained, the staff location was called Camp Seven. Bachelor teachers had barracks type quarters there, and held Saturday night revels. Asao Nakazawa, Mark Murakami, Tad Yamada and Paul Tekawa would cover windows with newspaper, spread blankets on the floor, and break out forbidden whiskey, together with salami, cheese, potato chips, pickles and canned goodies. Singing, dancing and general carousing went on into the wee hours. "We married instructors" said Shigeya Kihara enviously, "were not permitted to join them, to our chagrin." Kihara, along with Akira Oshida, Tetsuo Imagawa, Tom Tanimoto, Toshio Tsukahira and Satoshi Nagase, "had to entertain ourselves in more sedate fashion."

"Bud" Nagase was an electronics genius before that term was coined. He was a civilian when first encountered by Rasmussen, and "under suspicion by the FBI. His parents were locked up because they owned binoculars or something, but were completely cleared later," according to the Dane, who enlisted Nagase "so the FBI couldn't touch him," after Bud had given him some Japanese textbooks. The pair then decided it would be a good idea if Camp Savage had a radio station, so students could practice interception of Japanese broadcasts. It would also sharpen their language skills. Higher headquarters said "Impossible! There's a blind spot here. You couldn't pick up Japan!"

Rasmussen and Nagase found a local ham operator who said he'd talked to Japan daily for many years before the war. Nagase built a set just like his, and Radio Savage was in business. James Cullen, Tatsuo Tanaka, Sueki Murahata, Ed Okada and Robert Shiraga helped operate and maintain it. So did George Mizota, Satoshi Yuguchi and Frank Inami. MIS students listened in on Domei news broadcasts, changed these into *romaji,* then translated and distributed them. None had much intelligence value, but they did help estimate the tone of military and national sentiment inside Japan. Radio interceptors who got the basics at Savage, and more training elsewhere, did good work in New Guinea, the Phillipines, India and Burma.

Yutaka Munakata also had a special section— translation. He took men who'd completed the language course, gave them a refresher, and put them to work on captured documents as these came in. He also helped assemble teams, which consisted of three men strong in translation, three strong in interrogation, and three strong in interpreting, plus a team leader. Caucasian officers usually headed up each unit, an item that did not go down well with Nisei, although many developed deep and lifelong friendships with some officers. Nisei couldn't see why men who knew less Japanese than themselves, and often had no more education then some NCO's on the team, got commissions and they didn't. It was a real *shikata ga nai* situation.

Things started to go well on New Guinea, but the cost was high. One regiment of the 32nd, when relieved, was down to 200 effectives out of 1400 men. Makoto Sakamoto and Joe Yoshiwara went up to Guadalcanal from Noumea, and were joined by Hiroshi Matsuda and Terno Odow a few days later. All worked to get trapped Japanese to surrender, but found that dropping leaflets had little effect. Japanese who might have wished to surrender were too weak, from disease and starvation, to do so. On both New Guinea and Guadalcanal, nearly all prisoners taken were wounded, in shock, sick, starving, or all four. Only a handful lived long enough to be interrogated, and maggot-covered wounds became a sight familiar to Nisei. Information gotten from such men was less useful than that contained in diaries or documents.

* * *

Richard Sakakida got released by Manila authorities, who began to believe he might really be a civilian. He was told to report to Col. Nishiharu, of the 14th Army's legal staff. "You are being given amnesty," Dick was told, "providing you work for us."

Sakakida played his role to the hilt. He declined. "I have already been forced to do military work once," he protested. "I was captured, and tortured. What do you think the other side will do to me, an American citizen, if I'm captured again, by them? They'll shoot me as a traitor!"

"You have no choice," said Nishiharu, and took him into 14th Army headquarters as an interpreter. Somewhat suspicious, however, he billeted Sakakida in his own living quarters, so he could keep an eye on him. The Hawaii Nisei found that situation too confining, but got out of it by stealing the Colonel's Camel cigarettes until he got caught at it. He was summarily sent to bunk with three Japanese legal clerks. When they went out at night, so did he, but in a different direction. After a while Sakakida made contact with the "ROTC Group" of Filipino guerrillas, under a Major Tupas.

Sakakida then began gathering shipping information in the headquarters, and giving it to guerrillas. He fell under suspicion again, and a Maj. Matsunobe tried to trap him into admission of military status by handing him an American .45 pistol with orders to clean it. Sakakida followed orders literally, polishing the handle and barrel until they gleamed. He did not "field strip" the weapon, which would have given him away.

Continued careful reluctance drew from his captors that they wanted to land Sakakida back home from a submarine, as an agent for them. "What? And get tortured again? No thanks!" he told Matsunobe, and the major backed off. Sakakida focused on the stealing of shipping schedules, smuggling these out to guerrillas. They then got radio'd to Australia, relayed to Pearl Harbor, and broadcast to prowling U.S. submarines. Not once did the 14th Army suspect it was Sakakida who was damaging their resupply effort.

It's possible that MacArthur's interceptor-decoder team in Australia, or Nimitz's in Hawaii, came up with information in late February, 1943, of a major Japanese movement of troops from Rabaul to new Guinea, but Sakakida might have also lent a hand. He stole a copy of Japanese plans for a major movement of troops south, and handed it on to Filipino guerrillas. When 8 transports left Rabaul for New Guinea, protected by 8 destroyers, MacArthur's headquarters knew they were coming.

As he had with the two airlifts, George Kenney hurled everything he could, American and Australian, into action. Atavistic slaughter followed, with pilots and PT-boat gunners killing enemy soldiers in lifeboats and rafts. All the transports and half the destroyers went down. More than 3000 Japanese troops perished. Twenty-nine years later, via the *Pacific Citizen,* official publication of the Japanese Americans Citizens League, the American public got its first inkling of what Nisei linguists reaped in intelligence from the Battle of the Bismarck Sea.

An abandoned lifeboat from the sunken transport *Teiyo Maru* was found aground on Goodenough Island, north of New Guinea's eastern tip. In it was a document of immeasurable value—the Japanese Army's Officer List. Withan effective date of Oct. 15, 1942, it was the complete roster of 40,000 Imperial Army officers, from Hideki Tojo down to the most obscure company commander! It gave each man's rank, the unit to which he was attached, and the job he held.

Sidney Mashbir put every linguist he could spare to work on this, translating the *Kaisho* into *romaji* so Caucasians could read it. When the Nisei finished, and got copies off to Washington and elsewhere, the Allies had a running start on what every warring nation dreams of acquiring—the enemy's *order of battle*—what he had for troops. MacArthur, plus Nimitz and the Pentagon, now knew the composition of the entire Japanese army, together with the names of its units, large and small. Other information already on hand, or acquired thereafter, would establish the *locations* of all. Thanks to Nisei and other linguists in Australia, the American battle planners now had the guts of what it takes to fight a war successfully. It was thereafter possible to identify with increasing accuracy where which Japanese units were, and in what strength. MacArthur's possession and up-dating of this information helps explain why he lost less than 100 men at the water's edge in more than 50 amphibious landings, while the Navy and Marine Corps lost thousands in just a few. Proper use of the Order of Battle book saved thousands of American lives, and cost the enemy dearly.

As the second Savage class got cranked up, Nisei in New Guinea provided more valuable help to the 41st Division and elements of the Australian Army. One batch of documents, taken from the body of a sniper, revealed operating procedures in one area that let the 41st win two quick tactical victories. Interrogation of a captured Japanese runner revealed that forces blocking a vital road against the 41st had been radically reduced from the number earlier estimated. The 41st, and the Australians, quickly overran this opposition. And, after the Battle of the Bismarck Sea, one surviving POW revealed details of the antiaircraft defenses around Rabaul. MacArthur's air force suffered fewer losses when Nisei interrogators elicited this information.

* * *

At Savage, a certain degree of antipathy sprung up between Hawaii Nisei and the mainlanders, partly-due to long-held Hawaii prejudices, and partly to a snobbish attitude on the part of better-educated mainlanders. They quickly tabbed one another "Buddha heads" and "Kotonks." Journalists slavishly wrote what they were told, that the former appellation came from islanders having shaven heads like Buddhist monks, the latter being "the noise two Mainlander heads make when one of us Hawaii boys bangs them together!"

Neither explanation is true, according to Robert Honda, veteran of Burma. Nisei kids in Hawaii got called *Bobura-head* ("Pumpkin head") by elders when they goofed. They took the joshing appellation into manhood with them, condensing it to *bura*-head. Honda also traced the origin of Kotonk. It originated with Hawaii's prewar drafted Nisei GI's. One coined the pidgin word "K-nob," for knob. The fad caught on in the 298th and 299th Regiments. It spread to "K-nife" and "K-nowledge," then further, as Nisei strove for a separate identity in a sea of Caucasian uniforms.

In peacetime it was practice at Schofield Barracks for NCO's to refer to their juniors as "donkeys." Whimsical Nisei encountering mainlanders converted it to "K-donkeys," and applied it to their new associates. In time it got shortened to "K-donk," and eventually rattled out as Kotonk.

The attitude of mild mutual contempt didn't last long. Islanders and mainlanders circled each other and sniffed, but soon decided they needed to get along with each other. Few men could wade through a swamp of *Kanji* ideographs without help. Besides, a common area of agreement came into their lives—bitching! All complained about "Not enough rice!" in the Savage messhall, and all commiserated about the *extra* gear a linguist had to take with him to combat.

Each Savage graduate, after stringing knapsack, bedroll, knife, bayonet, weapon, canteen, grenades and ammunition bandoliers from himself, had to find room for three pocket dictionaries. Other team equipment included 14 more *thick* dictionaries, covering *Kanji* characters and their compounds; nautical terms; aeronautical terms; military terms; Japanese surnames; Japanese first names; plus a copy of *Webster's New Collegiate.* A portable typewriter had to be included, plus stationery, rulers, paper clips, pencils, pens, staplers, magnifying glasses, and various other office impediments. Nisei linguists soon came to agree with William Tecumseh Sherman, their war being a special and burdensome kind of hell. It was never easy to remain equipped with the clerical equipment that gave fellow GI's such laughs at first sight, so Nisei linguists observed a tradition handed down from Ceasar's legionnaires—what they needed, they stole. One way or another, MIS'ers scrounged up what got the job done.

* * *

A team headed for Indooroopilly while the second class was in session, led by Robert Pang and Donald Botting. Kim Hatashita was team leader. With him were Harry Umeda, Hideo Tsuyuki, Minoru Namba, Kaoru Nishida, Min Masukane, Ralph Kimoto, Kenneth Shimbu and Masaru Yoshioka. Another member of the team, Richard Hirata, made enough appeals, often enough, to be finally granted permission to visit his parents in Poston's concentration camp on the way overseas. By the time permission came through, Hirata was so disgusted that he'd gone to town to get drunk. He had to sell his watch, typewriter and some other possessions real quick, to raise the fare money, but Dick did become the first Nisei GI in uniform to enter that camp. Then he endured 58 hours of air travel to Australia, from which three members of his team came down with.ear trouble so bad they had to be hospitalized on arrival. Other members went on to New Guinea to serve with headquarters of the U.S. 6th Army, which came into being as U.S. forces in the Pacific grew. Yukitaka "Terry" Mizutari led another team to 6th Army. On it were Harry Fukuhara, Kengo Nagasako, Ben Nakamoto, Shoji Ishii, Yoshiaki Hirabayashi and Terry Teramoto.

* * *

Gen. William Slim headed British forces that had been chased, along with Gen. Stilwell and the over-rated "Flying Tigers," out of Burma, an area Slim hoped to retake without help from the covetous Chiang Kai Chek. One of Slim's more colorful subordinates, Orde Wingate, made a deep penetration thrust into Burma, moving well behind Japanese lines and operating there for months. His force tied up and distracted a large number of enemy troops, while blowing up bridges and doing whatever else would hurt the Japanese effort. Wingate proved that an enemy could be harassed by an airdrop-sustained force, although he lost one-third of his 3000 men making his point. His tactic would be repeated in Burma. Nisei would be involved.

Slim asked London for some Japanese-speaking help; and got told "we are just starting up some language courses at Oxford," so he welcomed news that Nisei were being made available to help in the China-Burma-India theater. Hundreds would serve there, although few fellow Americans in the States would learn of it.

By mid-February of 1943, the Pacific picture was brightening. The Japanese had evacuated all troops they could from Guadalcanal, physically giving up the island. In New Guinea, the Buna-Gona-Sananda struggle was over. MacArthur's engineers were hurriedly building or improving air bases for him, to cover further northwestern advances. The Australians, aided by the 32nd and 41st Divisions, had held out longer than the Japanese could. That spelled the difference, because both sides were at the trail end of very long supply lines.

Nisei proudly bore the flag that deserted them, at Savage Saturday inspections, following a week of hard studies.

On Guadalcanal only 600 POW's were taken, the Japanese leaving 25,000 dead while evacuating 13,000 in an operation that left the U.S. Navy with egg on its face. Now American troops began staging through Guadalcanal to the Russell Islands in preparation for taking New Georgia, further up the Solomons chain, as a first giant step toward Tokyo. MacArthur had already taken one, to New Guinea's north side.

* * *

As both sides paused for breath in the Pacific, and the Allied picture brightened in Europe, events began to overtake the Nisei. They were suddenly *wanted* by top echelon U.S. officers, and even more wanted by the desperate British in India. New plans began to be made for Nisei. The 11th Airborne Division was activated in North Carolina, with slots for Nisei linguists included on its TO. The 100th Infantry Battalion moved to Camp Shelby, Mississippi, for combat training. Word spread of a decision to form an all-Nisei outfit that would fight in Europe.

Reactionaries reacted, as reactionaries are wont to do. In a number of the camps, and especially Tule Lake, rocks and sticks came through the windows of families who let it be known they answered Yes-Yes to the infamous questionnaire. Few firebrands dared do anything physical to relatives of men who volunteered for active Army service, but families did get ostracized. It was *shikata ga nai* time again. There were certainly pro-Japan types in the camps, and they were active. It took years for anger to calm down, for such people and government authorities to forgive one another for earlier, now-understandable attitudes. In the overall picture, however, Nisei began to feel they *might* have a place.

* * *

Japanese reinforcements landed at Finschhafen, now threatened by MacArthur, while American ones arrived in the Solomons. The 43rd Division moved up to replace the Americal, which went to Noumea for rest and re-training.

Nisei were with both outfits, their positions respected. Another speeded-up class pulled out of Savage, slated for the 32nd Division and headed by Masao Matsumoto. He had with him George Suda, Yoshikazu Higashi, Harry T. Kubo, Fred Miyata, Shigeru Higashi, George Sugiyama, Kazue Takashima, Milton Tanizawa, and Masato Iwamoto. They, too, would learn to hate bully beef and hardtack.

At Port Moresby, amid daily bombings from Rabaul, Tom Masaharu Takata found time to collapse with malaria. James Fujimura and Kazuo Kawaguchi arrived to join the New Guinea Forces headquarters (an Australian-commanded organization) on the third day Takata was abed, and he was ordered back to Australia.

* * *

From Savage a team led by the man who said he never really "had to watch" his men, Sheldon Covell, headed for a special school in Pennsylvania, then out to India. The intrepid Harold Hanaumi was team leader. He had with him Richard S. Honma, Joe I. Ichikawa, Shigeto Mazawa, Ted Oda, Koichi G. Okano, James Ueno, Katsumi Baba, Eichi Nakazono (who'd gotten "lost" temporarily when Dick Hayashi's group raised enough hell for him to get emergency leave and visit his dying father in concentration camp, and who had then to be re-assigned), Harry Tsuchiyama and Samuel Umade. They were in the van of what became almost a mass movement of Nisei linguists into the Indian sub-continent.

Henry Kuwabara headed for India, too, and the enlisted version of an Order of the British Empire, on the team commanded by John D. McLaughlin. Leader was Fusao Uchiyama, and other members included Roy T. Takai, Hiroshi Osako, George P. Okada, Shori Hiraide, Joe Inafuku, Toshio Taniguchi and Hideo Imai. With them was Eiichi Sakauye, another Nisei destined for decoration by the British.

As the 1943 spring bloomed, top U.S. planners knew for sure the war was won. John Weckerling had taken on the job of giving Chief of Staff George Marshall, Army Air Corps chief Arnold, and Secretary of War Stimson their daily intelligence briefing. Solidly in the know, Weckerling gave the author details not publicly revealed before. Like Germany's having weakened even before Americans landed in Europe. And our knowledge of codes being so great that we could knock off Japanese shipping *at will.* Weckerling, in Washington, even knew which senior Japanese officers had abandoned their posts, leaving junior ones in charge, when American attacks impended.

Washington could see it was merely a matter of time when America would win the Pacific war. How was no longer a worry. Everything was rolling off production lines, including battleships and aircraft carriers, at a rate Japan could never hope to match. The U.S. Navy even unbent far enough to admit it needed the help of Nisei linguists, its University of Colorado and Harvard programs not getting out enough of the effective product needed. The Navy set up JICPOA (Joint Intelligence Center, Pacific Ocean Areas), which included a large pool of linguists. The Nisei contingent was kept away from Makalapa Crater headquarters, perhaps because enlisted men might catch a glimpse of the plush tennis courts and swimming pool senior officers had convenient to their bungalows. The Nisei were housed in downtown Honolulu, in what had been a furniture store. Per diem was paid them, which kept them away from military installations altogether, except when they were summoned to one. They ate in restaurants.

Tim Ohta led a team from Minnesota to Honolulu. On it were Hoichi Kubo, Jack Shigeo Tanimoto, Joe Fujino, William Nuno, Roy Higashi, Larry Saito, Dick Kishine, Richard Moritsugu, and Frank Mori. They got assigned to the 27th Division in time for the Marshalls invasion. Others would make that operation, with the 7th Division.

More than 100 Nisei streamed out of JICPOA to serve with the Marine Corps in invasions, often landing with the early waves. G. M. Neufeld, head of the reference section, history and museums division, at USMC headquarters regretted, on April 7, 1977, being unable to help the author with facts on this. "Little information is available on your topic as Navy policy during the War did not permit recruitment of Japanese Americans in the Marine Corps," he wrote the author. Nisei linguists were on "TDY" (temporary duty) with the Corps. Although a number of medals were awarded them by USMC generals, the Corps did not see fit to place Nisei on any official rosters.

* * *

Karl Yoneda, the longshoreman-political activist, wangled his way onto a team heading across the Pacific. Kai Rasmussen had called him in earlier, and apprised him that authorities knew of his Communist beliefs, but that Yoneda's services were needed and appreciated. Nonetheless, the Army intended to confine his services to the U.S. continental limits. Yoneda got to chuckle about that. He was part of a propaganda team that included Chris Ishii, an artist who'd worked for Disney Studios, who designed the language school mascot—a gopher, representing Minnesota, that tried its best to look warlike. Edgar Laytha, a magazine correspondent, was another member. Harry Akune's kid brother Kenjiro was on the team, as were Sam Sasaki and also Clarke Kawakami, the writer son of a writer. Clarke's mother was one of the first Caucasian ladies in America to become the bride of a Japanese. They had been drawn together by common humanitarian ideals. Koji Ariyoshi, Kenji Yasui, Masao Kitsuta and Alex Yorichi rounded off this talented group.

In New Guinea the 41st got a team from the December class at Savage. It was headed by John Tanikawa. He had Frank Ishida, James K. Sasano, Tetsuya Mayeda, John Sakai, John Mitani, Hisao Matsumoto, Shigeru Iba and Everett Sasaki along. All experienced the very worst of combat conditions, but the earth would rotate on its axis 13,000 times before more than a handful of fellow Americans got an inkling as to their wartime service.

More Nisei streamed out of Savage into the Far East, among them George Itsuo Nakamura, one of three MIS'ers to have the same first and last name. Also in groups that headed for Delhi, and often on to Burma jungles to fight alongside British, Chinese, and the fierce Kachin tribesmen were Toshio Abe, Harry Andow, and Harry Uyehara. The long voyage around the south of Australia, to avoid possible Japanese submarines, was also undertaken by Ryo Arai, Joe Ikeguchi, Henry Kimura, Richard Y. Koike, Tom Moriguchi, Shoso Nomura and others. Henry Kimura would be thrilled at meeting Jackie Coogan, the balding former child motion picture star, and scared from glider missions with Coogan in support of Orde Wingate's Chindits as they operated behind Japanese lines in Burma. Coogan flew gliders.

As seasick as anyone were Tom M. Tsuruda, Henry T. Tsuchiyama, Sadao Toyama and Kiyoshi Suzukawa. But, once all hands got settled in India, they found that war really did not necessarily have to be hell. Cooks and houseboys cost pennies a day. Food was cheap and good. Tom Osasa, H. "Slim" Takiue, Henry Kojima, and Amos Nakamura felt they might have found a home in the Army, until boredom and eyestrain set them clamoring, like ATIS men in Australia, for action up front. As stated earlier, however, not all Nisei claimed to be heroes. Arthur Komori frankly told the author that, once he'd gotten from Corregidor to Melbourne, he never volunteered to leave his rear echelon assignment. Not even once.

* * *

Doolittle's flyers had bombed Japan from the carrier *Hornet* in April, 1942. Some went down, and were captured. As rumors spread of what happened to them, Nisei were kept confined to camp for safety, and resented it. Others grew rebellious for other reasons. When one considers that no one at Savage ever had teaching experience before, but still had to produce qualified linguists at an ever-increasing rate, one can understand why tempers grew short and traditional methods of order and organization got discarded. MIS'ers remember being threatened with what could happen to their families if they didn't do their best, although they later softened in attitude at recognition of the oppression also being suffered by their "oppressors." Administration wasn't the best. No student got a 72-hour pass before February, and the day-night study, followed by four hours of Saturday tests, proved too much for many. Volatile Hawaiians, dismayed that friends were going to combat far sooner than themselves, developed a device for joining them. "Easy bruddah," one *bura*-head would tell another. "You and me make fight. Plenty *pilikia* (trouble)! Toss 'em out. We go Missasippy wid da rest a da boys. O.K.?"

The tactic worked until John Aiso caught on. After that, Hawaiians could hammer the hell out of each other all they wanted to, but they had to return to class. Sadao Munemori was an exception no one could handle. Kai Rasmussen finally put him on the stove detail, shoveling coal for a month, in the hope he'd change his mind about immediate transfer to the 442nd. The young Nisei persisted in his wishes, and Rasmussen reluctantly let him go. Munemori went to combat in Europe, sprawled on a German grenade to save comrades, and became the first Nisei to earn a Medal of Honor. Like all-too-many other Nisei decorations, it had to be awarded posthumously. A number of Nisei retained very bad memories of their association with the language effort. One, Tamotsu Shibutani, wrote a book focusing on these. He was not in the picture in 1943, however. The official MISLS school roster shows that a T. Shibutani was a member of the class that started just one month before the war ended.

* * *

Another good thing that happened to Nisei in the first half of 1943 was Gen. DeWitt's being *ordered* to rescind his edict barring Nisei in uniform from visiting the West Coast, so they could see imprisoned relatives. DeWitt got a shot in, the very day after he withdrew his order, by telling a House committee "A Jap's a Jap. They are a dangerous element, whether loyal or not." To DeWitt's credit, he later stated publicly that he might have been wrong, an action that, through 1978 at least, Earl Warren had not taken. DeWitt was eventually assigned to the Arctic, where he continued to distinguish himself for being undistinguished. He ordered the construction of a large base, and insisted on its being completed—in the wrong place, at the wrong time, for the wrong purpose. The elaborate structure had to be torn down. None of its cost was deducted from DeWitt's retirement checks.

* * *

Isoroku Yamamoto was shot down over Ballale Island on April 18, 1943, while on an inspection tour, a victim of American interception and code-cracking. So many sources have claimed credit for this coup that the author gave up trying to establish whether Nisei were involved, although they might have been. Tom Lanphier, the bored pilot who gave John Burden flying lessons in the Fijis, led the flight of P-38's that ambushed Yamamoto. Nisei would figure prominently in events surrounding the death of Yamamoto's successor, Adm. Mineichi Koga.

Again, May was a momentous month. Nisei linguists had become pearls of great price. Some got seized by whoever discovered them. Haruo Sazaki, at Ft. Custer, was placed with an MP company processing POWs arriving from the Pacific. George Kiyoshi Yamashiro (who later translated his last name, via a different reading of its characters, as Sankey) was in Australia doing counterintelligence work, having been snatched up in Hawaii earlier. Sazaki got to attend language school, but only after more POW work, overseas. On the 11th of the month, a landing on Attu, in the Aleutians, marked the first attempt to take back from the enemy American real estate he'd seized. The 7th Division, with Nisei assigned to it, was given the job.

More than 20 linguists from the Alaskan command were in on the operation. Besides those already mentioned as having been sent north, starting with Yoshio Hotta's original group from the Presidio, there were Jewett Kariya, Pete Nakao, Tadachi Ogawa, and Hiromi Wada. Attackers hit Attu from two sides, trying to link up and pinch off the enemy on a promontory. Not all Nisei got ashore during the battle. Most were scattered among the three dozen ships supporting the assault.

John White got ashore. He had with him Sam Sugimoto, whom he described as "tiny, but terrific!" and Yasuo Sam Umetani. When the campaign closed, the trio visited an enemy hospital encampment where patients had either been shot by superiors or disemboweled themselves when capture appeared imminent. A Japanese doctor had done the shooting of patients who were too weak to kill themselves. Umetani, a Kibei, wept bitterly while translating a letter the doctor left. It later appeared in a Sunday supplement, the *American Weekly*.

George Hayashida was with Gordon Jorgensen. They stunned White by showing up at his command post after walking across the island during a hail of fire. Jorgensen, and Umetani, showed tremendous courage by walking into caves and trying to get holed-up Japanese soldiers to surrender. "All I had was a flashlight and a .45," said Hayashida when telling how he had followed Jorgensen in, "so when about ten agreed to surrender after prolonged discussions, I breathed a lot easier."

Satsuke Tanakatsubo was teamed up with Howard Nakamura, a Kibei from Hawaii. Their own invasion got delayed a little when the destroyer they were riding had to run out of the harbor to dodge an air attack, then come back. "Suts" didn't get along very well with a Navy officer assigned, a recent graduate of the Navy's school in Colorado, and once told him "Dig your own foxhole!" although threatened with court-martial. He later refused to assist the martinet when the officer had trouble translating a document, claiming he was off-duty and not available. He finally relented when the Navy man couldn't get the job done, and disgustedly announced it was "only a quartermaster report!" Just before he made the landing,

Suts told Caucasian infantrymen at Attu what other Nisei had to tell other Caucasians elsewhere during the war. "Take a good look, and *remember me,*" said the Sacramento Nisei, "because I'm going in with you!"

Frank Otsuka and Mickey Kuroiwa were offshore during the fight, monitoring radio transmissions. Other Nisei at Attu did the same, hoping to detect any enemy move to interfere with the invasion. Shigeo Ito got ashore. When the battle was over, he got sent across the island to interrogate a POW alleged via radio message to be an officer. It was a long trek. Along the way, Ito noticed "how yellow the dead enemy bodies were against the white snow." He had to find shelter under a ledge when snow fell, and found himself sharing it for hours with three dead Japanese. The POW that Ito was sent to see turned out to be an NCO, most of whose buttocks had been shot away. Maggots covered the festering wounds.

Sam Sugimoto carefully wrote out seven sets of surrender instructions. John White dropped six of them on a trapped portion of the enemy from an airplane, but they were ignored. One thousand Japanese made a final *banzai* attack, their charge's momentum carrying through American command posts and a medical aid area. Pete Nakao rolled under a bed just in time to avoid the charging enemy, but his sheets and bedding got stabbed with bayonets as the Japanese ran amok. When their charge was finally blunted, half the enemy force blew themselves up with hand grenades. Only 28 POWs were taken at Attu, about 1% of the defenders. All the others died.

Back at Savage, some Nisei linguists moved east, instead of west. Jim Matsumura led Kazuo Yamane, Seishin Kondo, and John Kenjo to the Pentagon. The only other Nisei permitted in that structure at that time besides them was the repatriated Jimmy Hamasaki. The four naturally caught a lot of odd stares, and once while having coffee at a corridor stand were approached by a curious Caucasian, who asked if they were Indian.

"That's right." Yamane told his inquirer, who then asked "What tribe?"

"Osaka," he said.

The Hawaii grocer's son was not the only Nisei able to spin humorous yarns about his war service. Kiyoshi Hirano, 35 years later, told a story only one other Nisei could. A descendant of the Hojo clan that once ruled Japan for 350 years, Hirano did top-secret, ultra-sensitive classified research in a very stange place.

He worked upstairs from a fish market!

Chapter 7

The summer of 1943 found ATIS at Indooroopilly a paying proposition. George Kanegai had taken a headquarters detachment out there from Savage, none of them MISLS grads, to set up administration of a tent encampment for the growing number of Nisei scheduled to arrive. By that time ATIS had in its clutches a prize POW named Seichi Ogino, taken in the Tobriand Islands. Ogino had an even more powerful photograpic memory than "The *Kanji Kid,*" and John Anderton marveled at what John Shelton drew out of the man. Shelton continued to draw Ogino out for nearly two years. An Australian Army officer, Shelton was the son of a Russian. Born in Japan, he was undoubtedly ATIS's top linguist. ATIS learned that Ogino was disgruntled at remaining only a Superior Private when he'd been promised a warrant officer's commission. Shelton massaged his attitude daily. The man seemed to remember everything he had ever seen anywhere, and it turned out he had seen much in many places. Again and again a special query would come out from the Pentagon, like "Find out what Ogino knows about the Japanese forces on Formosa." The captured NCO would promptly give chapter and verse from some piece of paper he had somewhere seen before his capture.

Documents sent back to ATIS were revealing, as more were translated right behind New Guinea front lines. Japanese submarine and barge routes from Rabaul to various points in New Guinea were discovered, and ambushes prepared. The fact that the Japanese got any new

Mike Miyatake at Indooroopilly's tent city before going north to fight. Kazuo Komoto (left) gets Purple Heart.

supplies onto New Guinea at all is a tribute to the skill and bravery of the officers who brought them, including one man the author is pleased to call friend (Zenji Orita, co-author of *I-Boat Captain,* mentioned in the forepart of this book). Skill and bravery were not enough, however, just as they were not proving enough elsewhere. Japanese reinforcements rushed to Bougainville, New Georgia and other islands along The Slot between Rabaul and Guadalcanal fought well, but died in vain. American power in the Pacific was growing. Three new divisions, the 1st Cavalry, plus the 6th and 33rd Infantry, were heading west. Nisei would serve with all.

ATIS already had evidence of enemy atrocities. A photo had been found, of an enemy officer getting ready to behead a captive. The diary of one Kunio was also found, in which Kunio described his own finesse in wielding the sword during a decapitation. A POW named Kunio was later taken. When he completed the standard POW written questionnaire, "The *Kanji* Kid" leaped upon his use of an archaic, rarely-used, Chinese form for the character *kuni.* Anderton had taught cross-examination at Savage. Diary and questionnaire matched. As a result of John Anderton's observation, a commission was formed at MacArthur's headquarters, charged with collection of more such evidence and information. The file was later used in trying war criminals.

* * *

In Washington, the group headed by Jim Matsumura were hard at work on the Order of Battle file, a task of monstrous challenge. The Japanese Army Officers List, when translated, filled 14 file drawers. Keeping this up to date in Washington was an anger generator, because information from the Pacific arrived in a form that could baffle anyone who tried to figure where and how it had been derived. Kanji characters were not always "read" appropriately.

Dr. James C. Hepburn, a 19th Century medical missionary, developed a system to translate Japanese syllables into Roman letters. This was called *romaji*. (The author uses it for Japanese words in this book.) Yamane, Kondo and Kenjo could not always tell from the Roman letter versions what the original *Kanji* had been. It might have been any of many forms. It took a lot of backtracking to find which of the cards made from the original ATIS captured copy matched the *romaji* spelling of, say, Hidekazu Hashimoto, Captain, Imperial Japanese Army. Then "Whatsisname's" card, with other information, could be moved to the new unit he'd been just found to be with, or his unit could be moved to his new location as indicated by information from the field. Maintaining the Order of Battle file was a senses-dulling struggle, during which no clue could be ignored lest it prove the key to a major victory.

* * *

Kiyoshi Hirano didn't have it easy, either. He'd completed Middle School in Japan and became qualified to teach general subjects there, which he did until returning to the U.S. in 1939. Then he'd been a "schoolboy" worker while pursuing his American education. His work-and-study day ran from 6 a.m. past midnight. A "schoolboy" had to get his studying done in between completing household tasks that covered cooking, cleaning, dusting, ironing, shopping, bed-making and errand-running. This for room and board plus, sometimes, a few dollars. A man had to be really determined to achieve scholarship, to go the "schoolboy" route.

His doctor-employer gave him one week to get out when Pearl Harbor was attacked. Hirano made it back to Stockton from San Francisco by asking for a "bus ticket to Stockton *Chinatown*" when other Nisei at the depot were refused transportation. He kept the *San Francisco Chronicle* before his face while other Nisei were removed from the bus at the east end of the Bay Bridge. Hirano harvested beets on parole from an assembly center, and volunteered from the Amache concentration camp. He figured "I had better show some signs of loyalty. Otherwise, I had no future." After language school, Hirano was in infantry training at Camp Shelby when suddenly called back, alone, to Savage. Shortly afterward he found himself in New York with a phony cover assignment to *Yank* magazine while he compiled a special dictionary, two conversation books, and a military dictionary. He recalled that Japanese dictionaries he used did not have any equivalent for "subjugation" unless printed after the 1941 occupation of Indochina. Japanese military dictionaries given him to work with were so old they had no word equivalent for "paratrooper."

Hirano worked with Yutaka Namba, formerly of the 100th, a Hawaii Nisei who'd worked up to Staff Sergeant before the war. Namba attended Meiji University in Toyko, but hadn't finished. He did not have Japanese ROTC experience, as Hirano did. Hirano was qualified, by Japanese schooling, for a commission in the Imperial Army.

A mysterious telephone call took the pair from the Wall St. area where they had started working, to the RKO building, in mid-town Manhattan. There they volunteered for an unknown assignment offered them, rather than give up New York for Camp Savage. Next stop was the famous Fulton Fish Market. Hirano showed his I.D. at the second floor as instructed, and was stunned to be let into a completely-furnished extensive office space, when he had expected to see a loft. "Some professor from the University of Michigan was the only person there in uniform," Hirano said.

Hirano never learned what work Namba did. The Californian was given a mass of file papers from the New York office of the Mitsui and Ogura Petroleum Companies in New York. He was told to try to identify certain types and shapes of metals he'd never heard of before.

"Often it took a whole day of research to identify a single word!" Hirano said. Hirano couldn't be sure, but he may have been helping investigate how far Japan had come with research in nuclear warfare. He did come up with one enlightening piece of information in another area. Ogura Petroleum files showed that the Germans, who had years earlier stolen the secret from Standard Oil, refused to share with Japan their knowledge of the polymerization refining process for petroleum. As a result, Japan was using obsolescent methods of obtaining high octane gasoline for her aircraft, and continued stuck with them throughout the war.

* * *

In the Pacific, two American striking arms groped toward the northwest, Nimitz's from Guadalcanal and MacArthur's from eastern New Guinea. Imagine leaning a ladder against the left-hand side of this page. MacArthur's forces would be at the bottom of it. The rungs would be named Nassau Bay, Salamaua, Lae, Finschhafen, and on up. Do the same with another ladder. The rungs for Nimitz would be Russell, Rendova, Vella Lavella, New Georgia and Bougainville. At the top of MacArthur's ladder would be the western end of New Guinea. At the top of Nimitz's would be Rabaul. From these points, both would be ready to wheel north, or at least MacArthur could, while Nimitz struck into the Central Pacific, again keeping Japan off-balance. The two American commanders could protect their common flank while reaching for Japan's throat.

MacArthur's task was to climb the "lizard's back" of New Guinea's north coast. He had his 41st Division on the tail, working toward the rump. Hiroshi Tanabe, Pat Neishi and Albert Tamura were with the Jungleers, a name the 41st had given itself for Philippines fighting in 1899. It was working toward Salamaua, next Japanese base in line.

Gary Kadani spent most of June nearly 8000 feet up the Stanley Range with an Aussie unit, but did little good because no prisoners were taken. He was continually told that "We had one, but he tried to get away." In August, Tomio Munekawa was relieved by George Kayano with the 7th Australian Division. That same month Sidney Mashbir saw to it that Phil Ishio, Steve Yamamoto and Gary Kadani got warrant officer commissions. The trio was given $300 each for uniforms, and time off for a celebration. Yamamoto suffered sadness on return to duty.

"I had interrogated a prisoner," he said, "and caught him lying. When I faced him with this, he broke down, and started telling the truth, which included a lot of useful information. Then Colonel Mashbir gave us the time off. When I got back, the POW had committed suicide. He'd left me a note, saying he thought I was angry with him for lying, and that made him so ashamed that he had to kill himself."

The 41st landed in Nassau Bay, east of Salamaua, on June 30, surprising Japanese who were expecting an overland campaign. Before this, Aussie troops had flown into Wau, a highland gold mining area, and started down toward Lae. Arthur Castle was with them. MacArthur, once he had Milne Bay and the Gona-Buna-Sanananda areas in hand, was reaching out for Lae, Salamaua, and Finschhafen. He wanted to control the Huon Peninsula and the waters between New Guinea and New Britain, cutting the enemy's lifeline. His forces took Kiriwina and Woodlark Islands, near New Guinea's eastern tip, to build air bases for supporting his next moves, but MacArthur's troops then began to roll along at such a rate that by the time the bases were completed they no longer served their original purpose. Aussies and the 41st began threatening Salamaua from *two* directions.

PT-boats in New Guinea, armed with knowledge of Japanese barge supply routes from Nisei-translated documents, cut off a lot of Japanese reinforcements in New Guinea during July, and continued their field day into August. A mass attack of 164 planes against Wewak played hob with Japanese air strength on New Guinea. Things were really looking up.

On Sept. 5, an Allied air attack battered Nadzab airfield, and 1000 paratroops dropped on it shortly thereafter. Now troops could be landed to threaten Lae from one direction. One day earlier, the Aussie 9th landed on the near side of Lae. Kazuo Kozaki, known to his friends as *Hige-san* ("Mister Moustache"), landed with them. Zeroes strafed, pursued by P-38's. One or the other shot Kozaki in the stern. He saved an officer's life in the landing, and carried on for three more days before reporting his wound. Kozaki got the Purple Heart and a Silver Star, but shrugged off his alleged bravery by saying "Hell, I didn't want anyone to know *where* I was wounded!"

Sidney Mashbir made sure everyone did. When giving Kozaki his decoration before an assembled formation later, he announced "Sergeant Kozaki as we know, was wounded in the Hopoi section." All present knew that Hopoi Mission was the area of the invasion. It also was part of the "lizard's" rump.

* * *

Interesting things were happening to other Nisei, elsewhere, while this was going on. The 100th Infantry Division departed Brooklyn, New York, landed at Oran, North Africa, and soon went into combat. Hawaii induction stations were having to press their doors shut on the overflow horde of volunteers wanting to join the 442nd Regimental Combat Team and fight in Europe. Roosevelt and Churchill met in Quebec, and Orde Wingate convinced both that more deep penetration thrusts could hurt the Japanese badly in Burma. As a result, 14 Nisei would gain some fame but it could be only half-given to them.

Eddie Mitsukado led the detachment, Akiji Yoshimura and Herb Miyasaki with him. Russell Kono, Grant Hirabayashi and Jimmy Yamaguchi had no idea that the "eight-ball outfit" they were joining would become famous. Nor did Robert Honda, Roy Nakada, Roy Matsumoto or Ben Sugeta. The handful of Nisei were probably the only men, out of some 3000, who really were hand-picked for duty with the unit. Tom Tsubota, Howard Furumoto, Calvin Kobata and Henry Gosho made up the rest of the Camp Savage detachment. Each of the 14 volunteered after being told, individually, of a "perilous, short-term, one-time jungle mission, which expected 80% casualties." The rest of the outfit that came to be known as Merrill's Marauders was made up from cast-offs and garrison troops, the latter from the U.S. and Caribbean posts. No commanding officer lets his good men get away, but he'll happily volunteer all his drunks and other troublemakers. This appears to have been the case with mustering troops for the 5307th Composite Unit, Provisional, of which one member said, "It sounds like a street address in L.A. for Chrissakes!" The troublemakers, however, proved to be great soldiers.

Part of the unit left San Francisco in the *SS Lurline* on September 21, 1943. It was to pick up its "seasoned jungle fighters" in the South Pacific, enroute to Bombay, India.

* * *

With Attu secured, Kiska was next in the Aleutians. An excercise in total futility ensued. More than 29,000 American troops and 5,000 Canadian ones were assembled, plus some Eskimos and Alaska Scouts. Nobuo Furuiye served with the Canadians. He had to wear their itchy woolen uniform.

The invasion of Kiska was preceded on July 26 by a fiasco called the "Battle of the Pips," during which an American task force engaged *nothing!* A fellow Fire Controlman friend of the author's, who served in the battleship *Mississippi* during the shoot-up, said "We fired a million bucks worth of ammunition into a rainstorm!" Which is actually what happened. All firings were based on U.S. rickety radar. No enemy ships were sighted. None were found to have been hit later. Postwar checks showed that every Japanese ship was far, far away at the time.

For the Canadians, whose only battle experience in the Pacific to that date had ended in surrender at Hong Kong, the taking of Kiska was another bitter blow. Don Oka was with the Alaskan Scouts. He stood offshore in a ship, listening to tremendous firing ashore. Tad Ogawa, Ted Ishida and Shigeo Ito also participated in the invasion. All were certain from the noise, that a battle as bloody as Attu was taking place.

None was. After killing about 30 of one another, the

Americans and Canadians found there were no occupants of the island except for three yellow dogs and one cat. The Japanese, executing as slick a getaway as they had from the western end of Guadalcanal six months earlier, slipped off Kiska days before. They did leave the Nisei a gift, however, a cave full of food with a sign in Japanese that said, more or less, "Help yourself. This is not poisoned." John White's men did not seal the food caves as ordered by the task force commander. Instead, according to Shigeo Ito, "we partook voraciously. Such things as *tsukemono,* Mandarin oranges, *nori,* bamboo shoots, and so forth." White said there was "lots of rice, clams, and canned meat. The Nisei were their own chefs, and our intelligence detachment became the most popular unit in the command."

When this campaign ended, Shigeo Ito was among those who returned to the U.S. with some of the prisoners taken at Attu, the more experienced men being pulled out of the Aleutians for service elsewhere. Yoshio Morita was one of those left behind, but he didn't mind. In one of the hundreds of letters written from the field to Yutaka Munakata, head of the translation section at MISLS (which thick file Munakata graciously lent the author via John Aiso), Morita expressed gratitude for having "huts to sleep in, warm clothes, and wholesome food." He had a pretty good idea where Nisei who left the Alaska command were heading. Malaria, dysentery and dengue fever did not inhabit the Arctic.

* * *

Nisei were involved in another interesting operation kept quiet for 30 years, this one also inside the U.S. A special secret POW camp was established at Byron Hot Springs, California. Not many Pacific POW's got back that far, but those who did were treated well and milked gently of information. They included at first an engineering officer from the carrier *Hiryu,* sunk at Midway; plus survivors of a submarine, two cruisers, a destroyer, and other Japanese vessels that went down in the Aleutians and Solomons.

Joe Ryssin, born in St. Petersburg, Russia, was on the staff at Byron, famous for it shot springs spa. So was Matt Adams, an early graduate of MISLS. Joe Harada and Randolph Ideue were among Nisei who joined them there, although the staff did never become very large. The place featured a small hotel. Prisoners were kept on its third floor, interrogated on the second. Strategic information was chiefly sought, examples being morale of people back home, maybe where torpedo storage might be at the Kure naval base, or perhaps where the Yokosuka naval base machine shops were located. Old Japanese maps and charts were used, and prisoners asked to mark them, which they did.

Ben Yamamato, Harry Furushima, Clifford Sugimoto and Mickey Kuroiwa elicited information concerning Saipan, Guam and Tinian while these areas loomed up as imminent campaigns. Prisoners who'd been stationed at those places, or who passed through them on the way further south, were drained of pertinent detail. Whether POWs ever got to use Byron's hot springs, which Japanese love, does not appear in any report the author has seen.

* * *

The Russell Islands were taken not long after the Japanese evacuated Guadalcanal, and used as a training-staging area for further advances northwest. Parts of the 43rd Division landed on Vangunu and Rendova when New Georgia was invaded. Shig Yasutake ran a patrol across Vella Lavella with a battalion of the New Zealand's 3rd Division. When he got back he was offered his choice of OCS or a battlefield commission. Yasutake took the former, knowing "it would get me out of the muck and the dirt for at least a year, anyhow."

The 43rd language team was on New Georgia nearly three weeks when the enemy overran its command post, and Yasutake was "thankful for those mean Regular sergeants of the 7th Division, who made me dig a foxhole *deep*!" Bullets sprayed well overhead as Yasutake crouched in his foxhole. Landcrabs kept him company.

Lt. Mike Mitchell and Richard K. Matsumoto were elated with success the 43rd's language team was enjoying because, before the campaign, it had spent a lot of time familiarizing various regiments with the importance of bringing in "souvenirs" and other items taken off the enemy. The pair made arrangements to make broadcasts in Japanese, beamed at enemy forces in other islands, urging them to surrender. How effective these were was not determined, but they did confuse XIV Corps staffers on Guadalcanal, who didn't know where the friendly Japanese words were coming from.

The 43rd moved its command post to nearby Roviana Island the day after it was overrun, and among POWs later brought in was one who identified the location of enemy headquarters, near Munda airfield. Ted Kihara, Kiyoshi Nishimoto and the rest of the 43rd's team watched their artillery bombard it from Roviana, making the task of taking the airstrip easier for infantrymen. The 37th joined the 43rd on New Georgia right after that, just in time for Kazuo Komoto to get shot by a sniper. Komoto wore the Purple Heart while visiting his younger brother in concentration camp later.

* * *

Mussolini had been arrested by this time. Field Marshal Badoglio became Premier of Italy. Anti-surrender forces in Japan would later use Badoglio's name to label any one favoring surrender in the crucial summer of 1945. Haruo Sazaki moved from a POW camp in Wisconsin, with his MP detachment, to a larger POW camp on New Caledonia. Americans were becoming a little better at fighting the war, as each learned more. Troops now knew that a Japanese fighting man was no more determined than themselves, and that he could be made to surrender.

The typical fighting man was no more sophisticated than had been his father in an earlier war. Not the Caucasian fighting man, anyhow. On New Georgia, Mamoru Noji was sent into the jungle by Gene Wright to get whatever intelligence material he could from the wreckage of a downed Zero. Noji followed orders, gathering up charts, note pads, etc. He also took the dead pilot's parachute. During a work lull later, he and Shig Yasutake cut the parachute into the handkerchief-sized flags that Japanese soldiers liked to carry in breast pockets over their hearts. A little red paint, a few *Kanji* characters, and the supply of "souvenirs" sold out rapidly. Who could challenge the members of a team that actually returned battlefield prizes to soldiers as soon as they'd been checked for possible intelligence use? Authenticity was never questioned.

Throughout the United States, 30 years later, a lot of middle-aged men had probably pointed to their foot-square souvenirs, and boasted "I took that off a dead Jap, on New Georgia!" Unless they'd taken up Japanese in the interim, none could know that the *Kanji* characters Noji inscribed read "Do not buy this flag. It is counterfeit."

* * *

On Sept. 15 a force of Australians and Americans took Salamaua, and the next day Lae was taken. A *Yank* magazine correspondent swiftly wrote himself up as being the first American into Lae, but he was wrong. Arthur ("winner of honors") Castle rated that kudo. The Stanford graduate had come down the mountains with the Australian 25th Brigade. They slammed into Lae, chasing the Japanese out its other end.

While they did so the 21st Australian Brigade, having with it the *Yank* correspondent, moved into sight from seaward, opening up on the town with 6-pounders. Castle and his comrades took all that they could, before getting disgusted about getting shot at by friend *and* enemy. They ran up the Union Jack, and the firing stopped. When the jubilant journalist stepped ashore, he had no way of knowing that among the dirty, ragged and profane men in

One Nisei team in India included (above, l-r) Hideo Imai, Henry Kuwabara, Toshio Taniguchi, and Eiichi Sakauye. At rear (l-r) are Shori Hiraide, Joe Inafuku, Fusao Uchiyama, and George Okada. Below is view of Corregidor those Nisei who fought their way down Bataan peninsula got.

Digger hats on the beach was one tired Nisei from California.

On New Guinea the enemy was attempting several more *tenshin,* trying to pull his troops into concentrated forces after having earlier scattered them along the island's north shore. MacArthur was using every bit of intelligence he could gather, in figuring out ways to by-pass these Japanese strong points. On September 22, Kazuhiko Yamada landed near Finschhafen with the 9th Australians. He was joined by Roy Fugami and Hiroshi Kubota a short time later. The trio, like other Nisei who served with the Australians, were kept constantly puzzled by their allies' behavior. All had trouble understanding how the Diggers could treat them, the Nisei, in such openhanded, open-hearted friendly fashion, both on the continent and up in the forward area, while still fighting so viciously against the look-alike enemy. After one mountain clash, Japanese bodies were found to have no less than three bayonet wounds each. Too, there were those constant rumors of Aussies using captured enemy soldiers for bayonet practice, because the enemy had earlier done so with their mates.

Volunteers from Hawaii were arriving in Salerno, Italy, at this time, to flesh out the 100th, which had moved north across the Mediterranean to do more fighting. On September 29 the all-Nisei unit came under mortar fire, and Shigeo Takata got wounded. His was the first of 1703 Purple Hearts the 100th would be awarded. Next day the Japanese high command established a new "absolute defense zone" for the Pacific, readjusting the barrier beyond which Americans must not, at any price, be allowed to approach. The north coast of New Guinea—the rest of it, at least—was to be held, plus a line running through Rabaul and Bougainville, and then northeastward through the Gilberts and Marshalls.

Two dozen Japanese airfields were to be established on New Guinea, including seven already under construction or finished. Outer defenses would be held while inner ones were strengthened. The Combined Fleet would watch for a chance to engage in *decisive battle* with the U.S. fleet, said battle to take place outside the absolute defense zone. MacArthur's successes were having an effect, as were Nimitz's carrier strikes against Japanese posts elsewhere in the Pacific. Wake, Marcus, and the Marshalls were getting bombed by America's wide-ranging aircraft carriers. These were rapidly increasing in number since a decision had been made to forget about building any more useless cruisers of the *Cleveland* class, and instead use their hulls for medium-sized carriers. America was learning from her enemy, Japan having already started to convert midget submarine carriers and ocean liners to the task of carrying aircraft.

* * *

In the China-Burma-India theater, there were problems. Chiang Kai Chek avoided fighting as much as possible, wanting to preserve his military strength for a post-war showdown with the Chinese Communists. An American general, absolutely the wrong man for the job, kept fruitlessly trying to change Chiang's attitude, and pouted peevishly when he flopped. Vinegar Joe Stilwell would mutter his way off the pages of history, leaving behind him classic examples of how not to treat an ally, how not to fight a campaign, and how not to run a military command. Quick to win favor with correspondents by posing amid enlisted men, Stilwell had no time for the dull-but-vital paperwork associated with command. He frequently left his staff without a decision-maker because he preferred to be "up front with the troops." Stilwell displayed all the courage and fire it took to lead a company of infantry into combat, but his performance record indicates no wider scope. The man who led 14 Nisei and 3000 Caucasians into Burma combat, Charles Hunter, would develop an abiding hatred for America's senior officer in that theater of war.

* * *

Meanwhile, in Manila, Richard Sakakida faced more

problems. He had made contact with a batch of guerrillas known as the ROTC Group, and kept them fed with information about Imperial Army shipping schedules. These got results as prowling American submarines ran up scores along supply routes leading into or away from Manila Harbor. The guerrillas were growing too bold, however, and 14th Army headquarters was getting wise to them. Sakakida had warned the ROTC Group to move their center of activities out of Manila, but they ignored him. Finally, a bunch were captured and confined in Monte Lupo prison. Sakakida had to set them free. "It was a case of my neck, too," he told the author. "Anyone who got tortured, and cracked, was bound to implicate *me.*"

What to do? Sakakida had no idea until Mrs. Tupas, wife of the guerrilla group's leader, came into 14th Army headquarters asking permission to see her husband in prison. A Japanese captain routinely ordered Sakakida to approve her permit, using the hand stamp on a nearby desk. That gave the Hawaii Nisei an idea.

By that time Sakakida had gotten so accepted by Imperial Army members that he was assigned a regular turn as CQ (Charge of Quarters), a job requiring him to tend the barracks overnight though posing as a civilian. So, one night while office and sleeping spaces were deserted, Sakakida made himself a copy of the hand-stamp. He then dressed in a Japanese officer's uniform, assembled some more guerrillas, and marched them to Monte Lupo prison. Once inside, his force overpowered the guards, and released imprisoned ROTC Group members. "No others, though." Sakakida said, "It would have created too much of a row, if *all* the prisoners were released. The way we did it, we made it look as though the ROTC Group planned it for just their own people."

Which was true. Freed guerrillas took off for the Rizal Mountains, letting Sakakida breathe easier for a while. He was not suspected.

* * *

Italy declared war on Germany in October and the 1st

Cavalry Division, with which numerous Nisei would win commendations and awards, returned the hospitality shown it by Australians by staging a genuine Wild West rodeo for them. Next day, November 1, the 3rd Marines landed at Bougainville. The 37th Division began reinforcing them a week later. The 3rd New Zealand and American Division would also put troops ashore, letting the marines start moving out of action by Christmas Day. The Army then took over full command.

Joe Yoshiwara came back up from Noumea to join the 37th in November. Joe Iwataki arrived in Brisbane, where he luckily got an assignment that didn't require him to use his weak Japanese. Dick Hayashi had gone back to the U.S. from Noumea, where he had identified a POW as a survivor from the *I-17* submarine that shelled California nearly two years earlier. Hayashi started OCS, and was looking forward to serving in Europe, thus becoming the first Nisei to serve on both sides of the world. John Burden was relieved on Guadalcanal, and started back to Camp Savage. After wangling a set of courier's orders that let him lug along an unlimited amount of baggage, Burden loaded himself down with documents, publications, sample weapons, and a massive jug of *shoyu.* Soy sauce was in short supply in the States. Nearly all its Japanese-ancestry citizens were locked up and not near stores where they used to shop. Burden knew that the 5 gallons he lifted from captured stores would assure him a warm welcome among Savage staffers. Only trouble was, the stuff stank to high heaven!

"It's some kind of captured chemical," was Burden's explanation for getting it past various airstrip officers and flight crews, "I'm taking it back for analysis." No one caught wise until he got to Hickam Field, where a knowledgeable U.S. Customs officer sagely said, "That's a fine batch of *shoyu* you've got there, Captain." The container made it to Savage.

The XIV Corps now had an officially-designated language detachment, No. 165, in its headquarters, headed by William H. Fisher. His team was composed of Mitsuo Wakayama, Roy Fujii, Masami Tahira, Hiroshi Matsuda, Roy Uyehata and Tatsuo Matsuda. Its complexion had changed, and would continue to change. Pretty soon, in fact, when Roy Fujii and Masami Tahira were sent Stateside to OCS. Like Dick Hayashi, they were slated to join the 442nd in Europe. And, as asked, *keep their mouths shut* about their secret role in the Pacific. Members of the 442nd, who certainly did more than their reasonable share in fighting the war for America, unjustifiably ribbed, teased, and ridiculed MIS'ers as "armchair commando's" for decades. Until this book came off the press, 442nd men had no real way of knowing how much their brothers, cousins, in-laws and AJA neighbors contributed in the Pacific.

During November, Tom Taketa got a strange set of orders. No one's name appeared on them but his own. He set out not west but south; then east, crossing the Caribbean, Atlantic, and Sahara enroute to his assignment. A special unit of MacArthur's forces called the Alamo Scouts went to Fergusson Island, off eastern New Guinea, for special training. Richard Hirata, Phil Ishio and Kaoru Nishida joined them later.

Kenney's flyers smashed at Rabaul on Nov. 2. On Nov. 4, aircraft from American carriers hit the Japanese base. Navy instructions were "just beat 'em up!" and that was done. No heavy Japanese warships were left in shape to rush down and attack the Bougainville beachhead. Seian Hokama landed on Bougainville that day with a unit of the 37th, and in Italy the 100th crossed the Volturno River east of Monte Cassino, a place all would remember the rest of their days. Dye Ogata reached Bougainville on the 8th, and got buried alive in a bunker during an enemy air raid eight days later. He survived, and was awarded a Purple Heart. Tom Takata relieved Elbridge K. Okazaki at Dobodura with the II Australian Corps, and wrote a situation report into his diary. The illegal notebook is quoted here, from Tom's abbreviations.

"The Japanese 51st and 20th Divisions which were stationed in Lae-Salamaua areas were attacked by the 7th and 9th Australian Divisions, and American paratroops, and they were forced to retreat through Ramu Valley and Finschhafen."

Tom listed the 7th Australian as being at Dampier, the 5th at Lae, the 9th at Finschhafen; while part of the 1st U.S. Marines was at Milne Bay, together with 6th Army headquarters. The 41st Division was at Nassau Bay. To that date, the majority of fighting in New Guinea had been done by Australians, who were still hard at it, killing Japanese troops in the mountain areas, but the picture was starting to change. Americans were soon to do a lot more of the New Guinea fighting, and nearly all of it after this campaign. Roosevelt's military advisors had counseled that more ships, men and equipment could be dispatched to the Pacific, and 1944 was looming up as bright for U.S. Army forces. Finschhafen had been overrun on October 2, an action that took control of Dampier Strait away from the enemy. It had been his main supply route from Rabaul until that time. Now the strait could be choked off. The sea, as well as the sky, was being taken over by the Yanks and Diggers.

* * *

On Nov. 16, by invitation, John Aiso addressed a special forum at the Waldorf-Astoria Hotel in New York on "current problems." The Los Angeles attorney, whose brother Paul taught Japanese during the war at Boulder, Colorado and at Harvard University, and whose brothers Daniel and James would complete the MISLS, was right on the mark, and prescient. Introduced by Mrs. Odgen Reid, Aiso talked on the re-emergence and reconstruction of a postwar defeated Japan. His speech would have been a model for the Occupation that later occurred, so accurate were its recommendations. Aiso became a rare being—a prophet with honor in his own country.

* * *

On November 20, landings were made at Makin Atoll and on Betio, and islet in Tarawa Atoll, as preliminaries to an invasion of the central Pacific's Marshall Islands. Taking Makin wasn't difficult, since the 6500 Army men of the 27th Infantry outnumbered their foe 9-to-1, and the atoll wasn't really defensible, but Tarawa was another matter. A three-day blood bath ensued. It should make historians ponder for generations whether MacArthur's recommendation—that *one man* command the entire Pacific effort—shouldn't have been put into effect. The southwest Pacific's commander had offered to serve under any officer so-named, but top naval officers successfully fought off any attempt to unify leadership. When one examines what happened, one cannot but look with favor on Douglas A. MacArthur. There can be no doubt that his use of intelligence, like his use of air power, was superior to that of any other American officer, in any theater, during the war. One is reminded of the adage "criticism is mediocrity's tribute to genius." Where fighting was concerned, MacArthur certainly qualified in the genius category.

The American sea force at Makin and Tarawa totalled nearly 20 aircraft carriers, nearly a dozen battleships, 15 cruisers and more than 40 destroyers, a mighty force indeed. But Navy intelligence did an extremely poor job. No question of that. On the very night before the invasion it was learned that the "rifle barrel" Betio resembled was pointed 11 degrees off from what the Navy's chart showed. This was a piece of stupidity that could have been corrected from any one of the many thousands of aerial photos furnished the Navy and Marine Corps. No one seems to have bothered to check.

Nor was any shore scouting done, although the Japanese had no way of stopping it. They had no fast craft at what most reports mistakenly call "Tarawa," to chase off any submarines that felt like scanning Betio's shore defenses. Also, in its arrogance, the Navy rejected advice from an Australian who'd actually lived on the island, so its landing craft were caught on a tide that could have been watched for. Navy escort service was bad, too. It lost a carrier to a Japanese submarine.

Marines were slaughtered at Tarawa, over 3000 killed or wounded. Cymbal-clashers blared heroism. Again the USMC won headlines. There was no one to say that the 4500 defenders of Tarawa fought so fiercely (except for one the author interviewed, Tadao Oonuki, taken after waking from exhausted unconsciousness) because they knew what Marines had done to other island defenders 15 months earlier. Oonuki was one of the few Japanese who survived Betio. Careful examination of the facts as they later came to light make it conclusive that the arrogance and impatience of U.S. Navy planners needlessly cost American lives. Moreover, some of the top Navy officers were awarded high decorations. Most basked in glory for the remainder of their lives. Once a war is won, embarrassing questions don't get asked. At least, not until the public fever of victory subsides. The author must agree with the Japanese officer who said "winners get to write a war's history, while the losers are busy rebuilding their country." Rarely has a writer challenged the "party line" of the U.S. Marine Corps, except for William Bradford Huie. Even so doughty an individual as Harry S. Truman backed down after saying the USMC had a more effective propaganda machine than Josef Stalin.

* * *

Hate dies as slowly as it takes truth to be resurrected, it seems. Just before Frank Hachiya took part in the Tarawa invasion, and before Richard Moritsugu, Hoichi Kubo and Jack Tanimoto landed on Makin, an organization called NO JAPS, INC., was founded in San Diego, California.

* * *

On November 24, Leo Saito and Tom Takata relieved Calvin Kubota and Roy Fugami at Finschhafen. Harry Fukuhara joined them there after a while. With Howard Ogawa, Terry Mizutari, and Ben Nakamoto, he was getting set to cross Dampier Strait and hit Arawe, a peninsula on the south side of New Britain. The job was to be done by the 112th Cavalry Regiment, an orphan unit from Texas, and a part of the 158th Regiment, a cast-loose outfit of the Arizona National Guard. Some of the equipment they'd use was borrowed from the 1st Marine Division. In a number of respects, the southwest Pacific was still a makeshift war. A lot of admirals stood astride the supply line between U.S. ports of embarkation and where Douglas MacArthur's forces were fighting.

On December 14, after a terrific dinner they vomited all over one another during a stormy crossing, Harry Fukuhara's contingent got underway from New Guinea to invade New Britain. Enroute, all hands were ordered to use their helmets to help keep their landing craft bailed out. Harry lost his on the first attempt to assist. A wave snatched it away.

For the Seattle native, life was a mess. Working as a gardener in Glendale, California, he didn't even know where Pearl Harbor *was* when the lady of the house came out to tell him it had been attacked. Harry had volunteered four times before being given a uniform: once for the draft, which he found closed to him; another time as a linguist for the Marine Corps, which apologized but turned him down; a third for the Navy in the same capacity, going to enlist with a Caucasian friend, only to have his papers stamped "not acceptable"; and finally from Gila River after he'd been imprisoned there.

Once war started, Fukuhara knew no way to go but straight ahead. In New Guinea, one of his brothers could have been brought in as a POW, or one could be tied to the top of a tree, like other enemy soldiers were, taking a sniper's bead on him. Fukuhara's widowed mother, and three Fukuhara brothers' were in Japan.

They lived in a city known, at that time, to few Americans.

It was Hiroshima.

Chapter 8

Harry Fukuhara and other linguists with the Alamo Scouts hit Arawe Peninsula, on New Britain's south side, on December 15, 1943. Japanese air at once responded and, with Allied airpower distracted elsewhere in the Solomons and New Guinea, the attacking force had no cover. "All we could do was lie on the ground and pray," said Fukuhara. Foxholes couldn't be dug fast enough in the rocks to help, and there were no nearby caves or dense thickets for hiding.

Before this, and after the fighting had ended at Makin and Tarawa, the 100th Infantry celebrated Thanksgiving in Italy with an epidemic of diarrhea. Turkey sent up to their front line positions turned green enroute, but they hungrily ate it anyhow, with dire results.

Tom Takata, Paul Kuyama and Leo Saito were at Finschhafen, New Guinea. They had the novel experience of hearing their own side's artillery shells fly overhead. At the end of November a decision was made in a third theater of war, that Chinese troops trained by General Joe Stilwell would head into Burma for a place called Myitkina (which 14 Nisei would learn to pronounce "Michinaw"). The place, if taken, could serve two purposes. Its airstrip could provide cover for hundreds of transports flying "over the Hump," a route through the Himalayas made necessary by loss of the Burma Road to Japanese in 1942. That highway had been the only supply route to China's forces. Stilwell was running a new road into Kunming, China, from a place called Ledo. This, too, had to be protected from the Japanese. Orde Wingate would help, by making another of his deep penetration thrusts far to the south. This, it was hoped, would draw off Japanese who might otherwise threaten the new supply route to Chiang.

* * *

Susumu Toyoda's team replaced Dye Ogata's with the 37th on Bougainville during December, as the language intelligence effort improved in order and organization. Toyoda had Maxie Sakamoto, Seian Hokama, Yukio Kawamoto, Tadashi Uriu and Keiji Fujii, making up the 173rd Language Detachment. Joe Yoshiwara joined the team, and shortly had the chilling experience of trying to interrogate a POW who had only three-fourths of a head.

* * *

On the Asian continent, opinions differed on how the Burma campaign should be fought. The British needed to recover Burma, to regain face. Joe Stilwell wasn't enthusiastic about helping John Bull get back another colony, but the effort would give him a chance to test his contention that properly-led, properly-trained, properly-equipped Chinese could and would fight as well as any soldiers. Stilwell would get some proof, and Mao Tse Tung would provide more five years later. As for Chiang, he was quite willing to wait until MacArthur and Nimitz stepped ashore from the China Sea. He figured that the Japanese in China, then cut off, would have to surrender and thus his own forces might not have to fight at all. Only the constant nagging of Stilwell, who seems to have made the same mistake other Sinologists did in those days, mixing an affectionate contempt for Chinese with an inordinate hatred of Japanese, got any action at all out of the Generalissimo. It was not much.

* * *

Hisashi Matsuda, in Australia, poured his heart out to Yutaka Munakata in letters. He expressed regret about

Working in island government after successful invasion are (l-r, around table) Fumio Uchino, Tetsuo Sugumoto, Hiroshi Kobashigawa and Kazuo Nakamura. Arthur Swearingen and Hitoshi Miyamoto (below) did similar work.

trouble that broke out in the Tule Lake concentration camp and other places over the Yes-Yes, No-No questionnaire. In his Kibei's broken English, Matsuda managed to convey that, while Caucasian officers with him admitted to and praised the contribution Nisei soldiers were making everywhere, "only a few hundred are enough to change public opinion." Matsuda proved to be correct. With no news from the Pacific on what West Coast Nisei were doing out there, California newspapers kept Caucasian feelings flaming. The Board of Agriculture in California, concerned about harvests, voted for return of Nisei to their State and for fair treatment of AJA's, but Earl Warren, by then Governor, made new appointments to the Board. His beneficiaries combined to retract the Board's earlier voted decision.

* * *

Tom Takata again came down in New Guinea with one of his many malaria attacks. Steve Yamamoto moved up from ATIS to New Guinea, where he'd spend nearly all of 1944. Tom Taketa, who enjoyed a swim in the Arabian Gulf on his trip, arrived in Karachi, still in the dark as to his final assignment. Eugene Wright and Haruo Tanaka got recommended for citations in the 43rd Division, and Dwight D. Eisenhower was named supreme commander of the Allied forces in Europe.

On Christmas Day, the chunk of the Americal Division that had saved the Marines on Guadalcanal began relieving part of them on Bougainville, when the 164th Regiment took over from the 9th Marine Regiment. Next day the 1st Marines landed at Cape Gloucester, on the north side of New Britain's western end. This took the pressure off Harry Fukuhara's force, which all along had been a diversion anyhow. Jerry Yoshito Shibata, George Fukuhara, Tadashi Hamane, Shigeo Miyashiro, Kiyoji Sato, Albert Kanzaki and Tatsuo Yamane were with the northern, USMC, force. These two landings partially secured the western end of the long island. Rabaul, toward which other forces were advancing from the east, was now somewhat sealed off. So was Vitiaz Strait. MacArthur now controlled that and Dampier Strait, the watery highways that had to be his before he could increase his effort in New Guinea and prepare for jumping off toward the Philippines. It began to look as though the man the Navy seemed to treat as a greater enemy than the Japanese might really have a chance to keep his promise—and return.

Japanese forces on New Guinea felt the effect of all these actions. As 1943 ended, their 20th and 51st Divisions totalled 14,000 men in New Guinea. Two months later, only 9000 were able to assemble at Madang.

* * *

Edwin Kawahara, at this time, was trying to do a job everyone at Savage told him was important, although no one elsewhere seemed to agree. He had been selected in September, 1943, to lead a team out to get some more of those Hawaii Nisei. Earlier in the year, when Hawaii was asked for 1500 Nisei volunteers to fight in Europe, more than 10,000 men responded in just a few days, so more than 2600 were finally accepted. Rasmussen's staff took advantage of the emotional binge to snatch 250 of these for the school at Camp Savage. The men made up the bulk of the third class to start at Savage, in July, 1943.

To assist Kawahara, four men were carefully selected. One was Kenji Goto, a high school teacher from Kona. Goto "had to enlist at age 38, in spite of my age, to show an anti-Japanese school teacher, a so-and-so who'd come from Grant's Pass, Oregon, that my loyalty was beyond question!" Kenji's cousin, Yasuo Baron Goto, had also volunteered in the spring of 1943. Their mutual cousin-by-marriage, a *yoshi* named Gentaro Goto, served with the Imperial Army in Burma.

The third man on Kawahara's team was Benjamin Tashiro, no spring chicken either. He was 39, and abandoned a successful law practice on Kauai to sign up. Randolph Ideue of Honolulu was fourth member of the team, and its fifth member was Masaji Marumoto, a club-footed lawyer who did not let his infirmity bar him from completing infantry training—including the obstacle course—with younger men, so great was his determination. Marumoto had been a strong influence on Robert Shivers, local FBI chief, since their first meeting three years earlier, and was the single reason AJA's in Hawaii met less harsh treatment at the hands of government agents in the islands than Nisei and Issei did on the mainland. Shivers, on Dec. 5, 1941, had told Marumoto "There is going to be a war," adding that "for you Japanese-Americans, I think it could be the best thing that could happen." Shivers told Marumoto that no one would ever believe AJA's "unless we were given a chance to show our loyalty during the war." Shivers could do nothing to stop the removal, a few days after Dec. 7, of Marumoto and other AJA's from every Hawaii draft board on which they'd been serving.

Tashiro, Ideue, Goto and Marumoto were all well-known and respected in Hawaii. After war started they'd worked assiduously at helping other Japanese-Americans keep faith, adding to their efforts by weekend volunteer work with pick and shovel, clearing the weed-like *keawe* bushes from Hawaii's beaches to give defenders a clear field of fire in case of invasion. It was thought that a team made up of these respected gentlemen would be a recruiting success.

"And it was," said Edwin Kawahara, "although not as good as it could have been." The Army had goofed again. Due to administrative handcuffs existing because of the ever-present TO, the four men, who'd been found invaluable at Camp Savage, did their recruiting as T-5's, able only to wear two chevrons each. "We got 329 candidates sworn in," said Kawahara, "but had to turn away lots more because of family requirements. We tried not to take anyone who had a relative with the 100th or 442nd, because those outfits were suffering such high casualties in the Italy fighting." Kawahara probably gave Col. Farrant L. Turner, who commanded the 442nd, the idea of using *pidgin* over his European field telephones to confuse tapping-in Germans. As intelligence corporal in the 298th,

Edwin had initiated the practice there before the war started.

Kawahara claimed that many hundreds more candidates would have signed up, "if the Army had used its head. Imagine, sending men like Tashiro and Marumoto out to meet with people who knew and respected them, and giving them only a lousy *two stripes!*" he said. "The Army could have given them each *six,* if it wanted to, if only on a temporary basis!"

Kawahara's team arrived in the islands just before Tarawa was taken, and left just as the Marshalls campaign closed. He got a chance to speak with the idealistic Frank Hachiya during this period, Frank operating from the JICPOA unit, and the Oregon Nisei wrote in Kawahara's memory book his hope that a postwar reunion of all Nisei might be arranged. "Until then," Hachiya added, "may God speed you in your mission of restoring the democratic way of life to downtrodden people, and to achieve and cherish everlasting peace for ourselves and for other nations."

* * *

Rasmussen's school was being appreciated. Its staff now had 27 civilian and 65 enlisted instructors. The course was extended to 9 months from 6, and Savage began to take on a few bureaucratic tendencies as the pressure of war eased off.

* * *

The 5307th Composite Unit (Provisional) completed its training in India, and was ready to be put to use. The idea was that Chinese troops would thrust into northern Burma, retaking it so that the new road into Kunming could be completed. Far to the south, Orde Wingate and 3000 men were to chew up the Japanese strength with guerrilla tactics. Whatever was to the north of them would receive the same treatment from 3000 Americans under Frank Merrill, a protege of Stilwell's. Merrill's second-in-command would be Charles Hunter. A newspaper writer tabbed the unit "Merrill's Marauders" long before it ever encountered the enemy, and it retained that name after its numerical designator was wiped from Army lists. Japanese strength in Burma had increased by another three divisions in the six months before the Marauders got into action.

Going up the New Guinea ladder from Finschhafen, rungs can be labelled Sio, Saidor, Madang, Wewak, Hollandia and Aitape. MacArthur opened 1944 by landing part of the 32nd Infantry at Saidor. This cut off two enemy divisions, under General Hatazo Adachi, at Sio. The general hopped a submarine to Madang, and told his cut-off troops to head around the new American position and meet him there. An Australian force headed for Sio from Finschhafen, to keep the general's abandoned troops tied up, and was successful at it. At Pearl Harbor, the end-run by MacArthur that left enemy troops to "wither on the vine" did not pass unnoticed. Nimitz decided to bypass Truk, the feared-enemy fortress in the Carolines, and head straight for the Marianas. Rabaul, because of Nimitz's and MacArthur's efforts to that date, no longer had to be considered a challenge. It would continue to get pounded, by Army and Navy planes, but otherwise could be left alone. It was time to extend the American reach further toward the ultimate goal, Japan.

To do this required a blow to the right, followed by more blows to the left, keeping Tojo and company off-balance and in the dark as much as possible. Nimitz's next objective was to be the Marshall Islands. Taking these would brush aside the shield of Japan's outer defenses, and provide an opportunity to stick a knife into their belly.

* * *

Yutaka Munakata, when not trying to jam more Japanese into AJA skulls, probably got a better picture of the war than anyone, from the massive amount of mail he received. Fusao Uchiyama wrote from India his appreciation for the language part of the course, but disparaged the military training, "except for what we received at Shelby." His comment was valid since other MIS'ers later pooh-pooh'd the attempts of non-teaching Savage officers to "play soldier." One such, whom MIS'ers nicknamed "Dog Leash," had recently seen a Clark Gable movie in which aviation cadets sang heroically while marching to ground school classes. When his charges wouldn't sing, Dog Leash demanded to know why, and a voice from the rear rank responded "Cause we ain't happy!" The marchers had seen the same movie.

Fusao Uchiyama, whose men translated and interrogated until they could no longer stand it, and had to volunteer for front-line duty to break the monotony, also described the level of living that had so many Caucasian officers in India wishing they'd discovered war a lot earlier. He told how bearers or batmen "polish our shoes, fix our beds, do our laundry, etc." He noted life was a far cry from being restricted to Camp Savage "for having a loose button at Saturday inspection." Tea was served regularly to the Nisei linguists, in conformance with British custom, and they ate most meals at a selection of restaurants, hundreds of miles from enemy bullets. Uchiyama, quite happily married to a lady on Rasmussen's staff, made note of the fact that "lots of GI's would love to spend the duration here, in spite of the shortage of women."

Harold Nishimura wrote from Hawaii, where he was awaiting orders to head out into the forward area with an invading force. He was excited about his forthcoming marriage to the girl who had been waiting for him in the islands.

Cosma Sakamoto, described by more than one MIS'er as an "aging, scholarly legal type who did far more than his fair share in spite of his advanced years," also wrote from Hawaii. His letter was not cheerful. He told how Hiroshi "Bud" Mukaye and Lincoln Taira, both leaders of teams that were preparing in Hawaii to land anywhere with anyone, Army or Navy, at any time, were having trouble rounding up needed equipment, because of the bureaucracy that had sprung up on Oahu. Sakamoto lamented the slowness in getting work done "because an enlisted man has to be announced, and await his turn," at the various places necessary to visit. He thereby made one more point for the commissioning of linguists. "Wherever they go," he said, his friends found that "they have to look us up in the records, to make sure we are here." He also wrote his wish that the language teams could be fully equipped *before* leaving Savage. Sakamoto was cheerful, however, about the free movies and good swimming.

From India, Henry Kimura said little about himself, but told how H. "Slim" Takiue, Richard Koike and Howard Nakamura were away on a front-line assignment and what a good job his team leader, Harry Andow, was doing. Henry didn't mention two other team members, who found a new way to solve a mettlesome communications problem. Amos Nakamura and James Kimura had worked one out.

Teams formed at Savage usually paired a man strong in Japanese with one strong in English, for best possible results. This posed a problem for some Hawaii Kibei. They were strong in Japanese but, because of living in Hawaii, often did not obtain a good command of English. Free-wheeling Amos Nakamura, whose other name was Akimasa ("clear and strong") came up with the answer. He and James Kimura communciated in *pidgin!* Kimura would take a document, and translate it in chattered island patois. Nakamura then produced polished English prose from this, for higher-ups. A creaky system, but it worked.

* * *

More divisions kept coming. The 38th was now in Hawaii. The 40th and 93rd were soon on Guadalcanal, which had long since lost its glamor and glory. Guadalcanal was just another backwater staging base now, where Pvt. Joe Whalen of the 25th Division had run one of many thriving stills. "Death Island" had become Fun City.

In Italy, the Allies were ashore at Anzio. The 100th

was headed for the Rapido River, to color that stream with its blood.

The 6th Division left Hawaii for Milne Bay. George Hayashida had already met Eskimos. Now he met headhunters. James Hoyt and Robert Rhodes officered the team he led for them. On it were Kiyoshi Fujimura, Tom Matsumura, Theodore Takano, Minoru Hara, Hiroshi Onishi, Soshiro Baba, and Noboru Yamashita. Hayashida also had one of the George Nakamura's, whom he described as "quiet, totally dedicated, never complaining, and always ready to volunteer for anything."

Paul W. Aurell had the 24th Division's team when it landed on Goodenough Island to train for another landing further up the New Guinea coast. Some of the men with him were Ralph Kimoto, Hideo Tsuyuki, Kenneth K. Shimbu, and Seiyu Higashi. The men could hope, if Phil Ishio had told them about it, that Paul didn't suffer from the same affliction as his brother George. It had frightened the hell out of Ishio during New Guinea's early days, when they were pioneering the practice of front line linguist duty.

"George would talk in his sleep," said Ishio, "in *Japanese!*"

Every 32nd Division man within earshot would come to life, cock their weapons, and crouch deeper into foxholes until a drowsy Ishio assured them "It's O.K., fellows. That's just Aurell again."

* * *

Nimitz cocked his fist, and let go another right-hand punch. Landings started in the Marshalls on January 31, 1944. The Navy, after selling Tarawa short, tripled its shore pounding for this invasion, and the landings were less costly.

Howard Hiroki had the team of the 7th Division, which hit Kwajalein and Majuro. The 27th, and USMC forces, hit other islets. Mike Sakamoto landed with Min Nakanishi. The first thing he did was cry at seeing so many bodies and pieces of bodies, of Japanese everywhere. Mike tried to sing a Japanese song in their memory. George Matsui helped translate a batch of hydrographic charts that were captured. This work let the Navy identify a sheltered anchorage for a massive fleet. Others in on the action were Jack Mayeda, George Nakano, Frank Hachiya, and Kenichi Uyeno. Ben Honda, Sakamoto and Mayeda were stuck on the atoll with the garrison for two months after the rest of the team went back to Hawaii. Their main job was identifying captured foodstuffs that could be used to feed island natives, and to identify various writings on equipment nameplates.

Jesse Miyao had a real treat on this assignment. He was summoned to the flagship to interrogate some POW's and was stunned to be saluted, taken below for a hot shower, then ushered to the officers' wardroom for delicious food. He quickly concluded that the Navy thought all linguists were officers, so he "kept my mouth shut, and took full advantage of the situation. It was better than no showers, and eating nothing but K-rations."

The 27th Division was given Majuro and Eniwetok as targets, while marines hit other areas in the Marshalls. Hoichi Kubo, who'd seen the carrier *Liscombe Bay* blow up off Makin, went to a small islet after primary targets were secured, to persuade people there to surrender. He netted one warrant officer, the rest being civilians. "We had three bodyguards," Kubo said, "and soon found out they were more to watch us than guard us. It was O.K. with me. Two of the guys were non-drinkers and I got their beer rations." *Shikata ga nai* could fit many situations.

* * *

There was plenty of action for Nisei by this time. The Green Islands, in the Bismarcks, were taken, providing an airstrip that could hit Truk and Rabaul. Linguists went ashore with the 30th New Zealand Battalion. On the last day of February another landing was made, on Los Negros, in the Admiralties. A victory here would serve three purposes. Rabaul would be completely surrounded, and removed as a threat by aircraft pounding her continually from the Admiralties. A valuable Fleet anchorage would be in American hands. Another staging area, closer to the ultimate target, would become available.

A portion of the 1st Cavalry Division went as a "reconnaissance in force," to have a look at Seadler and Manus Islands, and stayed on their beachhead while reinforcements kept coming. Tom Sakamoto was with George Aurell on this operation, and got lucky the very first day. He translated a document for General William C. Chase, who could never remember his name, and called him "Sergeant Yokohama." It was a tactical order for an attack, set to take place in just a few hours. Sakamoto translated it orally, not daring to handle the wet rice paper it was written on, lest it come apart in his hands. As he did so, the 1st Cav's operations officer relayed his information directly to two offshore destroyers. They laid down heavy fire on the sectors Sakamoto told about. No attack came. A few days later, at command headquarters, Sakamoto noticed movement in tall grass only 50 feet away. At the general's order, Tom called out in Japanese "Who's there?" and "Surrender, while you have a chance!" For an answer, he got a grenade, so the headquarters group opened fire. Every member of a Japanese death party out to get General Chase (he had taken over one of their command dugouts) was killed or committed suicide. The Admiralties were soon secured, and Tom flew off to another invasion in New Guinea.

* * *

In Burma, other Nisei didn't have it pleasant, either. Grant Hirabayashi had a daily choice of starving, or eating his food and suffering the pangs of dysentery. A doctor with Merrill's Marauders finally decided Grant was allergic to something in the rations, and suggested he eliminate items, one by one, until the bad one was isolated. The unworldly lad from Kent, Washington, whom roughneck Roy Nakada had practically adopted as a younger brother, tried his best, but hunger took over. Like the other 13 Nisei, he ended up the campaign at the 100-lb. mark or below. Marauders clashed with the enemy dozens and dozens of times, rarely seeing him in any clash. Movement, or noise, was enough to make a target. Hirabayashi, like many others, tried for "that million-dollar wound that would get you back to the States," but every time he stuck his bared big toe out of a foxhole, reaction pulled it back when a mortar shell hit nearby. When the trick wouldn't work with a little finger, either, Grant gave it up.

On March 4 in New Guinea, the senior Australian general, George A. Vasey, commended Phil Ishio, Arthur Castle, Kazuhiko Yamada, George Kayano, Grant Ichikawa, Shunji Hasegawa and James K. Sasano, for earlier combat work there. Next day, in Burma, Roy Matsumoto proved how valuable Kibei were. He crept out to eavesdrop on a nearby Japanese force, overheard their plans for an attack, and squirmed back to help ambush it. When the first wave of enemy attackers went down, and the rest dived for cover, Matsumoto had an inspiration. In his best Japanese middle school ROTC baritone, he shouted *"Totsugeki!"* The disciplined remnants got to their feet and did charge, only to be wiped out. Matsumoto got the Legion of Merit after 54 enemy bodies were counted.

Thomas Tsubota had to be evacuated, along with hundreds of other Marauders, as exhaustion and disease decimated their ranks. Henry Gosho hung on, through 15 malaria attacks. Two days after Matsumoto's feat, Henry's first child, Carol Jeanne, was born. In a Colorado concentration camp. Her father had felt it to be the "safest place in America" to put her pregnant mother when he'd gone overseas.

* * *

A look at any Pacific chart at this time would show that Nimitz was reaching up past the right side of Rabaul, and MacArthur up past its left. Nimitz had spun off to the

Charles Tatsuda (front, left) with graduates of the parachute school. Some went to 11th Airborne, some to secret planning duties in Hawaii.

right again. He'd taken the Carolines, and then the Marshalls. Now he was aiming for the Marianas, straight north from New Guinea. MacArthur had to strike to the northwest, then reach out for the Philippines.

The pace of the war was quickening. Since MacArthur's next objective, Hollandia, was beyond the reach of his present air base, he was finally able to get temporary use of some aircraft carriers from Nimitz.

MacArthur decided to take no chances. His forces would also seize Aitape, an in-between site, just in case. He ordered the smaller aircraft carriers lent him to work on that target, while big carriers worked over Hollandia itself.

* * *

Haruo Sazaki saw 200 Japanese POW get shipped out from Noumea to a camp in the U.S. Bert Sueki Mitsunaga and 22 other Nisei finished parachute troop school. The Marauders began making mutinous mutterings when, exhausted, they were ordered to take a place called Shadazup. They had already taken Walawbum, the "one quick mission" they'd been told was all that would be asked of them. More than 12,000 Chindits were behind Japanese lines in Burma, doing a good job of tying down southern forces in that country. They were also giving General Kawabe second thoughts about his all-out thrust across Assam into India.

The Admiralty Islands were secured. MacArthur had by-passed 56,000 of the enemy around Rabaul, 31,000 on Bougainville and 8,000 on New Ireland, plus 12,000 Korean labor troops and 53,000 members of the Imperial Japanese Navy. It was as though the Allies had taken 160,000 prisoners. They were just as ineffective where they were as they would have been in any POW camp.

On Saint Patrick's Day, 1944, the Japanese invaded India. One week before that the 37th Division language team on Bougainville saved a lot of lives.

The Army continued a Bougainville campaign that would last a year. Susumu Toyoda had relieved Dye Ogata with a new team. He had on it Yukio Kawamoto, Joe Yoshiwara, Seian Hokama, Makoto Sakamoto, Keiji Fujii and Tad Uriu. Late in February the very first POW that Toyoda's team grilled came through with a jackpot for them, a payoff for work that earlier linguists had done. Their teachings persuaded Caucasian infantrymen to treat captives kindly, and by the time this one was brought back from the front he was absolutely congenial. He said he was part of the 45th Regiment, which was gathering to the north of the 37th for an attack. Before long the linguists knew *where* the enemy was going to attack, but not *when*. No one had a clue until one remembered what Akira Oshida had taught them back at Savage about the Japanese historic predilection for attacking on commemorative days. March 10 was Japanese Army Day. That had to be it! The 37th's perimeter was strengthened, and when the enemy came on the 10th he was mowed down. Infantrymen later told how they couldn't believe their eyes. They were thankful to the Nisei for the warning that saved so many of them.

One month later, Toyoda's team did it again, obtaining a map of the Japanese 23rd Regiment's disposition plus its proposed jumpoff point for a new attack. Noting that the enemy had started other attacks promptly at 8 p.m., the leader of Toyoda's team, Austin Bach, figured he'd follow the same pattern, and informed superiors of that.

There was just time enough to nail the Japanese 23rd Regiment before it moved out of its bivouac area, coordinates of which were hastily given to the 37th's artillery and the Americal's as well. A massive barrage was laid on, so great that it stunned American infantrymen, who "didn't know we had that much firepower!" Next morning the enemy's location was all wasteland, littered with dead bodies and parts. A patrol brought in one POW who somehow survived the holocaust. He was so frustrated he couldn't stop crying, over his having come all the way from Japan and not getting to fire even one shot.

This performance of Toyoda's team was a repeat of Shigeo Yasutake's on New Georgia with the 43rd about 6 months before. They, too, had shattered a planned Japanese attack by translating a captured copy of the plan.

* * *

The British were holding their own on Assam Plain against an all-out Japanese thrust from Burma. The Chindits were getting their job done behind enemy lines, despite having lost their leader when Orde Wingate's plane crashed into a mountain. Merrill's Marauders were at a place called Nhpum Ga, trying to block Japanese forces moving north against the Chinese, and on March 28 the column containing Robert Honda, Ben Sugeta, Roy Matsumoto and Roy Nakada was trapped there.

At Goodenough Island, preparations were made for a thrust against Hollandia. Saidor and Sio, two more rungs on the New Guinea ladder, had been climbed in January, and MacArthur planned to jump past the Wewak and Madang rungs. Across the world, the 100th arrived at Anzio as reinforcements. The battalion's ranks were not so thin now, Purple Heart veterans having returned from hospitals to rejoin their buddies in the fighting.

Different things had been happening to various Nisei. Tateshi Miyasaki became, on Vella Lavella, one of the Nisei linguists "captured" by friendly troops who mistook them for enemy soldiers, but although embarrassing it was better than getting shot. Miyasaki was cooking supper for himself and John Burden at the time. The rice convinced his captor Miyasaki was enemy.

Dick Honma, in India, made the mistake of buying some ice cream from a street vendor in New Delhi. Whatever was in it could have caused his family great embarrassment later, should anyone have asked them how he had died in the war. It nearly killed him. After hospitalization, Honma was back to duty.

Seian Hokama and Susumu Toyoda were awarded the Soldiers Medal on Bougainville, for saving the life of a war correspondent getting carried out to sea by a riptide while swimming. Both thought so little of the event that neither could remember the correspondent's name when interviewed.

On Bougainville, film star Gary Cooper came to entertain the troops. Herb Maruyama, Tom Osasa, Terry Yoshimoto and Min Watanabe were with the marines that landed there. Herb Maruyama wandered off, and was "captured," incredulous marines so proud of this that they displayed Maruyama to Gary Cooper as the first POW taken on the island.

* * *

Events were building up. Nimitz now had a massive fleet of aircraft carriers, plus all the escorts they needed. As carrier task forces, these powerful units roamed wherever they pleased. Admiral Mineichi Koga, based at Palau in the Carolines, got word that U.S. carriers were moving toward New Guinea. When other American carrier planes attacked islands in the central Pacific, the admiral decided he was sitting in a hot spot. Massive raids had already been made earlier that year on Rabaul and Truk, crippling both strongholds. Koga didn't want to get cut off from his forces if Palau was hit. He made a decision to move his headquarters to the Philippines. Specifically, Davao, on the island of Mindanao, ordering giant flying boats to accommodate his staff for the trip.

Before taking off, Koga made a decision. In his possession he had a copy of the Z Plan, designed and approved largely by himself, the grand scheme for protecting the Marianas against an American thrust from the east, which it was obvious soon would be coming. Like all Japanese plans, it was detailed and meticulous, with forces planned and weighed so that they would be in position—if all went well—to smash the oncoming enemy. Koga's chief of staff, Shigeru Fukudome, was with him.

Before boarding his plane, Koga ordered Fukudome to ride in a separate one, in case of accident. And, since he had the Z-Plan firmly planted in his own head, Koga gave

Fukudome a bound copy of it, the red cover bearing a "Z." Then both headed for the Philippines.

Enroute, Koga's plane was lost in a storm, and Fukudome's forced down by the same tropical disturbance. The chief of staff was captured by Filipino guerrillas, and his salvaged brief case checked. After exchanged radio messages with Australia, runners got the briefcase to the coast, from where an American submarine rushed it to Australia. There two Nisei would play key roles in putting the document to work for America.

They were Yoshikazu Yamada and George Kiyoshi Yamashiro.

Chapter 9

More forces were gathering to smash Japan, which was everywhere over-extended. Its foothold in the Aleutians was gone. All bases in the Solomons, Bismarcks, Carolines and Marshalls had been either lost or cut off. On New Guinea, forces that did engage got cut to pieces, and the rest were isolated. Even Japan's all-out thrust into India was fizzling. A new American division, the 77th, was in the Pacific. Another, the 31st, was on its way around from the Atlantic. Doomed Japanese garrisons, some of which had dabbled in cannibalism on natives and some captives, now plunged into the depths of practicing it on whomever died, friend of foe.

* * *

Nisei linguists were sometimes inspired, sometimes saddened, by sights they saw. Roy Uyehata and Hiroshi Matsuda, on Bougainville, translated for use in *Newsweek* magazine a poem of determination written by a Japanese soldier who'd died in the attack on their perimeter. Part of it went:

"To avenge our mortification on Guadalcanal
Will be our duty true and supreme.
Strike, strike and strike again
Until our enemy is humbled forevermore."

Here was *Yamato damashii!* This explained to American infantrymen why the Japanese had kept coming, through machine gun, rifle and mortar fire. The phrases used to exhort them had come from the Meiji era, when they'd been used to give Japanese a *peaceful* sense of national consciousness. It was from that era that the Issei sprung, the period when an all-out effort was being made to build a modern Japan. Issei left Japan before getting manipulated into martialism, so they had applied only the positive facets of these sayings and beliefs to the rearing of Nisei. Nonetheless, to Nisei linguists and the Japanese soldiers they opposed, duty stood before any other consideration. What Nisei had been taught at home, they saw the enemy apply—that a man must do his utmost for the land that gave him birth. The Yankee met the *samurai*—and found common bond with him.

* * *

It could not have been easy for Nisei to survive certain barbarities in silence. As intelligence specialists, they often had to help censor mail, keeping watch for any "souvenir" documents GI Joe might be sending Back Home Sally, in case these contained useful information. While doing this, they occasionally found fingers being mailed back to the U.S. They also heard of Caucasian soldiers sending Japanese skulls back home, for use as ashtrays. And they knew of some who smashed the jaws of the dead with rifle butts, to collect gold inlays. Harry Fukuhara put one mortally-wounded POW on a PT-boat at Arawe, for taking to New Guinea, and told the author "When he got there, he had no ears."

* * *

Stunned Caucasian friends who did *not* practice atrocities, just couldn't fathom the one Nisei were enduring. "Are you crazy?" Russell Sigwell, a Silver Star holder from Wisconsin asked Gary Kadani, after noting the Poston postmark on incoming mail. Kadani, Phil Ishio and Steve Yamamoto were commissioned on April 22, 1944. Sigwell had completed the local OCS course with them. "You mean to tell me," he growled, standing over the much shorter Kadani, "that you're a goddamned officer out here, while your mother and father are in a friggin' concentration camp? You gotta be out of your friggin' mind!"

* * *

One general described the campaigning in Burma as "like walking up and down the teeth of a saw!" True enough. Howard Furumoto, and Henry Gosho, enroute to rescue Ben Sugeta and others at Nhpum Ga, got up hills the same way other Marauders did—by grabbing onto pack mules' tails. Bob Honda kept a diary while besieged. Excerpts from it are chilling.

> "There are Japs all around us . . . they seem to sleep all day and crawl all nite, harassing us and keeping us from sleeping . . . it's hell!"

Another entry went:

> "At 11:30 they hit us with everything they got . . . I fire and fire in sheer self-preservation. Kill, or they will kill me. My whole body shakes, uncontrollably. Scared? I don't know. I cannot stop shaking. Stupid thing to do, but I counted 64 rounds of artillery."

Battalion C was enroute to rescue Honda's Battalion B. Chinese reinforcements had also been reported, but Honda's diary revealed everyone at Nhpum Ga "angry as hell because that force was already 15 days late!" A successful drop was made to the beleaguered Marauders on April 3, but they were puzzled when its contents included *harmonicas!*

Without any preliminary sign, the enemy suddenly withdrew. Rescuers broke through to Honda's unit on April 9. He saw Herb Miyasaki and Akiji Yoshimura not long afterward. His diary recorded "Man! They looked simply rosy!" Honda's diary doesn't record whether Furumoto and Sugeta did a celebratory duet together but, since Ben liked to sing and Howard insisted on lugging his Hawaiian guitar along throughout the whole campaign, it could have happened.

The Marauders moved on to take their second objective, Shaduzup, during the struggle for which an anonymous GI wailed "Where the hell are the *other* five thousand, three hundred and six composite units?" Nisei were already on record with their own wry sense of humor. Coming under Golden Gate Bridge on the *SS Lurline,* Akiji Yoshimura had been approached by a curious but friendly Marauder who thought the Nisei were turncoat POW's. He asked "How are things in your country?" Yoshimura looked over the man's shoulder, into San Francisco Bay, and said "Looks good from here." On the hill at Nhpum Ga, with mortars crumping all around, Roy Nakada delivered himself of Hawaiian pidgin irony with "Good fun, eh?"

The Marauders now had every right to be relieved, with Shaduzup taken. They had volunteered for one tough mission, but had completed two. Talk worked up about a "victory march" down New York's Broadway.

Joe Stilwell had other plans.

* * *

MacArthur's headquarters, after a series of messages exchanged with Filipino guerrillas, realized that the irregulars had bagged big game, possibly Admiral Mineichi Koga himself. A submarine was ordered to rendezvous with Z plan-carrying runners, and the thick packet was rushed to Australia. It didn't take Sidney Mashbir more than a brief look, to recognize what a find he had on his hands. It was Combined Fleet Secret Operations Order No. 73, dated March 8, 1944, and it detailed plans for protecting the Marianas Islands against an onrushing U.S. Fleet. It spelled out current status and projected strength, plus where Japanese surface and air strength were to be deployed by the end of April. Koga expected the Americans to show up in strength any time after that.

Mashbir at once got his top five translators together: John Anderton, Faubian Bowers, Richard Bagnall, Yoshikazu Yamada, and George Kiyoshi Yamashiro. The two Nisei did the final check. They pored over the end result, changing a meaning here, questioning a rendering

Dick Hayashi (above, left) joined Akira Oshida (seated) on MISLS research staff after combat wounds, Europe. At right (below) Kai Rasmussen gets well-deserved Legion of Merit from Clayton Bissell, Army intelligence chief.

there. Yamashiro differed with everyone on one major point in the translation. "I held out very strongly on this one item," he told the author, "and actually begged Colonel Mashbir to check it with the highest authority he could locate back in the States."

Mashbir did, according to Yamashiro, messaging Washington. Back came an interpretation. It agreed with Yamashiro's, and Mashbir himself operated the hand-cranked mimeographed machine to run off 20 copies of the 22-page translation. Copies # 5 and # 6 went to Nimitz's headquarters (the author has a reproduction of Copy # 9) and, after holding things up long enough to translate its own version, Navy intelligence finally presented it to Nimitz. He at once provided copies to every flag officer associated with the Marianas invasion.

In Australia, the printed translation was made into an ATIS report dated May 23, 1944. The next day, Yamada and Yamashiro were puzzled to find they had been promoted to Warrant Officer without explanation. By this time the Japanese brass had triggered the Z Plan in their usual fashion, via another order. This was called *A-Go,* an updated version of what Koga designed. Admiral Raymond Spruance, when he sortied against the Marianas, knew that the Japanese had 9 carriers, with 460 planes, to pit against the 956 on board his 15 carriers. He also knew what land planes his enemy had, and where, plus how to take care of them. He could thank Yamada, Yamashiro, and the rest of Mashbir's experts for this.

* * *

While Washington considered whether or not to make the 500-mile jump from Finschhafen, MacArthur completed his plans to execute it. They got approved, and on April 22, 1944, his forces moved in, generally calling Maffin Bay, Humboldt Bay and Tanahmerah Bay "the Hollandia area." George Aurell took over the I Corps team that day. It included Charles Y. Nakata, George Nakamura and Calvin Morimatsu. Nakata had a whimsical pen. His telling of an infantryman's tribulations would be hilarious, were it not so chilling.

The man hopped out of his foxhole after a grenade popped in, then scrambled back inside it just in time to throw another grenade out. When a third landed, he again rolled out just in time, as his foxhole got enlarged again. All the while bullets buzzed about him. When dawn came, he told friends "Some sonofabitch is trying to *kill* me."

A landing was also made at Aitape, to grab the airfield there. Part of the 41st went ashore at that spot. The rest of it hit Humboldt Bay, the only decent anchorage in the general area being covered. The 24th hit Tanahmerah Bay. A chunk of the 32nd came into Aitape next day. Thanks to prodigious work by Australian technicians and engineers, friendly aircraft landed soon afterward. In another 24 hours, three airfields at Hollandia were also taken. The 24th's team was led by Paul Aurell. He had Ralph Kimoto, Richard Hirata, Hideo Tsuyuki, Kenneth Shimbu and Seiyu Higashi.

Tom Takata had gotten sick enough on New Guinea to rate leave in Australia after getting out of the hospital there. He missed this campaign, but embarked on a lifelong one. He fell in love with Sylvia Joyce Look You, the half-Australian daughter of a Chinese doctor. They later married.

With the 32nd Division at Aitape were Shigeru Higashi and Masato Iwamoto. Raymond Gage, with the remainder of the team, joined them 10 days later, when the rest of the division did. It had been occupied for more than three months, several rungs down the New Guinea ladder, at Saidor.

Yoshikazu Yamada had been at Saidor, too, with the 9th Australian Division. Norito Kawakami, Masao Torai, Mamoru Takanishi and Hiroshi Kubota also served with the 9th at various times. So did Roy Fugami, Henry Hikida and James Tomatsu Kashiwada. They remained as unsung in American histories as their Australian "cobbers" did. Digger friends have never been given, in American writings, the credit they deserved for their struggle in New Guinea and elsewhere.

John Tanikawa, the WWI veteran who tearfully implored Harold Hanaumi to take him overseas with his team, went into action with one of his own. The 41st's leading linguist now had two officers, Robert Heilbroner and James Mize. Nisei teammates included Hisao Matsumoto, James K. Sasano, Harold Tanabe, Albert Y. Tamura and Everett Sasaki.

With this one bold stroke at Hollandia, MacArthur had cut off another 40,000 Japanese. Now he had left behind him more than 200,000 of the enemy, who became totally useless to Japan's war effort. In time they were written off by both sides, left to survive whichever way they could. General Hatazo Adachi ground his teeth in frustration as Australian troops nibbled at his isolated ones, keeping them too off-balance to make a concentrated dash in any direction.

* * *

Back at Indooroopilly, war could seem far away to men who spent their days bent over diaries and documents that were sometimes difficult to read. A bit of blood, dirt, or stuck flesh could change the shape and meaning of a *Kanji* ideograph for these men. Harry Sekiya, Robert Ohama, Tsuneo "Cappy" Harada, George Hatakeda and Joe H. Ikuta were among them. Others who interrupted work only to holler "Hey, Sarge!" at one of the more qualified NCO's who operated as "language checkers," or to look questioningly at a senior for reassurance while interrogating a brought-back-from-the-lines POW, were Maynard Matsunaga, Kazuo Inouye, Lad T. Miura, Peter Nakahara and Joe Hideo Iwataki.

But, there were some compensations for flying a desk. Like the Roma Cafe, in Brisbane. There Richard Omori, Hachiro Kita, Iwao Shimamoto and Sadao Takahashi could, like other Nisei, enjoy the kind of fare they'd liked best at home—Chinese food. It might have been confusing to Ken Ota, Frank Tomita, Harold Migishima and Masao Uyeda to eat in a terrific Chinese restaurant that had an *Italian* name. To Nobura Yoshimura and George Sugimoto it probably seemed more a fitting name for a pizza parlor. No matter. Once Nisei got the cook to prepare rice by *steaming,* the way they liked it best, they made the Roma as popular in Brisbane as they had John's in Minneapolis.

Few men got to leave Indooroopilly for the front lines at this time. They had far more value right where they were, behind a desk. Their experience was needed more there, at the moment, than up front, especially since more and more men were already arriving as teams. Captured documents started to arrive by the jeepload. They would total 20,000,000 pages worked over by ATIS specialists at war's end. Each page had to be examined by top linguists, called "scanners," and handed out as relative importance seemed to dictate. Translators then translated, calling on "checkers" as needed. When an item looked "hot," it got special, concentrated attention.

All of this had to be done at a never-slowing pace, very difficult to maintain. It's hard to keep even the most willing of human beings enthusiastic over pieces of paper. Sidney Mashbir did what he could. He made sure his men were kept as informed as far as security would permit. That helped. He also kept watch for any intelligence victory, small or large, that would give his men proof that Indooroopilly's work had positive results elsewhere, and keep them hustling.

Besides the Roma Cafe, lovely beaches weren't too far from Trent City. Many Nisei got "adopted" by Australian families, being invited to dinner, and frequently put up at vacation cottages when on furlough. There was also a convenient racetrack, frequented regularly by Dick Oguro. He made sure to stick close to Ernest Watanabe, whom he described as a "hotshot handicapper." Watanabe's very high IQ might have been asset for picking winners among the bangtails. In any case, it helped make sure that the pair of friends always had money.

In Europe the 100th celebrated May 1, Hawaii's "Lei Day," with a big bust, streaming strings of beer cans about their necks while doing the hula. Breaking out of the battered Anzio beachhead on May 23, they entered Rome on June 5, one day before the Allies landed in Normandy, and finally combined with the 442nd on June 11. The 100th veterans didn't like being made *part* of a newcomer outfit at all, and said so.

* * *

In Burma, over the protests of their angry temporary leader, who said none was fit to fight, the Marauders were given a third mission—taking the lightly-defended Myitkina airstrip. Charles Hunter, who took command of the outfit when Stilwell's protege, Frank Merrill, had his first heart attack in the jungle, and who continued when a second one followed, began developing an abiding hatred for Joe Stilwell. It would explode into an expository book 19 years later. The Marauders staggered on and, after a heart-breaking struggle against heat, malaria, dysentery, steep hills, plus a mite typhus that killed almost as many of them as the enemy did, finally took the airstrip on May 17. *Now*—maybe—they could get the hell out of there and go home!

Such was not to be. An incredible foulup followed. Blame must be laid at Joe Stilwell's doorstep. As senior American officer in the theater, it was his task to replace his fighters with fighting men. He didn't. Off the planes arriving at Myitkina came Army engineers, none trained for combat. By then nearly 2000 of the Marauders had come down with illness or wounds (some of the latter self-inflicted). Only 1310 men had made it to Myitkina airstrip, and of these 679 had to be lifted out in the next week. Hunter drove the enemy off the airstrip, then had to watch the troops who had helped him do it fly away to hospitals.

Stilwell then gave an order that still stuns historians. The completely worn-out one-fifth of the original unit was given a *fourth* mission—taking the town of Myitkina itself. This was naked insanity. Planners had estimated that the 5307th Composite Unit would suffer 85% casualties. It had already incurred 80%. Only one out of five originals was left. How could they be expected to do the job?

"Stilwell" might yet make Roget's Thesaurus as a synonym for "bull-headed, unreasonable, angrily-insistent." In the rear, Marauders were tumbled out of hospital beds and sent back, a phony emotional appeal about their "buddies at the front" that might have been lifted from the script of a very bad movie, being used to inspire them. Some were hardly able to stand, much less fight. Doctors with enough guts to brave the brass sent nearly all of them back as soon as their planes touched down. A makeshift Chinese-American force finally took the town on August 3, but only 200 Marauders were in on the end. Among them was *every Nisei physically able to make it!* All 14 had survived the action without wounds. In spite of illness, they had to see the campaign through. Charlton Ogburn wrote of the Marauders. He said that, while he and other Caucasians could tell themselves they were fighting their war for survival, the Nisei had "only the value of an idea." That impelled Grant Hirabayashi through the campaign, although he could have been hospitalized and out of it right at the start, something he declined to do.

* * *

Back in the U.S., a group of 23 other Nisei were also making a special mark. They finished parachute training. Charles Tatsuda, Mitsuo Usui, Yasuo Umezu and Akira Abe all had relatives in concentration camps while each was making his five qualifying jumps. Yutaka Munakata, at Savage, got a letter from Charles Tahara, which told about Takeshi Fujisaka showing "aggressiveness," and John S. Nakahara "teaching Japanese to Caucasian officers."

Tatsuda flew to New Guinea with Akira Abe, John S. Nakahara, Kazuo Yoshida, George T. "Parson" Ito,

Lawrence Kiyabu, Tetsuo Koga, Yasuo Umezu, Norman Kikuta and Clarence Ohta.

Mitsuo Usui went with Bert S. Mitsunaga, Roy Y. Yamanishi, Takeshi Fujisaka and Charles Tahara to Seattle, after a lot of fun stomping around Savage in jump boots before envious eyes. With the other "glamour boys" were Harold Hayashi, Ritsuji Sodetani, Harry S. Shimada, Robert Kimura and Richard L. Saito. All, plus Mas Mita, William Naito and Richard Y. Suehiro embarked for—of all places—Hawaii!

Home! But was it? Although 12 of the 13 men came from there, none appeared heroic or glamorous in the eyes of relatives. They could only do their duty and clam up, suffering this silence for many years. How could they tell anyone, with security almighty, that they had an office only two doors away from General Simon Bolivar Buckner at Schofield Barracks? How could they even hint that they were playing key roles in topmost secret planning for an invasion—many months in the future—*of Okinawa?*

The 13 did no more jumping from planes. It was maps, charts and documents for them from then on, but any military intelligence officer will agree that each was worth 100 parachutists, minimum, in terms of total contribution to victory. Pound for pound, the 23 Nisei paratroopers may have been the most effective troops in the history of warfare. Totted up, they weighed not much more than a ton.

* * *

MacArthur lost no time making his next move. On May 17, after a group of British and American carriers combined to raid the East Indies, distracting Japanese naval forces with this thrust in the north, he put troops ashore in the Wakde-Sarmi area, another rung up the New Guinea ladder. MacArthur and Nimitz were working well in combination. A Japanese counterattack on MacArthur's new intrusions was launched, when he moved into Biak only 10 days after the Wakde-Sarmi thrust, but the admiral who succeeded Mineichi Koga was thrown off-balance when American forces were sighted approaching the Marianas from the east.

Kon, the sea attack against MacArthur, was called off. *A-Go,* an up-dating of the Z plan, was kicked off. Yamada and Yamashiro, working with Mashbir's other best men, had provided Admiral Raymond Spruance with everything Admiral Soemu Toyoda, new commander of the Combined Fleet, did *not* want him to know. The results of the *A-Go* order doomed Japan.

* * *

An avid student of history, MacArthur knew well the principle of applying maximum force at the right place at the right time, employing every scrap and means of intelligence in preparing for it. Near the back of the "bird's neck" portion of the Vogelkopf was Biak. He needed to take it. While doing so, he kept pressure on at other places, too. Nisei learned names like Afua, Toem, Sawar, Maffin Bay and the Driniumor River, as MacArthur fed in elements of the 6th, 24th, 31st, 32nd, 41st and 43rd divisions, as well as the 158th Regimental Combat Team. The enemy was overpowered where possible, isolated where not. Nisei linguists got shuttled to where they were needed. Besides the divisions, headquarters of I Corps and 6th Army needed their help. So did Australian units. It was getting to be more of an American show at last, because Australians and Americans were getting in position to fight separately. Up to then, an Australian general commanded all Allied forces in New Guinea, but an American commanded whatever portion was American whenever such portion was on an *all*-American mission. This was then referred to as Alamo Force.

* * *

Approaching the Marianas, Spruance flung nearly the full force of his airpower against one or two outlying Japanese airbases at a time, overpowering them. He then concentrated on Saipan, Tinian, and Guam. These tactics not only smashed the spider's web Mineichi Koga had so carefully woven to entrap Spruance, but also gave its center a good bash. Landings were made on at Saipan on June 15, with Tinian following nine days later. Guam's turn would be July 21. The beaches got a good battering this time, by an admiral with enough guts to close in and do the job—Richard L. Connolly. Before long, however, it was revealed that Navy intelligence hadn't done much.

For more than 40 years, a series of U.S. naval officers had held the cushy billet of Guam's governor, but still the island had not been accurately mapped. And, although native Chamorros sailed back and forth to Saipan and Tinian regularly for those four decades, nothing had been ascertained about the state of Japanese installations there. When soldiers and marines hit the beaches, they were starting almost from scratch where useful intelligence was concerned.

* * *

Another Army division, the 40th, had been put into action by MacArthur before this. It moved out of Guadalcanal in April, and took positions all around the western end of New Britain. Lt. Richard Child had the language team, and Terno Odow was its leader. The 40th fought no major battles. Moffet Ishikawa, Kay Futamase, Mike Hori and Kay Tamada chiefly had to battle heavy rains and mud. With Hisashi Komori, Shogo Yamaguchi and Shizuo Tanaka, they whiled away part of their time on New Britain as they had on Guadalcanal, by listening to Zero Hour. Beamed from Tokyo at midnight, it featured a girl who called herself Little Orphan Annie. The team had acquired a shortwave radio on Guadalcanal, ostensibly to monitor Japanese traffic. Late at night, an atmospheric freak let them pick up a St. Paul station. "It filled us with nostalgia," Ishikawa said. He also told that the team was happy at having pyramidal tents, and "real cots to sleep on." Foxholes were still required Ishikawa said, "but when we dug them in our particular bivouac area, we hit water a foot below ground level." By staying where it was, the 40th helped contain Japanese forces isolated at Rabaul.

* * *

The Americans landed on Saipan on June 24, and infantrymen were glad to meet no air opposition. The 2nd and 4th Marine Divisions hit first, and the 27th Army Division followed them in. Before this, Spruance's flyers had hit all airfields that might have sent attackers against his landing force. His carriers had roamed to the north and the south. What they did not smash were handled by land-based bombers. With the translated Z Plan in hand, spots that might send airborne help to the Marianas were checked off, one after another. Their runways and installations were wrecked, their aircraft shattered.

Ships of the Imperial Combined Fleet, coming through and around the Philippines, were ambushed, two carriers getting sunk by awaiting U.S. submarines. Spruance held back, staying at the extreme range of Japanese carrier aircraft, and when enemy planes were enroute they got ambushed, too. The Japanese pilots were far less experienced now than American ones, who also outnumbered them better than two-to-one. American flyers had trouble staying out of one another's way as they tried to run up their personal scores. Newspapers called it The Great Marianas Turkey Shoot. It actually was an ambush-and-slaughter, a tactic that goes a long way toward ending any war.

Service rivalry came to a head on Saipan, when a Marine Corps general had the 27th's commanding officer relieved of duty. Arguments raged for years about this incident, but it boils down to the fact that the 27th was using Army tactics, while the 2nd and 4th were using Marine Corps tactics. The marines, after all, had only one function—that of shock troops. They were not trained for sustained campaigns, but only to storm ashore, smash away at the enemy for as long as they could, as hard as they could, then backtrack to the beaches while Army infantrymen passed through their ranks to finish the job—no matter how long the campaign might take. On Bougainville, and New Georgia, the Army was still finishing up campaigns marines had started. Its pace was slow and solid, and the 27th's was similar. It must be said that each service simply functioned differently. To say otherwise would be to cast aspersions on brave men.

On Saipan with the 27th was Tim Ohta's team, the same crew he'd taken from Minnesota to JICPOA at Honolulu. Ben Honda was in Hawaii, assigned to no team at the moment, when he got "loaned" to an artillery captain. He and George Matsui were awarded the Silver Star on Saipan, for "talking" enemy soldiers and terrified civilians out of caves where they had holed up. Jesse Miyao got snatched up at Honolulu, too, for a special task. Without a word to say about it, Miyao led a group of "shanghai'd" Nisei out to Saipan, about 20 of them. These soldiers had recently joined the Army, or had gotten drafted into it, and were not yet finished basic training. They were arbitrarily ordered to Saipan because they could speak Japanese. Miyao took them out there, and they went to work managing civilian and POW camps for the island's new military government.

Hoichi Kubo got the Distinguished Service Cross on Saipan. Before he did, he encountered a chaplain carrying a rifle, who claimed he was going to "put the fear of God into those Japs, one way or another!" He also got a little girl and her younger brother out of a hole in the ground. "Where's your father?" Kubo asked her, and learned that the naval bombardment got him. "Where's your mother?" elicited that Army artillery had killed her. All Kubo could do was pass the two children on to camp people.

Kubo interrogated one POW who told him a *banzai* attack was planned, but the information was of little help. The 27th took a clobbering because, although it called to the beaches that it was short of ammunition, none was brought forward. A baker wielded a Browning

Kenji Yasui (l), P. Melquist, later editor of *Sunset* magazine, with Karl Yoneda and captured battle flags.

Automatic Rifle in stemming this Japanese rush, Kubo said, and a colonel sat behind a machine gun.

As the fighting wound down into wiping out pockets of Japanese holdouts, Kubo and others made daily pickups of prisoners. He used POWs to help him, sending some into caves as messengers. Finally, near the sea cliffs, Kubo's unit happened upon an extra large cave. He sent three POWs in and, after a while, they came out, saying that some Japanese soldiers had a large group of civilians in the cave, holding them as hostages.

"I'm going in!" Kubo told Lt. Roger Pear. Giving the officer his .45 pistol, the Maui native slid down a rope into the cave. He talked to the civilians, and began herding them out. A Japanese sergeant interrupted him, saying "You're a spy!"

"I am an American!" Kubo shouted. "My grandfathers fought with the 5th and 6th Divisions! I am here to take out the non-combatants."

His opponent was taken aback on learning that Kubo descended from fighting men of Hiroshima and Kumamoto. They sat down to confer, and Kubo shared his K-rations with the obviously-hungry Japanese soldiers. After more than 100 civilians left, helped up the cliff by American GI's hauling on ropes, Kubo went outside to see how things were going. He heard someone shout "Roger Pear's been shot!" He turned about, and stormed back down into the cave.

"Someone shot that man," he said to the soldiers, "who saved all of your lives!"

Earlier, the Japanese soldiers had questioned Kubo about how he, with Japanese blood, could serve in the army of the United States. He quoted to them a dictum from their own schoolbooks. Nearly 800 years before, in Japan, Shigemori Taira was urged by his father to lead forces against an Imperial faction. His quandary resulted in an oft-quoted palindrome, which in *romaji* reads *"Ko naran to hosse ba chu naran chu naran to hosse ba ko naran."*

When Kubo uttered it, the Japanese soldiers gasped,

bowed, and apologized. In that moment they knew why all Nisei had to serve the U.S.A. "If I am filial," Kubo had quoted, "I cannot serve the Emperor. If I serve the Emperor, I cannot be filial." Shigemori Taira, Hoichi Kubo, the Japanese soldiers in the cave, and all Nisei in uniform were bound by the same centuries-old precept —that a man's loyalty goes to the higher authority. Taira disregarded his father. Nisei opted for their native land.

When Kubo, angry over Pear's shooting, asked "Is there not a *samurai* among you?" four enemy soldiers asked him to wait, while they climbed down to recover the lieutenant's body. Upon bringing it up, they surrendered themselves.

Kubo had lived up to his name. A girl was stillborn, and a boy died young, so when Kubo was born his parents wanted a *tsuyoi* (strong name) for him. His maternal ancestors soldiered from Kumamoto, his paternal ones from Hiroshima. The "scholarly" reading of Hoichi was forsaken for the one that meant "great cannon."

Ben Hazard was commissioned after studies at Michigan before schooling at Savage. He didn't get assigned a language team until the Saipan campaign was nearly over, and didn't meet the other MIS linguists until then. Ben had his problems with the Army. An orderly had taken to the laundry, and picked up for him, one shirt while the 27th was practicing landings on Maui before coming to Saipan. Long after the Saipan campaign was over, a thick sheaf of documents caught up with Hazard. Endorsed by no less than three generals, it was a complaint Hazard satisfied by getting the garrison force finance officer *to deduct thirteen cents from his pay!* It seemed he'd forgotten to pay for the washing of his shirt.

Before that, Ben enjoyed a fringe benefit. Ordered to Aslito Field after it was captured, to check for documents, Ben and his escort squad found documents concerning aircraft engine ball bearings that proved to be strategically significant. More importantly, so far as they were concerned, they found the Japanese garrison's abandoned beer ration, which Hoichi Kubo and the 165th

Regiment had, in their haste, missed. Frustrated Japanese troops spotted Hazard, knew what he'd found, and opened up with long-distance small arms fire. Hazard and his squad braved the bullets long enough to stuff their jackets full of beer, then snaked on their bellies behind a building to enjoy the warm Kirin.

* * *

Tinian was an easier campaign than Saipan. Japanese made air attacks on it from Okinawa, and even tried long-range flights from southern Kyushu, knowing Tinian to be a perfect base for the new, long-range B-29 Bomber rolling off American assembly lines.

Don Oka got sent to Tinian from JICPOA, with Sam Isokane, Nobuo Nagata, and Yukio Kawamura. They were concerned mainly with rounding up civilians, and herding them into camps to be cared for. George Inagaki came over from Saipan while Oka was on Tinian, to lend a hand. Don didn't know it until after the war, but in one of the numerous *kamikaze* strikes made against Tinian while he was there was his brother Takeo, who died.

* * *

The Guam campaign was preceded by 30 days of Navy bombing and bombardment. No Marine Corps official history mentions it, but two teams of Nisei hit the beaches with the leathernecks. Lincoln Taira led a team with the 3rd Marine Division. On it were Ryoichi Okada, Eddie Fujimoto, Stanley S. Shimabukuro, Henry Uyehara and Yurikichi Ikehara. Kenji Uyesugi, Tadashi Nomura, Ichiro Obikane, and Shoichi Yamamoto made up the rest of the unit. When the campaign was over, they folded up their equipment and quietly accepted reassignment to the 1st Cavalry Division. War was war. It didn't matter who you fought it beside.

Also in the Guam campaign were Nisei attached to the 1st Marine Provisional Brigade. Though the USMC history division had no record of it, all were cited by the

Marine Corps. They were Thomas T. Osasa, Minoru Watanabe, Terry Yoshimoto and Herb Maruyama, who had earlier been with the Corps on Bougainville. This time, however, the marines did not "capture" Herb.

"Ours To Hold It High" was the motto of the 77th Statue of Liberty Division, which also landed on Guam. Lt. Harvey Daniels was in charge of the language team, and Shigeo Ito from the Aleutians was its leader. The pair usually worked out of division headquarters with Aki Hayashi, Jim Sugimura and Eddie Fukui. The regiments had two men each: Kunio Endo and Vic Nishijima with the 305th; Frank Mori and Mac Miyahara with the 306th; and Tetsuji Yamada and Mitsuo Shibata with the 307th. They were a congenial group, having worked together in Hawaii. There Eddie Fukui had met and become engaged to Elaine Kato, whom the group delighted in calling Pee-Wee. When the campaign was over the team reassembled in a rest area, drinking their first beer since leaving Hawaii. It made them slightly high, and some Nisei broke into Japanese song. Years later, at a reunion of survivors, they wondered "how we never got shot!"

* * *

No enemy airpower or seapower of any significance barred the way of the Army and Navy taking the Marianas. The campaign, in fact, cost far less in casualties than anticipated, and Nisei are entitled to a goodly share of the credit for that. In this campaign, more Nisei became cave-flushers, their task being to inform hidden civilians or enemy soldiers that they'd better come out, or else they'd either get killed or sealed up. Hoichi Kubo told the author "Hell, Joe, I've been over-publicized!" referring to his Distinguished Service Cross, "Plenty of guys did what I did, and some did a hell of a lot more!"

Kubo was right, but few war correspondents noticed. It was easier for hundreds of journalists who got "simulated" rank that sat them at captains' tables, to settle for one splash. Getting more news would require following Nisei around, and taking the same chance they did—of getting shot at any moment. Before landings in the Marianas started, men of the 41st Division were flushing caves at Biak, where they had landed on May 27.

Chapter 10

In China, there was trouble with Chiang Kai Chek. Despite being given hundreds of millions of U.S. dollars in loans, arms and equipment, Chiang was proving an obstreperous ally. Joe Stilwell was no help. Although Chiang's second-in-command, he kept referring to the man as "the Peanut." Stilwell finally became so troublesome that Chiang insisted Roosevelt call him home. Roosevelt did.

Before that, and after, certain problems still existed. It was America's intention to take Formosa eventually, then land near Canton, using the coast of China as a staging area for the final massed assault on Japan. Trouble was that, in spite of being at war with Japan for many years, Chiang's troops were drawing little Japanese blood. Unless more fighting got done on the Asian mainland, Japanese forces would be able to meet the arriving invasion with full strength.

Japanese under arms in China and Manchuria were an X factor. Other areas could draw on the millions there for reinforcements, and had done so. The process could be slowed or stopped by some action on the mainland, but Chiang wasn't helping. Maybe the Communists would.

The Reds, fleeing annihilation by Chiang's forces in 1934, had made their way to northwest China. Word was that they were showing real patriotism in fighting the Japanese. So, overriding Chiang's dilations, Roosevelt insisted that Chiang stop restricting Americans to his Chungking capital, and let them go north for talks with the Reds. On July 22, 1944, the first contingent of what was called Dixie Mission landed at Yenan. Remainder of the party arrived 16 days later. One of the special 18 personalities freed from Chiang's clutches for this assignment was George Itsuo Nakamura, of Arroyo Grande, California.

The Dixie Mission didn't get off to an auspicious start. The plane carrying the first contingent crashed, on landing.

* * *

At Delhi, the Red Fort was beginning to look like the Honolulu YMCA, as more Hawaii Nisei showed up to do translation and interrogation. Hajime Minemoto had come out. George Fujitani and Sadao Miyashiro, too. So had James Tatsumi Okita, Takeshi Sakai, Sachio Shigeta and Edward Nakamura. The pidgin of James Wakamiya, Izumi Yoshizawa and Hitoshi Miyamoto must have rung oddly on the ears of India's beggars.

Agra was not far away. If they felt like seeing the Taj Mahal in the moonlight, Shoji Yoneshige, Taisuke Yamagata, Ralph Toyota, and Edward Miyagi could. Curry became palatable to Shoji Fujishima, Nisao Mikuni, Harry Akitake, Masaharu Okinaka and Toma Tasaki.

Masato Sugihara had a team that included Bob Kimoto, Ernest Hashiwase and Yoshinobu Tanabe. Like many other Nisei who had duty in India, they also got duty in China, returning home with disgusted tales of "draftees" for Chiang's army, roped neck-to-neck, being dragged off to basic training.

* * *

The 1st Cavalry had taken the Admiralties, including Manus Island, and were getting ready for their next move. When the group that would join them from the Saipan fighting arrived, they'd learn that Noboru Yoshimura, Jack Nagano, Minoru Namba, Ernie Hirai and Paul Aurell had received commendations for the Admiralties action, Hirai once "talking" an enemy soldier out of a bunker only 50 yards from his command post.

Down in New Guinea, Harry Fukuhara lost another friend. Fukuhara had made short trips with a PT-boat around New Britain, entering Arawe Peninsula coves at night and calling out in Japanese. Whenever he got an answer, gunners on the PT-boat would open up. "There I'd be," Harry said, "beautifully silhouetted between a pair of twin .50's. They were air cooled, and you might just as well have turned on two searchlights, for the glow they gave off." He gave it up.

Ken Omura was swimming one day, and got caught in an undertow. He drowned.

Back went the team to Finschhafen when they finished this mission, and everyone went back south except Fukuhara, Yukitaka Mizutari among them. Gene Uratsu came up with Shoji Ishii, Naotsuzuku Miyasaki and Yoshiaki Hirabayashi, but after the next landing Harry got sick and was evacuated. Mizutari, known to his friends as Terry, volunteered to come back up and take Fukuhara's place. Within a few days, a sniper got him. He died in Kiyoshi Fujimara's arms.

* * *

Noemfoor and Sansapor, if taken, would complete domination of New Guinea for MacArthur. Before that, Hiroshi Tanabe's team with the 41st was relieved by "Cappy" Harada, Noboru Yoshimura and others. Tanabe was so exhausted that when he got back to Hollandia he slept completely around the clock, after which he and Albert Tamura grabbed a Sydney-Melbourne leave offered them. Uratsu made the Noemfoor landing with "Smiley" Muranaka, Harold Nakamura and Robert Nakamura, who had joined him with the 158th.

The 168th RCT landed at Noemfoor, behind the "head" of the Vogelkopf, on July 2. The 6th Division landed at Sansapor, the bird's "eye," on July 30. By the end of the first week of August, MacArthur was ready for his next big move. On September 15, he was going to take Morotai, in the Halmahera Islands, while Nimitz's forces would take the Palau Islands. This would leave MacArthur poised southeast, and Nimitz east, of the Philippines.

* * *

Teichiro "Timmie" Hirata had volunteered from his Konawaena High School teacher's job, and 40 students tried to enlist with him, of whom 18 were accepted. He showed up in India with a language team that included Charles Kunio Tanaka, Thomas Haga, and Toshio Kamei. Two of his men, Wallace Nagao and Haruyoshi Kaya, were assigned to the 26th British-Indian Division for a campaign. Saburo Watanabe, George Maeda, Harry Ito and Nobuo Kawata were the other members.

There were other teams in India, too, large ones. Their job was to do radio interceptions. Sanji Shirai was a team leader. On his were Chuck* Kisao Hironaka, Torao Ikeda, Ken Murakami, Munaki Morimoto, and Kiyosh Ishibashi. Oldest member of the team was Yoshio Shitabata. The youngest was Mark Akisada. Others included Robert Honke, Hajime Minemoto, Kenneth Moriji, Sachio Shigeta, and Edward Sumida.

Sumida was one of seven brothers, of whom six wore the uniform of Uncle Sam. Harry didn't get in, but he did work for the Army in Japan after the war. Richard served with an engineer unit, Layton was with the 100th, Haruo went to Okinawa with the occupational forces, and

---

*Trying to identify individual Nisei is a harrowing job. Some legalized their nicknames. Others were known only to their friends as "Yosh," although they really might be Yoshio, Yoshiharu, Yoshikazu, etc. Sorting out Nisei, especially those totally intent on *Americanizing,* is a chore that at one point almost had the author throwing up his hands and quitting. Establishing who was who became nearly as difficult as getting any to talk. It may have been one of the reasons several other writers had given up on this project.

Raymond served in a later, Korean, conflict. Makoto, or "Maxie," ended up with the most interesting assignment of all the Sumida's.

At Vint Hill Farm Station, outside Washington, D.C., a very special unit was at work. Here Nisei were "reading Hitler's mail," so to speak. The British had stolen, before the war, one of the Enigma code machines the Germans used for their top-secret transmissions, and named all traffic decoded from it "Ultra." Japanese codes, of course, had already been broken, and were continually broken. In Turkey, a special station intercepted what Maj. Gen. Hiroshi Oshima, the Japanese ambassador to Berlin, was sending to Tokyo, and relayed it to Vint Hill Farm Station. Makoto Sumida, Tatsuji Machida, Francis Ogoso and others, including Naomitsu Kitsuiwa, translated, working with decoders. The White House often knew, before the Imperial Palace did, what Hitler's generals had told Oshima. Nearly three and one-half decades would pass before this achievement was made public, and even then the Nisei were not mentioned. One result of Vint Hill's work was an extremely-detailed description of Germany's "Atlantic Wall," the barrier invading Allied troops would have to breach, in order to get a foothold in Europe. Oshima had been taken on a long tour of this system of western defenses, and sent a lengthy report of what he saw to Tokyo. Thanks to men like Maxie Sumida, top American army officers studied the report just as avidly as top Japanese ones did. At the same time.

* * *

Nimitz wanted the Palaus for a staging area. He planned to take only Angaur and Peleliu, isolating the large Japanese garrison on Babelthuap at the northeast end of the island group. His intelligence people, however, did not do the kind of job MacArthur had come to expect of his own people. The 1st Marines landed at Peleliu on September 15, 1944, expecting to clean up the place in four days, according to one USMC general, so the 81st Division was sent ashore at Angaur, slightly to the southwest.

Don Okubo was cousin to the Onishi brothers who'd fled the shores of Pearl Harbor on December 7, 1941. He hit the beach at Peleliu with the marines. Ichiro Obikane, Edwin Fujimori and Hisashi Kubota were on his team. They dug in near the shore, and waited for some POW's to be taken so they could question them.

There weren't many, for a good time to come. The Navy paid the price for a very poor intelligence job. Ten days of bloody fighting saw 4000 Marines, most of them in their teens or early twenties, killed or wounded. The 1st Marines took such a beating that a regiment of the 81st had to be pulled over from Angaur, to reinforce them.

James Kai led the 81st's language team. His officer was Philip Beaufoy. With Hiroki Takahashi, Frank Kubota and Shiuso Chojin, they operated from division headquarters. The rest of the men were paired, at regimental level; Robert Sakai and Shiro Sakaki with the 321st, Saburo Nakamura and Tomio Ichikawa at the 322nd, Masao Abe and Kei Kitahara with the 323rd. Lachlan Sinclair was with the team at the outset, his place taken by Beaufoy when he had to return to JICPOA.

"We bobbed around on the waves for hours, before going in," said Tomio Ichikawa of the Angaur landing and his seasickness. He and Saburo Nakamura had six bodyguards *each,* "who even followed us to the latrine." Ichikawa's written Japanese was not really strong. He had difficulty with the *sosho* in diaries. When under pressure, sometimes the best he could do with documents was, in his words, "make a guess."

When his regiment moved over to help the marines, a sniper hit Masao Abe, and Shiro Sakaki then went with the 323rd to take Ulithi Atoll, later the Navy's biggest Pacific anchorage. Sakaki found a native "who spoke excellent Japanese, so we had three-way interpretation." Kei Kitahara assisted in moving all the natives to one islet in the atoll, the Navy taking over Mog Mog for

1st Cavalry Division language team, off-duty in Manila. Below (l-r) on Okinawa are James Iwamura, Jerry Katayama and Bob Sugimoto with real, not "manufactured" flags.

beer parties of visiting crews. Then they joined a commando-type mission to take Ngulu, halfway between Ulithi and the Palaus. Their Japanese-speaking native guided them in through a mine field. The pair went back to Peleliu, where they began to talk Japanese, natives and civilians out of caves. One of the first prisoners had maggots in his ears.

Kei Kitahara came down with jaundice, and had to be evacuated. Sakaki carried on. He saw an enemy soldier who had committed suicide by holding a grenade to his breast. "What a gruesome sight," said Sakaki. "His ribs and chest were blown apart like an LST's doors wide open." When one caveful of soldiers resisted, firing back with captured American weapons, Sakaki saw satchel charges thrown in at them. When these had no effect, flame-throwers were called into play, and did the job. That weapon either burned a man to death, or took all the oxygen out of his air, suffocating him.

"The Japanese ate pretty good, compared to our C-rations," said Sakaki, telling how he feasted off a case of captured canned *sukiyaki* for a week, washing it down with whiskey made from "C-ration raisins, fruit bars, etc., which cost me 30 bucks a bottle!"

Hiroki Takahashi interrogated one officer who was caught swimming toward a nearby island, his 700-year-old *samuari* sword dangling from his neck. Other GI's looked on goggle-eyed as Takahashi and Shiuso Chojin let the officer give a weapon-brandishing demonstration of his sword technique. Another officer was caught when, filthy from hiding in a cave, he tried to purify his body in the ocean before committing suicide.

Jimmy Kai, interrogating prisoners, picked up reflections of the marines' raid on Makin in 1942. He learned that Japanese soldiers on Peleliu and Angaur had been told that, if captured by the Americans, they'd have their penises cut off and be subjected to other tortures. Kai's group captured a Japanese paymaster, who told them where some money was buried. They dug up one of the two crates and, when an officer decided to keep the money "as a souvenir," those of the language team who could grabbed a big handful each before surrendering the loot. After the war, upon taking up Occupation duties, they found the money could be spent. Kai knows where the other crate is, to this day, but at 1978 rates it's probably not even worth the cost of its container.

The team stayed in the Palaus a good while, then moved down to New Caledonia with the 81st for rest and recreation. Kai gave Shojin three of his four beers when they had a party to celebrate Shojin's award of the Silver Star, "so Shiuso had seven, to celebrate."

It is worth noting that seven Nisei members of the 81st's team had families in concentration camps at the time they participated in some of the war's costliest fighting. The Palaus were a blood bath.

* * *

Noboru Murakami had another team in India. It included Morris Taketa, Hisashi Nakagawa, Errol Nakao, Harry Uyehara and James Nose. They found the work largely dull. Few interrogations were fruitful, because POW's brought in were too sophisticated, from earlier grillings done closer to the front.

Some captives even waxed whimsical, giving the POW camp at Delhi a "Hogan's Heroes" air. Pugnacious Harold Hanaumi, reading a roster of new POW's one morning, blew his top. He ordered the newcomers lined up, and asked each his name, getting answers like "Masashige Kusunoki, Iyeyasu Tokugawa," etc. These wise guys, noting that the Japanese spoken by some of the Nisei was faltering, had been saying, in effect, "I'm Paul Revere. He's George Washington."

The other four men on Murakami's team were Herbert Ujimori, Norman Ueno, Frank Takao, and Hank Nakakihara. Like hundreds of ATIS in Indooroopilly, they would go home after the war with few combat stories to tell, and it's hard to be heroic in front of family and friends when one spends a war scanning documents.

The Nisei in India mostly had to settle for the knowledge they had done their part to win the war, that part being to do what they were ordered to do, no matter how dull.

* * *

"Jungle rot" afflicted nearly every soldier, of any nation, who served in New Guinea, but two examples best illustrate how it could affect a man, and, in one case, especially a Nisei.

Gary Kadani's case was not unusual. Until penicillin arrived, he suffered from the ailment continually, especially in the groin area, to the point where nearly any movement caused chafing. Skin could not be scratched, lest it come away in large folds, on one's hand. Kadani was finally taken in a jeep to Port Moresby, where penicillin did the job. He paid a price for earlier treatment, however. An Australian medic had arrested Kadani's ailment to some degree by having him smear himself with a substance called "Whitman's Ointment." As a result, Kadani's groin, abdomen, and upper legs "turned black," according to him, "and stayed that way until about 1949!"

Gene Uratsu's experience was a little different. During the Wakde-Sarmi operation, he contracted some kind of dermatitis all over his body. Medics finally told him the only cure was to go swimming in salt water every day, and bake himself in the hot sun. Gene followed instructions, but after a few days of this treatment was "captured" by two GI's of the 158th RCT. Protestations availed nothing until an officer recognized the naked Uratsu, and he was released. He stayed on in the jungle campaign, but later learned that his two captors "were given R&R to Australia, for being alert."

* * *

MacArthur wanted the island of Morotai, part of the Halmaheras. It would put his heavy bombers within range of most of the Philippines. It would also let him stage aircraft onto Philippines airfields as fast as he captured them. Taking airfields was a must in any MacArthur operation.

Morotai was to be Kazuhiko Yamada's last combat operation. He'd been to Buna with Arthur Castle and Phil Ishio. He'd gone to Goodenough Island with Ishio, Gary Kadani, James Tsumura, Steve Yamamoto and Kazuo Kawaguchi. He had been in combat with the 32nd and 24th, and the Aussie 7th and 9th. Then he led a team ashore at Morotai.

Mike Miyatake had gone to Afua, at the head of the Driniumor River, to help Henry Morisako when his friend came down with dysentery. There he met Masao Yamamoto, whom he described as "very small, and very brave." Mike could not keep up with Yamamoto during re-supply airdrops. The smaller man kept jumping in and out of foxholes, amid enemy fire, to gather food and ammunition. "Twice was enough for *me!*" Mike said.

Richard Ishimoto went in with the XI Corps team. Others on it were George Sugimoto, Satoshi Nishijima, Tom Yamada, Hirotoshi Yamamoto, James Tanaka, Casey Kawamoto, and James Yasuda.

The 31st Division's team included Yoshito Shibata, George Y. Fukuhara, Kengo Nagasako, Tadashi Hamane, Albert K. Kanzaki, Tatsuo Yamane, Shigeo Miyashiro, and George Z. Kobata.

* * *

Tom Taketa, in India, found himself assigned to a strange outfit—the 1st Air Commando Unit. It was headed by a colorful character named Philip Cochrane, immortalized by Steve Canyon in his comic strip "Terry and the Pirates," as Flip Corkin. Taketa did not get immortalized, but he did get a Bronze Star. The only Nisei attached, Tom was doing radio intercept work for the combination of gliders, transports, fighters and medium bombers that backed up Wingate's unit and Merrill's Marauders. Tom listened in on Zero fighters that were attacking one of the Commando's flights. The enemy pilots carelessly spoke in "plain" Japanese, saying enough so that Tom could not only identify their squadron, but where it was located. Cochrane laid on a bombing strike, and later supply flights were not harassed.

George Taketa could be proud of his kid brother. So could their imprisoned parents.

In Burma, things had begun to go well. The Japanese 18th Division's units withdrew from Myitkina. Karl Yoneda's team moved in, and he began "hog-calling," trying to get holdout enemy troops to surrender. He then interrogated 31 of those he helped capture, and wrote a survey of the effort. It had some surprises. For one thing, Yoneda learned that surrender leaflets had no effect on Japanese soldiers engaged in combat, only when they were on the defensive. Otherwise, leaflets were ignored. Sentimental Japanese music, Yoneda found out, could have a devastating effect, especially if coupled with factual news in leaflets. Enemy soldiers were starved for news and, when leaflet information was confirmed by Japanese sources, they were psychologically better prepared for further attempts to induce their surrender. Yoneda also learned that all propaganda had to be "more Japanese," with well-known proverbs an excellent device about which to build statements.

Henry Gosho worked with John Emmerson, of the U.S. State Department, broadcasting to enemy soldiers from the rig on the back of a jeep. He had to stand up on the jeep to man the speaker, however, and made an inviting target. Asked how Japanese soldiers usually reacted to his broadcasts, Gosho said, "With a few rounds right through the loudspeaker."

Kenji Yasui, of Yoneda's team, got the title "Baby Sergeant York" during the mopping-up operations around Myitkina. He once swam to an island in the Irrawaddy River and passed himself off to 17 Japanese soldiers as "Colonel Yamamoto, with orders for your surrender!" A Kibei, he put them through close order drill, then had them push a raft back across the river, with him on it, to surrender. An inveterate gambler from Los Angeles, Yasui was a master bluffer. The Japanese found that out. So did the soldiers who'd made the mistake of getting on the same troop transport to India from the States with Yasui. He disembarked with their money.

Frank Tokubo was an eyewitness to Yasui's feat. A man who'd, for safety reasons, put his wife into the Amache concentration camp with their baby daughter, Tokubo had fought his way through non-combatants to Myitkina. He'd done three weeks of POW interrogation at the Red Fort. Then he worked with a man named McKenzie who'd come out from Washington for the express purpose of getting strategic information from prisoners about the Mitsubishi Aircraft factory at Nagasaki. Tokubo did that for five weeks, pumping Nagasaki POW's. His elicited information may have been added to what was collected for targeting that city the following year. Frank had been itching to "get to the front." His watching Yasui operate was the closest he'd come to that date. He'd get closer.

Frank Tokubo's case resembled that of some other Nisei. His older brother Tsumoru was interned, and treated so badly that in anger, he renounced his U.S. citizenship when a wartime law made that possible. Tsumoru did not recover it for many years. A younger brother, Harumi, was in Japan with the rest of the Tokubo family, and neighbors looked upon them with "cold eyes" when the war started because the entire town of Itsukaichi, Hiroshima-ken, knew Frank was in the American army. While Frank was still in Burma, Harumi volunteered for the *Tokko Tai,* the kamikaze corps, feeling he had to do something to dispel the suspicions of disloyalty that neighbors had about the Tokubo family.

* * *

In Australia, Mac Nagata worked hard to get permission for Tom Takata to get married, and succeeded. In New Guinea, copies of the July 31 overseas edition of *Time* magazine were getting pretty ragged from being passed around. It contained heartening news about what the 100th and 442nd were accomplishing, and MIS'ers wistfully wished someone would take notice of themselves. They'd been in combat a lot longer.

Now and then someone did, but if a news photographer took a picture of a Nisei linguist, it was confiscated and destroyed. Higher-ups didn't want the Japanese to know Nisei were working against them. MacArthur himself feared that, if captured, Nisei would be tortured, and that their relatives in Japan might be, as well. MacArthur wrote these reasons in his own hand, when disapproving of one of the many ATIS requests for duty in the front lines.

* * *

The war in New Guinea, the Solomons and the Bismarcks was winding down, as it was in the Marianas, but you couldn't really tell if you were there. The marines and war correspondents were long gone, but surviving enemy soldiers weren't. Harry Tanaka did quite a stint with Australian forces, starting in the summer of 1944. So did Tsutomu Shigeta, Larry Mizumoto, and Noboru Miyage. They were engaged in "mopping up" operations, a euphemistic phrase for work that can get you just as dead as the first day on a beachhead can. General Hatazo Adachi realized his cause in New Guinea was hopeless, but he and his soldiers intended to take as many Allied troops with them as possible, if they were going to die. It meant that many less would be able to approach and threaten sacred Japan.

* * *

The Marauders were now out of business. Some of the Nisei went to India, some to China, and three went back to the U.S. for officers' training school. They barely made it through the course, said Herb Miyasaki, "because we were so damned weak!" He, Bob Honda, and Russell "Kats" Kono had gotten back to the U.S. Howard Furumoto, Akiji Yoshimura, Eddie Mitsukado and Roy Nakada weren't so lucky. They were commissioned in the field, and had to stay in the Far East. All had the coveted Combat Infantrymen's Badge. All wore a homemade shoulder patch designed by one of the Marauders but not approved by the War Department, whenever they felt like it. Before leaving Myitkina, Bob Honda and Grant Hirabayashi had helped Won Loy "Charlie" Chan scan captured documents, and to interrogate some of the "comfort girls" captured with the Japanese at Myitkina.

* * *

Comfort girls may have had some Nisei wondering whether the enemy's ideas on how to wage war might be more compatible with the average infantrymen's wishes, but the linguists did turn use of them against the enemy. A document, picked up on Guadalcanal, helped. Later discovered to be in the *gosho* handwriting of a senior Rabaul staff officer, it was the officers' and enlisted men's schedule—with prices—for use of comfort girls at the New Britain base. It listed hours for each, and even had the menstrual period for each girl plotted, so that a customer could decide upon the day, as well as the hour.

This document was thoroughly analyzed, to develop when the maximum number of senior officers would be patronizing the girls. An air strike was then laid on for that hour. After that, according to John Anderton, "Japanese leadership at Rabaul was never the same."

* * *

It was now time for MacArthur's great stroke—his long-promised, long-awaited return to the Philippines. Leyte Island had been substituted for Mindanao, along with other changes in American plans. No longer would Formosa be a target. Instead, the Philippines were to be taken, while long-range bombing strikes kept hitting Japan proper from the Marianas. Later, Iwo Jima would be a target because it was on a straight line with Tinian and Tokyo, and after that Okinawa. That island, instead of Formosa or the China coast, would be staging area for the final assault on Japan.

Meanwhile, the Driniumor River campaign in New Guinea was wrapped up. The enemy retreated toward Wewak after losing nearly 10,000 men. The MARS Force, in Burma, was activated, as successor to Merrill's Marauders. It would be striking south, toward Lashio, in an attempt to recapture and restore the old Burma Road. With the Japanese now on the run out of India, this might not be easy, but intelligence reports indicated that enemy troops retreating from the Assam Plain might not make much of a foe. They were dying at an unbelievable rate, of disease and starvation.

Karl Yoneda found he had become the first Nisei to become enrolled in the Veterans of Foreign Wars, in San Francisco, although what the VFW's national headquarters might have said about the big publicity splash if they'd known Karl was a Communist has never been reported.

Command posts on New Guinea were not generally threatened, by this time. Nisei actually got to grow some vegetables in little plots around headquarters. Back at Camp Savage, instructors were doing the very same thing. It was the only way, on both sides of the world, that Nisei could obtain the kind of vegetables that went with the Chinese and Japanese food they preferred to prepare—grow them.

* * *

A new organization had been started, at Camp Ritchie, Maryland, better known to the world later as "Camp David." It was PACMIRS, for Pacific Military Intelligence Research Service. Jim Matsumura, Seishin Kondo, Kazuo Yamane, and John Kenjo were transferred 60 miles, as part of the cadre developing it. Lachlan Sinclair joined it later. In Europe, the 100th crossed the Arno River in Italy, heading for an assault on the Germans' Gothic Line. In New Guinea, an 8th Army had been formed. Tom Takata reported from Australia to the 33rd U.S. Division at Finschhafen. He knew something was up. So did all the other linguists who were gathering with various units. Ralph Saito left Pearl Harbor in *USS George Clymer,* a transport, as part of the headquarters staff for the new XXIV Corps. American strength in the Pacific continued to grow.

* * *

U.S. carrier task forces began to pound the Manila and other areas on Luzon, northernmost island of the Philippines. Guerrilla activity picked up so much, when Filipinos grew so sure that "Makassar," as Japanese in Japan would also later call him, was about to return that, the Imperial 14th Army headquarters had to declare martial law.

In late September, Masaru Yoshioka activated the 178th Language Detachment with the 24th Division on the same day that Gen. Tomoyuki Yamashita was transferred from Manchuria to the Philippines. The "Tiger of Malaya," who had taken on a British-Australian force three times his size and defeated it, accepting their surrender at Singapore, had been buried in the hinterlands by a jealous Hideki Tojo. Now Japan was counting on him to save the day, by stopping MacArthur in his tracks.

By this time, nearly 4500 Japanese bodies had been counted in the Hollandia area, not all of them dead from wounds. Many had starved. The enemy was paying an awful price for long, thin supply lines. Planes and submarines had snipped them, and MacArthur's infantrymen had taken over their nearest key points.

* * *

Nisei were, again, shuttling around as the action picked up. Amos Nakamura joined the British Army in India. Morris Taketa and Hisashi Nakagawa got assigned to it, too. They stayed with the 14th British Army's 33rd Indian Corps all the way to its taking of Rangoon, Burma. George Hayashida and Minoru Hara joined 6th

Army headquarters staff at Hollandia, and Masao Matsumoto landed on Bougainville with the 2nd Australian Corps headquarters. Dick Oguro and two other Nisei got sent to Hollandia from Aitape, and Kenneth Yoon, a Korean, arrived in India. Yoon and a Chinese-American, Kynsul Lee, were part of a special, polyglot team sent out from Savage.

Kazuo Komoto headed a 12-Nisei team that joined the 475th Infantry Regiment, part of the MARS Force, which may have gotten its name via a narcissistic whim of the general who led it. His name was Arms. Gene Wright, of the 43rd and Yoshikazu Yamada, who was now with the 112th RCT, got to meet. In India, Timmie Hirata was listening to the World's Series on radio, while planners in Australia were going something entirely different. Still drawing upon knowledge gained via capture of the Z Plan, and its translation, ATIS had figured out, with only one error in name as it proved later, every ship that could come through Surigao Strait, or San Bernardino Strait, to fend off the strike that was planned against Leyte Island.

* * *

To sap Japanese strength, and to interdict airstrips through which enemy planes might be staged from homeland factories to front line airfields, powerful U.S. carrier strikes were made on Formosa and other places. These were quite successful, but the Japanese citizenry didn't think so. Various Japanese commanders lied. They claimed to have sunk 11 carriers, and 6 other warships of the U.S. striking force. As a nation, Japan celebrated. Yamashita, in the Philippines, thought that Leyte could be defended, rather than concentrating everything on Luzon. He, too, had been led up the garden path.

* * *

On October 20, 1944, Nisei with four U.S. divisions hit the beaches at Leyte. Others were with the two infantry and one airborne division held in reserve. Still more

Karl Yoneda (left) with "hog-calling" equipment, used for inducing an enemy to surrender. Henry Gosho did similar work, nearly got shot.

were at Corps, and Army headquarters. Others were with radio interception units, ready to go to work as soon as they could get set up.

As much as anyone, the Yankee *Samurai* had made it possible for Douglas A. MacArthur to keep his word. He had returned.

Chapter 11

While some Nisei were streaming toward Leyte Gulf for the invasion of the Philippines, some on the other side of the world left Marseilles, France for a town they'd never heard of but would always remember—Bruyeres. The 442nd was about to write in blood a chronicle of American history. In the U.S., one Nisei made a bit of history himself. It was Kazuo Yamane. His contribution came from noticing something a lot of other people hadn't.

Yamane was among those moved from the Pentagon to Camp Ritchie and PACMIRS. Col. G. F. Gronich let him have leave, and he got married on October 12, knowing he'd been selected for a secret special assignment about which he was given no details. Yamane enjoyed a week's honeymoon in New York, then went back to Ritchie, where carloads of documents awaited translation. Fingering through them, several weeks later he spotted one that should have had greater priority than *Routine,* which was how Navy intelligence experts at Pearl Harbor marked it before shipment on to Washington.

Yamane took the document to Col. Gronich, who made people unhappy by cancelling their holiday leaves and putting all to work on Yamane's discovery. The Hawaii Nisei had stumbled across the Imperial Army's *ordnance inventory*! Through the U.S. Navy's hands at Pearl Harbor had slipped the amounts and types of every weapon in the Japanese home islands. Furthermore, the inventory listed their condition, locations, and quantity, plus where spare parts and other materials in the Japanese weapons network could be found. Strategic planners could add new targets to the B-29 list, and Yamane's find was also used with stunning effect at the war's end. Yamane kept his find to himself until telling the author about it, although he undoubtedly realized more and more over the years what a find he had made. Still, he made light of it, preferring instead to tell how the Navy got so angry at the courier who flew back and forth between Pearl Harbor, who kept ribbing its intelligence experts about their foulup, that he got shangai'd out of Ritchie and sent overseas. Yamane went overseas a while later, on a very special mission.

* * *

Just before the Leyte invasion, three Pacific Nisei were awarded Bronze Stars.* Shig Yasutake got one for work done around caves at Munda. Richard K. Matsumoto was given one for his speedy translation of captured documents that got put to quick and successful tactical use on New Georgia. Haruo "Slim" Tanaka was awarded his for work done at Aitape. There Tanaka pioneered use of a POW to bring more POW's, in spite of a policy forbidding him to get within enemy target range.

* * *

Three Nisei were in Panama at this time, another strange place for any to be. Yoshio Ogata was as puzzled about his assignment as he had been when the FBI locked

---

*Little space is given in this book to listing medals and awards won by MIS'ers. For one thing, they mean little to the public 35 years after the fact. For another, American military awards have since become cheapened, often being given out for much less than they were a generation ago. Too, the military services have actually competed with one another in giving them out. Heroism is not a numbers game. Suffice it to say that Nisei in the Pacific, like those in Europe, earned decorations on a scale far out of proportion to their numbers.

up him for three days on Sand Island, Honolulu, at the war's start. He'd been released when someone explained to government agents that it had *not* been a Japanese army uniform Ogata was wearing on December 7, but his high school clothing. Unable to speak much English, Ogata had only returned from completing Middle School in Japan during the summer of 1941. His buttons and cap confused an informant.

Three attempts to volunteer finally paid off. Ogata, after MISLS, served at Bolling Field in the nation's capital, translating "JAM Tins." This was the name given nameplates on Japanese aviation equipment. From them, strategic intelligence was developed. One example was learning that Japanese aircraft were numbered *in sequence* by manufacturers. This made it possible to ascertain how many of a certain type might still have to be faced, and which ones were no longer being made.

* * *

The Leyte landings commenced on October 20, 1944. They are covered elaborately in books by other writers. Nisei linguists were with the mighty force reported by enemy observers to include more than 100 troop transports alone. MIS'ers were part of the 7th, 24th, 32nd, 38th, 77th and 96th Divisions, as well as the 1st Cavalry and 11th Airborne, besides various Army and Corps staffs. General idea was to take Leyte, then asault Luzon— northernmost of the Philippines—while putting the squeeze on islands in between, like Mindanao, Mindoro, and Palawan. Every area taken had to provide airbases for attacking the next, MacArthur being a total believer in airpower. He also bought intelligence *in toto* as a vital function of command. By using it in the Philippines, as elsewhere, he kept the cost of each victory at a minimum.

The 96th landed at Dulag. Warren Higa had the team, under Allen A. Beach. "I went in with the third wave," said Tom Masui. "Frogmen went first, and the scouts second. The line companies were in the fourth wave, and believe me, I was scared as hell to be out there *in front of the fighting men!"* Herbert Yanamura and Akira Ohori were on the team, as were Takejiro Higa, Yoichi Kawano, and Osame Yamamoto. Like Rudy Kawahara, Takeo Nonaka and Fred Fukushima, they had taken jungle training in the Kaaawa Valley on Oahu's north side, and had been heading to invade Yap when the 96th was diverted to the Admiralties. There they spent a few days climbing coconut trees and drinking beer before heading for Leyte.

The 1st Cavalry landed at Tacloban. It also had to capture nearby airstrips as quickly as possible, and it did. Besides the men who joined it after fighting with the marines on Guam, the 1st Cavalry language section had the services of William Dozier, Yoshikazu Yamada, Noboru Yoshimura, Hakumasa Hamamoto, Hiroshi Miura and Terasu Yoshimoto. Hiroshi Miyake and Minoru Namba were in the scramble, too, and what a scramble it was. So anxious were top commanders to have documents and diaries seized, then translated as quickly as possible, that some Nisei team members rarely saw the others after October 20. Kai Rasmussen's dream had come true. Proof was everywhere of how valuable Nisei linguists were. They were in such demand that every general wanted to "own" a few. In Panama, Yoshio Ogata actually waited for months, having been told that a general would be coming through the Canal enroute to the Pacific fighting, and especially wanted the Nisei on his staff. The general never showed.

Richard Ishimoto was with X Corps. So were Tom Yamada, Morley Miyake, Tadashi Uchigaki, George Sugimoto, Henry Morisako, Satoshi Nishijima, Fred Nishitsuji, Tom Hadomato and Casey Kawamoto. Others who served with X Corps, at Leyte and onward, are listed in this book's Appendix, the task of tracking them down were they served with various divisions and regiments as needed proving almost impossible.

Every American fighting man at Leyte, or near it, held his breath for days while the naval aspects of the campaign were fought out. The Japanese Fleet was on the prowl, determined to smash the landing force. Enemy plans were well thought out, and very nearly worked.

The Leyte invasion was protected by a massive surface armada that included old U.S. battleships not useful for much more than shore bombardment. Roaming east and north of the troop transports was a powerful carrier task force, by William Halsey. Against this four Japanese thrusts were coming, one strictly a diversion. Two were coming around the south of the Philippines and up through Surigao Strait, to fall upon the massed transports. One was coming through San Bernardino Strait, in the center of the Philippines, to poise a northern second pincer over the landing force. Meanwhile, down from further north was coming a carrier task force that really wasn't a carrier task force. It had practically no aircraft. It was bait, to draw off Halsey.

In Pentagon files today, as well as in the strategic military intelligence files of other major nations, are "psychological profiles" of foreign generals and admirals. Some contain notations like "Prefers head-on attack," or "Extremely cautious unless absolutely certain of victory," and so forth. During the 1941-45 war, both sides had these.

The Japanese one on Admiral William F. Halsey must have been right on the mark. Halsey, except for a mild hit-and-run air raid on the Marshalls and Gilberts nearly three years before, had commanded at no major sea victory. He was in the hospital when Frank Fletcher won at Midway, and down south out of the picture when Raymond Spruance succeeded in the Marianas. Japanese strategists knew Halsey was chafing at the bit, and played on that. Their decoy carrier task force sucked Halsey out of position completely (he spent the rest of his life angrily justifying why he took the air cover away from MacArthur's soldiers), and the wolf got in among the sheep. The Center Force of the Imperial Navy was blocked from wrecking the Leyte landings only by the bravery of Americans in thin-hulled "jeep" carriers and destroyer escorts, which fought it off.

An ambush again took care of the Southern Force. Z Plan knowledge, carefully followed up, allowed American PT-boats, then destroyers, to bushwhack the Southern Force, and ancient U.S. battleships to finish it off. Japanese intelligence was good. They knew their man, Halsey, well enough to conjecture that he could be drawn toward the opportunity to achieve fame. They exploited this. The use of American naval intelligence at Leyte Gulf left much to be desired, but when a war gets won no one asks questions of the victors. Halsey was hailed as a hero, and Bureau of Ordnance torpedo specialists were never called to account for refusing to adapt a captured German torpedo when the one they insisted on using wasn't working and got American submariners killed by the gross. Those are the breaks of the game called war.

* * *

The XXIV Corps had two language teams operating from its headquarters in the Leyte campaign. One was headed by Joseph Bothwell. On it was Jerry Katayama, whose family was in a concentration camp. Others were George Kozuchi (who also turned out to be one of those manufacturers of "genuine Japanese battle flags"); James Ogisaka, "whom nothing bothered,"; Thomas Higashiyama; Ralph Saito; Akira Tanaka; and Ted "Legs" Nishiyama. Some members found chunks of flesh missing from the thighs of dead bodies after the initial invasion. They couldn't tell from this whether cannibalism had been practiced by Japanese soldiers, or by local natives whose diet was usually vegetarian. Dan Nakatsu, James Iwamura and Robert Sugimoto enjoyed a chicken dinner with the others, followed by cake and ice cream, on board the Navy transport the night before landing. The 306th Language Detachment wouldn't have another hot meal until Christmas Day.

* * *

Work done by Nisei that has never received reasonable recognition was in the field of aircraft technical intelligence. Rikio Koga led a team to New Guinea for this. On it were Karl Akama, Hisayoshi Ueki, Jack Wakayama, Thomas Takasone, Toshimi Yamada, Isamu Sugiyama and Thomas Yoshikawa. They were to work on shot-down or captured enemy aircraft. They did, and sometimes sent back to the Pentagon useful, even vital, information.

Dan Tamotsu Nishimura had another team that went out at the same time as Koga's. On it were Norito Nagao, Warren Adachi, Jay Kaneshiro, Tatsuo Yamamoto, Shigemitsu Nakashima, James Yoshinaga, James Hozaki, Takeo Takata and Clarence Ohta. Some of the men did this type of work on New Guinea, then went on to do more of the same in the Philippines, but not all. Men of both teams either bored with the work or not feeling they were doing a useful job, volunteered for the infantry, something any GI will tell anyone that no *sane* GI would do. But, like most Nisei, the volunteers felt they had to prove themselves the equal of any when it came to demonstrating patriotism. A lot would get their chance—on Okinawa.

* * *

The 6th Army had some of the old pro's, as they now could call themselves, with its headquarters. Staff linguists included Spady Koyama, Steve Yamamoto, Tsuneo "Cappy" Harada and Minoru Hara. Koyama was the kind of man who hangs tough. He later made a career of the Army. In New Guinea he had gotten a POW, Yoshio Takayama, to cooperate with him. A *sumo* wrestler, Takayama worked like a "trusty" seeing that 600 other prisoners maintained health and sanitation standards.

When LST 552 was still offshore at Tacloban, a *kamikaze's* bomb got it. Cappy Harada and Spady Koyama were wounded. Koyama had to be evacuated. He arrived in the Admiralties naked except for what corpsmen had wrapped around him. He got all the way back to Spokane before arriving at facilities where an operation could safely be performed. Koyama came out of an anaesthetic to "Wake up, Irish!" He found a grinning nurse pointing to the names on five empty pint bottles of donated blood. In gratitude, Spady later named a son John Patrick, making him probably the first Gaelic Nisei in Spokane. Homecoming was kind of a triumph for Koyama, badly injured as he was. From New Guinea he earlier answered a letter to a Spokane newspaper with one of his own. When the writer complained of seeing "Japs" on the streets of Spokane (which was outside the evacuation zone), Koyama wrote and proposed to change places with him, offering the irate citizen a New Guinea foxhole.

* * *

The 38th Division didn't come in to Leyte right away. It followed the others by about six weeks. Its language team was first class, being loaded down with combat veterans. Arthur Castle was with it, as were Yoshikazu Higashi, James Tsumura and Lincoln Taira. James Fujimura and David Kato, of the original Presidio class, were members. So were Tomio Munekawa, Ichiro Obikane, Masao Nagahiro, Kiyoji Sato and Albert Tamura. Besides Charles Tatsuda's, the 11th Airborne had another team. On it were Robert Kimura, William Naito, Mitsuo Usui, Takeshi Fujisaka and Tetsuo Koga. Some of the men had come from the secret planning for Okinawa at Pearl Harbor.

* * *

Nisei were busy in the China-Burma-India theater of war. The shy Grant Hirabayashi interrogated "comfort girls" captured at Myitkina, with Won Loy Chan. A lad of religious bent, totally out of place in the roughneck Army, even Hirabayashi had to admit that the Japanese had some novel ideas for fighting a war. A picture of him and "Charlie" Chan at Myitkina reminded the author of a cartoon showing two Roman legionnaires coming out of a city they've just helped destroy. One is carrying loot, the other has a struggling female slung over a shoulder. The second is saying to the first "The pay is lousy, but fringe benefits are terrific!"

Frank Tokubo had talked, fought, conned, and big-dealed his way up to where he wanted to be, "the fighting front!" He worked with the MARS Force as it headed toward a place called Bhamo. Tokubo went on wide patrol swings around and behind the army, accompanied by Kachins, the fierce mountain tribesmen who loved fighting and hated Japanese. With him was a *kendo* expert from Hawaii, Hiroshi Nakamura.

Others with the MARS Force were Art Morimitsu, Angel Hirano, Tom Tsuruda, Tony Uemoto, James Araki, Paul Miwa, James Okita, Toma Tasaki and Gilbert Nagata. Yutaka Nakahata was also with the group as it combined with the Chinese 30th and 38th Divisions along the border of Yunnan Province. "Over the Hump" flights were now refueling at Myitkina, instead of getting attacked from there. Tonnage flown to Chiang built up at an unbelievable rate.

Fighting alongside Chinese units could have complications. Tony Uemoto became another "captured" Nisei when Chinese surrounded him. They wouldn't even permit him to leave his foxhole for four hours.

Somewhat to the north of the MARS Force, Shigeto Mazawa found fighting with the Kachins confusing, too. Volunteering from a desk job in India to serve with the OSS, Mazawa was told he'd be parachuting into the Burma jungle. Without a bit of training, he did just that, working with British, Americans and Kachins behind Japanese lines. What confused him were several massive, black balls of some strange tarry substance. When he asked what it was, Mazawa got told "Opium." It was the coin in which Kachin mercenaries got paid.

* * *

A goodly number of Nisei saw a lot of service with, but were reluctant to talk about, the Office of Strategic Services (OSS). Much of what the OSS did in the 1941-45 war was so tied to British operations that some of its operations may not become public until Great Britain's Official Secrets Act is further modified. (As did the British kept-secret-until-the-1970's fact that Franklin Roosevelt, working through William Donovan, who became head of OSS, broke a host of American laws by dealing with William Stephenson, a Canadian engaged heavily in espionage and counter-espionage for the British, long before the U.S. was actually at war.) The author did learn of Nisei who worked with the OSS, but only one would discuss what he did. Since *YANKEE SAMURAI* was not planned as an expose, I saw no reason to inquire further of others, especially since so many Nisei have worked in intelligence for the U.S., some in uniform and some not, right through the Vietnam war.

Nisei known to have engaged in OSS operations in the China-Burma-India theater of war are: Fumio Kido, Wilbert Kishinami, Richard Betsui, Junichi Buto, Edward Arida, Shuichi Kumagai and Tom T. Baba. There was a rumor that Hideo Imai, and possibly others, disembarked from a submarine in Burma for some cloak-and-dagger work, but investigation yielded no documentation. Perhaps a younger, more dogged writer will have more success. Also with OSS were Ralph Yempuku, Shuichi Kurahashi, Charles Matsunaka, Takao Tanabe, and Susumu Kazuhata. There probably were others.

* * *

From what has been written thus far, it should be clear to anyone that the Pacific was practically crawling with Nisei in uniform, although only a handful of America's civilians knew they were there. Had the civilians known, they might not have believed it. They certainly wouldn't have believed that Jerry Katayama, Art Morimitsu, Pat Nagano, Kan Tagami, Roy T. Takai and Paul Bannai were only a handful of the hundreds who served in the Pacific while their parents or relatives were locked up in concentration camps that featured watch towers, guards, patrol dogs and other aspects American motion pictures then and since showed as existing only in Nazi Germany.

Some Nisei, circumnavigating the world to get home, saw Pyramids (above, left). Harold Nishimura and Yasuo S. Umetani (above, right) were in Attu campaign. Harry Oka and Conway Yamamoto (below, left) liked enemy guns silent. Nisei visited Taj Mahal before jungle combat.

But Nisei—the people described by author Bill Hosokawa as "The Quiet Americans," did serve. And none more quietly than those who worked with radio interception units. Torao Ikeda, Kiyoshi Ishibashi, and George Okamoto were part of Timothy Pietsch's team in the Calcutta area. They manned headphones round the clock, worked at busting Japanese codes, then listened for "one-word" signals the enemy carefully cloaked with routine transmissions. The Nisei had to pounce on these when detected, then draw on information gathered from other intelligence sources, to inform higher-ups of what the enemy was doing.

Don Kuwaye was in northeast India with a radio reception team when Leyte was invaded, and wondering what the hell he was doing there. He'd started the war on leave in Maui, and spent the first six months of it with men of Portuguese, or Hawaiian, or Asian extraction, patrolling beaches, before getting shanghai'd first to Camp McCoy, then to Camp Savage. Before coming overseas, Kuwaye'd gotten a pal, Juichi Miramatsu, to countersign his will. On Kuwaye's team were Takeshi Sugai, Robert Honke, Haruo Akitaki, James Araki, Shoji Yoneshige, James Wakamiya and Thomas Sasaki. The most exciting thing that had happened to them thus far had been visiting the Pyramids during a stopover at Cairo, Egypt, on the way to India.

* * *

A number of Nisei worked in counterintelligence in the Pacific. Their full stories may never get told. Arthur Komori did that kind of work, but so did many others who may never get recognized, because of inherent modesty and security restrictions. One who did work in Australia, and also in Leyte, was William T. Hiraoka. He had been picked up at the same time Kiyoshi Yamashiro (known later as George Sankey) was, on December 2, 1942, and flown to Australia from Honolulu in a Pan-American gull wing two-engine seaplane.

Suicide planes, dreamed up by a Japanese naval officer on an impulse just after *kaiten* (suicide manned torpedoes) had been officially announced as part of Japan's naval effort, rained down on American forces at Leyte. Six escort aircraft carriers covering the landings were hit on the same day, Oct. 26. It was no way to celebrate the eve of America's Navy Day. The 40th Division was relieved on New Britain, and began training for the next area of attack—Lingayen Bay, on Luzon Island. In Europe, the 442nd Regimental Combat Team headed out to rescue a battalion of the 36th Infantry Division, of which the 442nd was a part. The Texas unit had been nearly completely surrounded by Germans. In China, a Japanese thrust began that overran General Clair Chennault's forward air bases, which sort of destroyed his claim to be capable of subduing Japan with a few dozen long-range bombers operating from China.

* * *

Nisei were still operating with the Australians. Dick Oguro, Roy Takai and Yoshio "Ace" Fukai were in the mop-up operations around Aitape. Harry Toshio Tanaka, after wrapping up at Lae with the Australian 1st Army, moved to Jacquinot Bay, New Britain, with its 5th Division. Minoru Hara had become convinced, by then, that he could spot Japanese who had practiced cannibalism "by looking into their eyes. They had a definite animal look to them." Authorities were puzzled that Gary Kadani could say "I have no home," when they told him he was being given a chance to go home, but Kadani's irony rang true. He went back to the States, got married, and divided his honeymoon time between two concentration camps; visiting his new in-laws in Gila River for New Year's, after spending Christmas in Poston with his own folks.

* * *

Howard Moss, better known as "Mike," had the 7th Division's team when it landed at Dulag. His leader was Bud Mukaye (whose name sometimes got spelled Mukai).

Aging Cosma Sakamoto was on this team with Noboru Yamada, who came down with dysentery and got evacuated. Min Ichinose, Thomas Hamada, Sam Rokutani, Frank Masuoka, Futoshi Inaba, Harold Nishimura and Gus Hikawa made up the rest of the unit. Plus Frank Hachiya, who flew out from Pearl Harbor to take Yamada's place.

Main aim on Leyte was to drive across the island and take Ormoc Bay, the only port through which Japanese reinforcements from other islands might come. The 7th got across, and was joined by the 96th south of Ormoc. The enemy moved troops south to meet this threat, leaving the way open for a landing behind him by the 77th.

Shigeo Ito, team leader for the 77th's language group, nearly got killed—again—when the enemy shelled his command post. Jim Sugimura interrogated the highest-ranking POW taken by the 77th to that time—a captain with both legs shot off. The 77th's commander, scheduled to link up in a pincer with the 11th Airborne and 7th Divisions, got off one of those puerile messages that somehow get transmuted later into historic utterances, "Rolled two 7's into Ormoc," his communication read, "Come 7, come 11!"

Frank Hachiya refused the offer of a relief so he could return to Hawaii, preferring to stay and finish the campaign. On December 3 he wrote Baron Goto "I'll not be back in time for Christmas, as I had hoped. Instead, celebrate it in some muddy foxhole with can of GI rations." Hachiya took the war seriously. He knew what it meant to men like himself, who had twin loyalties. His mother and younger brother were living in Japan. Hachiya spent Christmas in combat, all right, and New Year's on an operating table, from which he was lifted dead. He'd been shot while moving up to the front, a place where he did not have to go without plenty of escort and assistance.

The 32nd Infantry Regiment, to which Frank was attached, was moving along two parallel ridges when it ran into enemy fire. It called for his help, to "talk out" the resistance. Frank hurriedly headed down the valley between the two ridges on December 30, but a sniper got him before he reached his destination. Hachiya died three days later, the bullet having passed through his liver.

A proposal for Distinguished Service Cross was made in Frank Hachiya's behalf. It was still being processed when the American Legion Post of his home town, Hood River, Oregon, removed Frank's and 13 other Nisei names from the town's Roll of Honor. When this became known, editors nationwide had a field day pontificating. Members of what Gov. "Kissin' Jim" Folsom of Alabama once referred to as "the heroes' union" re-painted the names in, amid the thunder of the press, the new paint making its gaffé all that more obvious. So much so that a 1978 search of the Hood River public library files could not unearth, for use in this book, a photograph of the embarrassing "new" sign, that later appeared in the paper there. One can only conjecture what action town-wide shame might have prompted.

* * *

In November the man who might have warned the U.S. about Pearl Harbor was hanged. Richard Sorge, who'd become privy enough to Japan's top secrets to let Russia know Germany was going to attack her, met his death at Sugamo Prison, a place that would become well-known to Frank Tokubo, Sohei Yamate, and plenty of other Nisei. By that time, MacArthur had lost a total of 2135 Americans killed, and 10,735 wounded in all the New Guinea campaign plus the Palaus. In the Palaus alone, the Marine Corps casualty lists came up to about half that number, a horrific price for one bit of real estate. Newspapers in the U.S. were growling about the high cost for victory the USMC was paying. Writers wondered aloud, and in print, whether the U.S. could afford a Marine Corps that spent young men as though an inexhaustible supply of them existed. The murmuring would become a roar, within a few months. Masaru Yoshioka made a landing on Panoan Island, in Leyte Gulf. He was busy for 12 days interrogating 45 POW's who'd survived the Battle of Surigao Strait by swimming ashore from sinking Japanese ships. Yoshioka's work won him a commendation.

* * *

Nisei were with the British Army at that time. Toshio Taniguchi was with Eiichi Sakauye when the latter saved a British officer's life and was awarded the British Medal, enlisted equivalent of the Order of the British Empire. Hiroshi Osako, at Imphal, talked to the first POW taken there. He developed information encouraging to his superiors, that the Japanese were in no way equipped to advance any further into India. Osako and Roy T. Takai were served tea at the proper British hour daily, even close to the front. By an orderly. Few other GI's, Nisei or not, could boast about having a "batman." Haruyoshi Kaya and Wally Nagao were with the 26th British-Indian Division. Hisashi Nakagawa was with the 2nd Division.

Henry Kuwabara was with the 36th British Division. He also got a British Medal, "for obtaining information that enabled British forces to capture Japanese strongpoints at Hopin and Pinbaw" in Burma. Others who served with His Majesty's forces included Harry Uyehara, Isao Kumabe, Frank Takao, Amos Nakamura and Herbert Ujimori. The British Army also got a lot of assistance from 60 ½ inches of truculence known as Harold Hanaumi.

* * *

Frank Tokubo was in north Burma, getting all the action he could handle, twice getting shot down in L-5 spotting aircraft while trying, with a loudspeaker, to convince enemy troops that they should surrender.

Karl Yoneda was busy turning out "white" propaganda—pamphlets that included photos of fleets of B-29's enroute from Tinian to bomb Japanese cities. He also turned out "black" propaganda—hand-written notes describing how awful conditions at the front were. These, written in Japanese, were sent to addresses taken off Japanese soldiers. It was hoped they'd damage homeland morale. Yoneda grinned when recalling how his work sometimes had to be toned down. He'd often work in something about overthrowing the Emperor, only to be told "No, Karl, no! We're going to *need* the Emperor, after the war is won!"

Nisei linguists with the MARS Force encountered David Akui. He had captured the war's very first POW, and was also found among Merrill's Marauders. Now Akui was helping win the final Burma campaign against the enemy.

* * *

On Leyte, Tom Masui just missed being a hero, but it was not his fault. Early in December, Tom learned that a coordinated Japanese attack was soon to be made on airfields around Burauen, which the Americans had seized. An infantry attack would simultaneously be made overland. Also, Japanese aircraft would crashland on the three airstrips, some of them carrying infantry. With all this, Japanese paratroopers would descend. The enemy high command knew these airfields were precious, and it wanted them back.

Masui's information apparently never got to the staff intelligence officer of the 96th Division. Yasuo Umezu told how the sky lit up, and how it was "pretty, watching the tracers shooting in the air" as the enemy paratroopers came floating down. The Japanese plan didn't work. One way or another, the infantry and airborne attackers were cleaned up in the next few days, but only after putting a thorough scare into the Americans.

The Japanese high command, in spite of General Yamashita's sentiment against the tactic, kept reinforcing Leyte. More and more individual ships, plus convoys, and fleets of small craft, kept trying to put troops ashore at Ormoc, on the west side of Leyte. American submarines and aircraft raised hob with them. The 11th Airborne blocked off the enemy's movements in the Leyte Valley, so that the 7th Division could move ahead with its attempt to seize Ormoc.

* * *

In mid-December, the 24th and 31st Divisions made landings on Mindoro. Once the airfields on this island were taken, Leyte would be shut off from all further reinforcements, and Japanese forces there could be overwhelmed. The Army was hard at work, its job far different from what was expected of marines. GI's had to hang in until the job was done. There would be no relief for them, unless it was more Army infantrymen. American histories seem to have glossed over the fact that the Philippines campaign was no short-term enterprise, like Tarawa, Guam, Saipan, Tinian and Peleliu. MacArthur's infantrymen had a 10-month long row to hoe. Besides the enemy, they met nearly every tropical ailment imaginable along the way. And, especially in the southern Philippines, more rain than any human being could possibly want.

Walter Tanaka and Sho Onodera, both now commissioned for their services as combat infantrymen in New Guinea, showed up on Leyte. Each had a 10-man Nisei linguist team under him, and Walt had to try to show a little dignity. There would be no more selling of "genuine Japanese battle flags" with *Kanji* characters that said things like "Your mother wears Army shoes." And no more taking, as James Tsurutani had, all clothes off and lying on the ground, so that a Caucasian buddy could stand over you, bayonet at the ready, having pictures taken that would show the folks back home how he (the Caucasian) had "captured another Jap!"

Robert Fukuda, Floyd Yamamoto and others got onto Leyte with their air technical intelligence team, trying to glean from wrecked enemy aircraft information that might save some of their buddies' lives in future battles. And, in other areas, more Nisei continued their quiet work with radio interception units.

Ken Sekiguchi had such a team. On it with him were

Yoshiaki Nakamoto, James Okada, Stanley Kimura, Henry Kaneshiro and Kazuyo Uyehara. They went straight from San Francisco to New Guinea, but stopped only a while before moving north in support of the infantry in the Philippines, where Yukio Tamura later joined up with them.

Another such team, with Goichi Shimanuki, Herbert Kawashima and Sanji Shirai on it, started in the Assam Plain, then went into Burma, supporting the MARS Force right through its campaign. Teams like those Sekiguchi and Shimanuki were on had plenty of problems. Equipment was never really dry, and there were all kinds of problems due to moisture getting into circuits. When equipment was working well on any given day, eyes rolled toward heaven, and thanks were muttered.

* * *

They got tired of the publicity after 30 years or so, but it was an AJA family that had more sons in uniform than any other in America. The Nakada family merits notice here. James, John and Minoru were MIS'ers, and Stephen was on the MISLS staff. Yoshiano worked with the OSS. Saburo and Yoshio served in the Pacific, while George and Henry were with the 442nd in Europe. No Nisei war story in the Pacific can be told without mentioning this family.

* * *

The 6th Army spun off chunks of its linguist detachment just before Christmas. Tsutomu Umeda took a team to the 24th Division. Yoshito Shibata took one to the 31st, and Harry Fukuhara, now recovered, took one to the 33rd, which moved up from New Guinea to Morotai. MacArthur had put as much power into the Leyte campaign as he was able. All had begun to go well there for him. Now it was time to cast an eye further north. His "old dependable," the 32nd Division, had done its share of the battling in the southern Philippines. Now he would call upon it, and all the others, to repeat their fine performance elsewhere. He had returned, but the lengthy island chain was far from recaptured.

* * *

Camp Savage had become too small a place to handle the language school as it grew. In late 1944, the MISLS moved down the road to Fort Snelling. No one was any crazier about accommodations there than they had been at Savage. They quickly dubbed the tarpaper shacks in which they slept, six men to a hut, the "Turkey Farm." Katsumi Onishi, on the staff, regretted not getting out into the battle area, which is what he and his brother Harold wanted, but there was a bit of compensation. His brother, then he, then a friend named James I. Nagai had each been selected as the best all-around student in each of their classes. Katsumi was delighted that "one small fishing village" could produce three outstanding students for the course. They taught others Japanese.

* * *

The 81st also saw service in Leyte. Hiroki Takahashi told how, on a reconnaissance mission, he encountered Filipinos who shouted at Caucasian soldiers to hang the Nisei, thinking they were members of the Japanese army. Rocks were thrown, even after it was explained to Filipinos who the Nisei linguists were. The 81st's commander had to order his language team back to his headquarters, and keep them there, for their own safety.

* * *

Koshi Ando, James Harada and Shizuo Tanakatsubo were in on the Mindoro landing. Harry Akune showed up on that island a month later, with the 503rd Parachute Infantry Regiment, a unit that fought mostly as foot soldiers in the Pacific. Meanwhile, forces were getting poised for a long jump and thrust. When MacArthur got ashore where they were going, he would be back on old turf. What he had in mind next was the taking of Luzon. That included

Manila, Bataan, Corregidor and other places full of bitter memories.

It would bring bitter fighting, too, even though most of the world would ignore it while watching the Allies close in on Germany. But Tomoyuki Yamashita had over 250,000 men—who had faith in him—that MacArthur's forces had to defeat if the Philippines were to be taken. There were some 30,000 in the Clark Field area, between it and Lingayen Gulf. MacArthur intended to land at the same place the Japanese invaders had in 1941.

Another 80,000 of Yamashita's troops were in the mountains east and northeast of Manila, and he had better than 150,000 under his direct command in the northern part of Luzon, centered on Baguio. This was the "winter capital" of the Philippines, high in the cool mountains.

* * *

There was still lots of mopping up to be done on Leyte before top American commanders could stop worrying about it. Stanley Shimabukuro helped ease their concern with an unbelievable, almost superhuman, effort.

Three American divisions had hammered against the Japanese 1st Manchu Division, one of Japan's best, for five weeks in central and northern Leyte. An idea of how fierce the fighting was is indicated by the fact that only four POW's were taken during that time, while 15,000 Japanese soldiers fought and died where they stood. The 1st Cavalry finally broke through this enemy outfit, and began descending into the Ormoc Valley. The road to complete capture of Leyte was now open—if.

It was now vital to know what forces still protected Ormoc. Rumors were coming in about a massive new enemy reinforcement through that port. Word was that it included a whole division of fresh troops, equipped with tanks. William Dozier had with him Stanley Shimabukuro, the only linguist allowed at the division's front line headquarters, because of what Filipinos might do if they sighted any Nisei. A few POW's were brought in, plus stacks of documents taken from enemy command posts and corpses. Dozier interrogated prisoners for 36 hours, without a break, but he credited Shimabukuro with the really rewarding effort. He was lavish in his praise of the Kibei, saying "captured letters and notebooks the *hakujin* and Nisei could make no sense of, he could read, even though parts of words were obscured by rain, sweat or blood."

By sunlight, flashlight and lantern light, Shimabukuro poured over *sosho* for 51 hours, without rest or breaks. He handled diaries, letters, messages and reports, quickly grasping the essentials of each. The results Shimabukuro got were immediately radioed to Corps headquarters. The attack continued, and Ormoc was soon taken. Victory on Leyte was complete.

What Shimabukuro had done was tell his superiors almost exactly how many men of the reinforcements sent actually got ashore; how many were lost at sea as victims of American ships, submarines and aircraft; and how many enemy troops were at locations Shimabukuro indicated on maps. This let the 1st Cavalry finish the job without needing further reinforcement of its own. Stanley Shimabukuro's name probably never caught the attention of Douglas A. MacArthur, but the quiet linguist made a vital contribution to planning. What he did made it possible to continue the war unabated on Leyte. Some troops there were freed to move on to Luzon, instead of being held up waiting for reinforcements they really didn't need.

* * *

The New Year opened brightly. Some top U.S. commanders were sure it would be the year in which war ended. In Europe, anyhow. About the Pacific, however, they could not be certain. Japan still had perhaps two million troops in the field, and probably that many again in the home islands. True, it was obvious that the Emperor's domain was on its last legs. Hundreds of thousands of his troops had been cut off, behind MacArthur's advancing forces. U.S. airpower had almost completely blanketed all war areas, and that coverage would soon be total. The

Nisei at JICPOA lived and worked in downtown Honolulu, not wanted at Navy headquarters, but managed to find relaxation between invasions.

road to the Japanese homeland was wide open. There appeared to be nothing that could stop the oncoming juggernaut. In three short years, the entire face of war had been changed. It was Japan that was now on the defensive, but the fighting spirit of her troops still stood high.

There were three effective barriers to Tokyo, now: the northern Philippines; Formosa; and Okinawa. The second one was eliminated when the Allies decided not to try to take it. It was replaced by Iwo Jima when it was decided that this volcanic island must be seized. Iwo was needed both as a massive fighter base so bombers hitting Japan from Tinian could have escort, and so that the B-29 bombers and their valuable crews would have a reachable haven if they got shot up badly in the skies over Japan.

MacArthur hit the first barrier, after Navy aircraft carriers had done all they could in preparation, on January 9, 1945. He sent in the 6th, 37th, 40th and 43rd Divisions. The 1st Cavalry, the 25th and the 23rd would follow them. War would now be waged on the terms MacArthur liked best, with his ground troops well-protected from above.

One more giant step had been taken when the first troops landed at Lingayen Gulf. A lot of other steps would have to follow, but Manila was now only 100 miles away.

Chapter 12

Before leaving New Guinea, Walter Tanaka had faced up to a major crisis in his life. He had done everything he could to dissuade his angry and disappointed father from renouncing the U.S. and returning to Japan. This was not easy to do while soaking wet in a foxhole with the enemy shooting at you. The moisture on Walt's face was more than rain when he read what he feared was his father's last letter on a painful subject.

America had disappointed him, Tunejiro Tanaka told his son, as he recounted the family troubles. He intended to go back to Japan as soon as he could. But, he had other ideas concerning Walter. "When a tiger dies, he leaves his skin," Tunejiro wrote, quoting an old Japanese adage, "but when a man dies he leaves only his name. America has rejected me, and I am going back to my native country, Japan. You, however, are to stay in America. It is your country. Defend it. I charge you not to do anything that will dishonor my name."

* * *

Nearly 40 suicide boats tried to attack the U.S. invasion force in Lingayen Gulf while MacArthur was putting troops ashore. All were destroyed before they could do any damage. As the 1st Cav, 6th, 25th, 33rd, 37th, 40th and 43rd Divisions plus the 158 RCT began to hit the beaches, they suffered little from air strikes. What was left of Japanese air strength was being evacuated from the Philippines. Formosa and Okinawa were now the key places to be defended from Allied air attacks. Yamashita's troops could hide from aircraft in the Philippines jungle. His troops outnumbered MacArthur's, on Luzon, about 4-1. It was his job to make the American enemy pay a terrible price for the Philippines, and thus perhaps open the door to a negotiated peace. With one hand Tokyo was continuing to fight the war, while with the other she kept trying to seek out avenues to peace. At the highest levels it was well-known that the war had been lost when the Marianas fell.

What MacArthur had to do now was invade at Lingayen, drive inland, spin right and head for Manila. More landings would have to be made, south of Lingayen, and still others to the south of Manila. The idea was to drive across Luzon, splitting Yamashita's forces. That would also cut off Yamashita, who had pulled back into northern Luzon, from any supplies or reinforcements. From then on it would be a battle of attrition, once Manila was isolated.

* * *

Susumu Toyoda had the 37th's team at Lingayen. He almost lost one of his men, Yukio Kawamoto, when a landing craft hit a sandbar on the way in. The 37th drove for Clark Field and Fort Stotsenberg, capturing them by the end of the month, and then wheeled toward Manila. Keiji Fujii and Yukio Kawamoto were told to catch up with division headquarters anyway they could. They hitchhiked. The motor convoy the pair got into made a short stop at an abandoned brewery just outside the city. A lot of GI's enjoyed something few GI's did—beer by the helmetful!

Harry Fukuhara had the 33rd's team, having been transferred from 6th Army. He had Ben Nakamoto, Shoji Ishii, Toshio Ogawa, Marshall H. Taira, Yukio A. Tanaka and Terry Teramoto with him. The 33rd didn't land until Feb. 10, when it relieved the 43rd. It had been pretty busy making sure all of Morotai had been cleaned up.

Minoru Hara's first POW when he landed at Lingayen with the 6th Division was a civilian, later hanged as a spy. His second was a shot-down pilot who said AA from the invasion forces was so heavy that he couldn't get low enough for an accurate bombing run. With Shizue Kunihiro, Hara later had an assignment on Bataan Peninsula. There he saw ammo and hand grenades spread out on the edges of foxholes, ready for use, where retreating Americans had left them three years before. Hara was also part of an old-fashioned bayonet charge at a place called Munoz, but his group found itself with such an abundance of ammunition that instead they shot the enemy soldiers, who were poised for hand-to-hand combat. Hara was then stunned to see a fellow GI, knife in hand, rush up to a Japanese soldier who was gripping a stomach wound—*and cut off the man's rank insignia for a souvenir!*

* * *

It is not the purpose of this work to tell the story of a war but, rather, the story of Nisei in a war. It is probably best, therefore, to simplify the Philippines campaign, which was actually very complicated. But, one can try.

Leyte was necessary for a foothold, and Mindoro to protect it, the idea being to shut off the enemy in the southern Philippines, then eliminate him. Landings at Lingayen, north of Manila, had essentially the same kind of objective. Luzon had to be cut in half, so that Yamashita would be without new help. Manila had to be taken, so that no aid could get to him from there.

Then other areas had to be attacked—like Palawan, Mindanao, Cebu, Negros, Panay, etc.—with each garrison isolated and then destroyed. All had the option of surrendering, but MacArthur's troops didn't expect any to exercise it.

The success of the Philippines campaign hinged on good military intelligence. A lot came from guerrillas who had become very active. Much of the rest came from POW interrogations and document translations done by Nisei linguists. It seems profitable to cover the Philippines from some of their points of view.

The 6th, 37th, 40th and 43rd Divisions hit Lingayen Gulf on January 9, with the 25th and the 158 RCT landing there two days later. Fred Stanton and Morris Smith were with the 25th's language team. Leading it for them was Fred Odanaka, who'd been with the outfit since Guadalcanal. Stanton, a long time later, remembered with favor George Sakaguchi, Henry Suzuki, Shinji Okamura, Grayson Hagihara and George Kitajima. His notes reminded him that "Masayuki Hashimoto was our best all-around man, although he turned all colors one time from drinking some local rotgut." The 25th's team made a series of valuable contributions to the division's success, mostly in the form of captured and translated maps that gave details of enemy's defenses.

* * *

Gene Uratsu was with the 158 RCT. So were Harold Nakamura, Robert Nakamura and Reynold "Smiley" Muranaka. They got commended by the 43rd Division, with whom they worked, during the push through central Luzon. They also took part in a later operation, south of Manila, and Uratsu got his second Bronze Star. Gene Wright had gone back to the States and a spot with PAC-MIRS by this time, joining his efforts there with those of "Charlie" Chan and Phil Ishio, as well as other Nisei like Tadao Ito and Joe Masuda. His place had been taken by Roy Little, and some new Nisei had joined the 43rd along the road from Bougainville through New Guinea to Luzon. They were Sam Y. Matsumoto, Midori Inouye, and a fellow who would certainly not be mistaken for an Irishman if you met him—Michael Ohara. The 43rd saw the war to its end in the Philippines, fighting right up through the surrender announcement.

* * *

The 11th Airborne made a beach landing at Nasugbu, southwest of Manila, and fought its way overland by foot toward that city. Then it, like a Nisei outfit on the other side of the world, got done out of being first to burst into a major city because of lack of transportation. The 100th was short of Rome, awaiting trucks, when a rear echelon outfit rolled past it to become first in Rome. The 11th was similarly delayed, letting the 1st Cavalry Division run off with the honors. Not that the 1st Cav. didn't deserve it. Getting into Manila was no easier from the north than the south.

* * *

In Burma, the MARS Force had life no easier than troops did in Luzon. Members had to resort, at times, to frisking enemy POW's in the hope of obtaining some food. Ben Hirano wrote Munakata from the Marianas, but "couldn't say" what kind of work he and other Nisei were doing. He might not have wanted to say if he could, because Nisei were closely connected with some bombing missions over Japan. A few were flying in specially-equipped B-24 bombers that went north ahead of the B-29's, and listened in on the Japanese air defense circuits. Harold Nishimura, down south with the 7th Division, told about Leyte mopping-up operations, and his letter showed sadness over Frank Hachiya's death. Torao Ikeda, in Assam, wrote of his amazement at the variety of things sold in India's bazaars, pointing out that farmers in the U.S. had never been able to offer such a variety of crop products together with hard goods. "Everything" he said "is for sale here."

* * *

Back home, the Supreme Court had overturned the War Relocation Authority's right to keep loyal citizens locked up. Raymond Sadamune, on Leyte, greeted the news with mixed emotions. His father, Kakuichi, was released from Poston but his brother Alfred had been reported wounded in France, where the 442nd had rescued the "lost battalion" of the 36th Division. The 442nd men were made "honorary citizens of Texas" by that State's grateful governor.

Akira Abe was thankful that the weather on Luzon was drier than that on Leyte, but not every soldier agreed with him. It was hot, dry, and sometimes dusty. Ken Uyesugi and the 1st Cavalary got to Santa Tomas University, where many Americans had been imprisoned, after getting word that all there might be slaughtered. There Ken had perhaps the most unique experience of any American GI in the entire war. He had to "talk" 66 Japanese soldiers into surrendering, and failed at it because their leader felt to do so would bring *haji* (shame) on Nippon for him and his men to lay down their arms. A strange deal had to be made. The 66 Japanese holdouts released their few hostages, in return for which all 66 left Santo Tomas fully-armed in formation (except for their wounded, who were carried on carts), marching out and away from the immediate fighting. Chances are that all Japanese later perished, but they did not perish in Santo Tomas—or surrender. Uyesugi had gotten a first-hand look at *Yamato damashii* at work.

* * *

Clarence Ohta and John Nakahara were among those who made a combat jump with the 11th Airborne, to clear the way from Nasugbu to Manila, but it was a rank amateur, Harry Akune, who made the most exciting parachute jump of any Nisei in the war. He did it without being qualified in any way, except to have guts.

Harry had been with 6th Army headquarters when he came down with dengue fever. A medic mistakenly identified him as a POW, but when he got that straightened out and was released he went to a rest area on Mindoro. He there learned how massive the Japanese influence on the Filipinos had been. All the young girls knew how to sing *"Shina no yoru"* (China Night), a very popular Japanese song before, during and after the war. Harry was asked if he'd make a parachute jump, and said "Sure." He was then told he'd be landing on Corregidor!

The idea was for the 503rd Parachute Infantry Regiment to make a drop onto The Rock, at the entrance to Manila Bay, while a battalion of the 24th Division assaulted it by sea. Akune was turned over to a sergeant for "training." The NCO stood Harry in the doorway of a tent, had him jump out, and said "Terrific! One more time, Harry!" Akune repeated the process, was told "Fantastic! You're ready to jump!" Shortly thereafter he found himself floating down on Mindoro. He was told to "land like I was drunk," so it would relax him, but said "I swear I felt my chin hit the heel of my shoe when I landed!"

Others got Harry out of his chute, but he was shocked, numb, and had hurt his ankle. The only medic available was a dentist who taped up his foot "like he knew what he was doing, then told me to take some aspirin and drink from a 5-gallon can that was there." Harry followed orders and his head nearly exploded. The can was full of alcohol, mixed with orange juice. In a few minutes, Akune felt no pain at all, and was just a little regretful when mission orders came through a week later. He was briefed, and told his job on Corregidor was to get his hands on Japanese documents as quickly as possible, then translate them. For a while, after that, Harry felt like he was in a comical movie. When he had to stop in a field enroute to the airstrip his jeep left without him. Once on board the aircraft, an officer who had two weapons denied Harry one, saying "If I don't need both of these after we get down, I'll give you one."

"I'll never forget him," Harry said, "He was a jerk!"

The aircraft was going to make three runs, to disembark three "sticks" of paratroopers, because Corregidor's length was too short to drop all in one run. Akune wondered if he'd miss it. As it turned out, dozens of jumpers did.

Akune almost missed, and a pull on his parachute risers that kept him from falling in the ocean almost impaled him on a shattered tree. Akune landed the wrong way, backward, and slid down an embankment on his backpack board. Had he landed properly he might have been skewered. He scrambled up the slope, to find "a whole line of guys, all pointing their guns at me!" One recognized Harry, "a guy with glasses so thick I never knew how he did become a jumper!" and he was saved. He made his way to an established command post, on Corregidor's "Topside," and translated documents nearly all day and night.

The Japanese commander at Corregidor got killed early in the fighting. That took some spirit out of the Imperial Navy men who were in the garrison, although they did continue to fight. Many blew themselves up, often taking Americans with them as they did so. Akune was attacked by one POW, who seemed deranged, but other paratroopers shot him. Harry then feasted on captured crabmeat and beer until food supplies were dropped to his unit. He stopped an American Navy man who visited the island from cutting off a prisoner's ears by saying "Go get some from a *fighting* Japanese!" Harry startled one POW by sharing food with him, and saw a wounded one get just as startled when an American, on an adjacent stretcher, save him a light from his cigarette. He later declined an interview with the *New York Times* because his family was in Japan, and an enraged officer "punished" him by assigning him to a rear echelon senior command that kept him out of action for the rest of the war.

* * *

The XIV Corps staff hit Lingayen beach head on Jan. 9, with William H. Fisher in charge of its language team. Operating with senior officers, and on down to regimental level as required were Eugene Hattori, Shig Inamasu, Yoshimori Morinaga, Harold H. Nishimura, Shigeru Shiozawa, Kazanobu Tamura, George Tokunaga, and Toru Yamada. Their campaign took them down to Manila, and through the cutting off of enemy forces on Bataan Peninsula.

Arthur Castle had a brother, California, working as a battalion surgeon with the 442nd in Europe when he landed with the 38th Division near Subic Bay, later to become a major U.S. base in the Far East. Castle's force quickly captured a small village well-known to American sailors, Olangapo, then circumvented a Japanese strongpoint at ZigZag Pass by climbing over a hill and onto Bataan, grabbing clumps of grass as Marauders had seized mules' tails in Burma.

Part of the 24th suffered severe casualties at ZigZag Pass, the place the 38th avoided. Masaru Yoshioka was with its team, headed by Tsutomu Harry Umeda. Others were Tatsumi Kimoto, Minoru Namba, Hideo Tsuyuki, Richard Y. Hirata, Kenneth K. Shimbu and Yoshiaki Hirabayashi. MacArthur's veterans from New Guinea were getting a real workout.

* * *

The 40th Division wrapped up its New Britain operations, and made its way to Lingayen, landing there on January 9. It was in on the fighting toward Manila, but got pulled out to seize the island of Panay, where it landed on March 18. Cleaning up that area, the 40th landed on Negros, a neighboring island, 11 days later. Moffet Ishikawa got lazy on Negros, didn't dig a foxhole, and barely missed dying during a sudden Japanese attack. He made Joe E. Brown's eyes bug out when the comedian arrived to entertain the troops but found only Ishikawa and seven other men on hand. The rest were away on patrols. Indignant fellow GI's, all Caucasian, began writing letters to their hometown newspaper editors, when they learned Ishikawa's family was in the Heart Mountain prison camp.

* * *

John Tanikawa and the 41st came up from New Guinea to help. It landed on Zamboanga on March 10, and found out that the monkeys did have tails, after all, there. The Americal Division came up from the south also, landing on Cebu on March 26. The 186th RCT landed on Palawan at the end of February. Slowly, and at less cost than elsewhere, the Philippines were falling back into the hands of the U.S. Only in the north, where Yamashita held out, was combat as severe as it had been in earlier campaigns.

* * *

At Vint Hill, things were going far less well than authorities thought. At a level where they were in the know, some Nisei felt the war was pretty much won and that they were spinning their wheels. Masao Tanino spent the time from January, 1945 teaching Japanese to Caucasian officers, a lot of whom had begun to think in terms of Occupation duty after the surrender they were sure was coming. Ishizo Tanimura was surprised, as had been Morio Nishita, senior NCO of the unit, when Nisei were given work in cryptanalysis. It actually stunned them. Tatsuji Machida, Francis Ogoso and Naomitsu Kitsuiwa felt their work was no longer essential. They got disgusted when, suddenly, nearly all of the senior and most proficient NCO's were reassigned out of the place. Word later filtered back that it was because all either were Kibei, or had relatives in Japan. Many of those who remained had relatives in concentration camps. That seemed to have no negative effect on a man's security rating.

* * *

An island named Iwo Jima found itself almost directly on the route between the B-29 bases in the Marianas, and Tokyo. It had to be taken, so that fighters could be based there to escort the massive bombers, and so that the bombers themselves might have a refuge if damaged. When it became obvious that MacArthur would take the Philippines, all right, even if it required time, the decision was made to by-pass Formosa and settle for a smaller target, Okinawa. It would be the staging area for a final assault on the Japanese mainland. First, however, Iwo

Dugout flushing could get a Nisei a bullet or a grenade in response to surrender urgings. Below, on pass from New Delhi headquarters are (l-r) Roy T. Takai, Norman Ueno and Fusao Uchiyama. Hundreds served in CBI area.

Jima must be taken. A large number of Nisei were to be involved in that enterprise.

* * *

IX Corps headed up the 77th and 81st in the Philippines. Colgate Dorr had its team, led by Yukio Taniguchi, son of a Big Island grocer in Hawaii. With him were Kenneth Kihara, Gary Shibuya, Hiroto Mukai, Bill Oshita and Gulstan Enomoto, plus a man with a name like the leader's—Yukiwo Taniguchi.

Enomoto had six kids at the time he volunteered, and five more after he got home. His Japanese name, Toshisuke, meant "ocean of help." His father may not have been far off the mark selecting it. John Tanikawa had four kids when he left for Australia and New Guinea, and James Yoshinobu had a bunch when he stepped ashore at Iwo Jima in February, 1945. In India a man with a bad heart, and five kids back home was Charles K. Tanaka. Nothing daunted Nisei who intended to serve, especially those from Hawaii. Mainlanders, too, fudged on the qualifying tests for MISLS, dozens arranging to memorize the page they'd have to read, just before the testing.

* * *

The 32nd Division would finish its fighting in the Philippines, totalling more than 13,000 man hours in a combat situation, something no Marine Corps unit has ever been able to claim. Milton Tanizawa was with it when 32nd finished up at Leyte and headed for Luzon, where it fought on down to Manila. Ken Ohta, Kiyoshi Umibe, Charles Imai, Tom Kadomoto, and Masami Fujimoto were still with him.

* * *

No Caucasian could possibly understand the mental workings of a Japanese soldier, nor perhaps the thinking of wartime Japanese, without reading and digesting Emperor Meiji's "Rescript to the Soldier." Although he certainly did not write them all, the first "restored" Emperor issued a series of pronouncements, edicts and urgings that materially motivated nearly all the Issei who had left their homeland for America.

Rescript to the Soldier reads like it had been written by one of the men who signed the Constitution of the United States. Maybe Douglas A. MacArthur had read it before "Duty. Honor. Country." was inscribed in stone at West Point. Who can tell? Drawing upon this Rescript, nonetheless, military and naval instructors of Japan inculcated in their juniors a sense of purpose few other nations have inspired. Knowledge of Japan, passed on to them by their parents and accented where necessary by Akira Oshida and other members of MISLS staff, made Nisei linguists aware that "a true Japanese does not lie." This gave them a weapon for breaking down captives. It was not difficult to make a POW remorseful, and to understand why, when caught in a lie as one in Australia was by Steve Yamamoto, a POW might kill himself. Or, break down and talk. Staunch loyalty to a code, or one's country, is an admirable quality, but when not combined with a strong sense of military intelligence security it can be a glaring weakness, to be exploited by those who have studied it.

* * *

The British 14th Army had crossed the Irrawaddy River in Burma by this time, striking toward Mandalay. The Burma Road was re-opened before February 1, and supplies really began to pour into China. Henry Kuwabara, Hiroshi Osako, Harry Uyehara, Iwao Kumabe, Frank Takao, Hisashi Nakagawa, and Morris Taketa were still with various Tommy units. So was Harold Hanaumi, who had people convinced by his attitude that he was actually personal bodyguard to Major General Gracey, commanding the 20th Indian Division.

Hanaumi had gotten bored and disgusted with behind the lines work, and being hospitalized. He liked Arnold Dadian, whom he considered "more a gentleman than a soldier," but was glad to get to the front. Things like translating a work called "Imperial Army Paratroopers," only to find out in the process that it was a novel, irritated Harold. But there had been rewards. Like getting a tip from the front where about 150 enemy soldiers were hiding, verifying this, and being part of laying on a strike by bomb-carrying P-47 fighter aircraft. Hanaumi helped make the body count, afterward.

Just as he'd raised hell with fellow Nisei who'd been conned by Japanese POW's giving phony names, Hanaumi tore a strip off the British soldiers who woke him at 2 a.m. to do an "emergency translation for General Gracey." He was given a small black notebook, read the first line in it, and hit the ceiling. Hanaumi was still chewing out staff members when General Gracey walked up behind them. After Harold's explanation, the general laughed, and the redoubtable Hanaumi went back to sleep.

"Since I left Japan . . ." had caught the eye of a British officer who knew some Japanese. He'd become excited, convinced he was onto something hot, so he had Hanaumi awakened. Harold immediately recognized that this was but the opening words to *Aikoku Ko Shinkyu,* a sentimental Japanese song.

* * *

Los Banos and Cabanatuan prison prison camps, in the Philippines, had been re-taken, but when Yoshikazu Yamada—now commissioned—led a team into Cabanatuan he met none of his old buddies from Mindanao, who were still at Del Monte when he'd been evacuated with a bad back from a truck accident nearly three years before. He did find traces of friends in camp records. Some were dead.

* * *

John White, who led a Nisei language team in the Aleutians campaign, had taken a photo intelligence course at Camp Ritchie, location of PACMIRS, and then went to the Current Intelligence section of the War Department's G-2 staff. He had hopes of visiting the grave of his brother, who had been killed with the 33rd Armored Regiment, so he volunteered when he learned that a Japanese language team was needed in Europe.

Dave Itami, Kazuo Yamane and George Urabe were the Nisei assigned to the team but Itami, a former newspaperman, had made himself so valuable with his expertise that it was decided to freeze him right where he was. Pat Nagano was given his spot.

A Navy officer, Arthur English, was the fifth member of the team when it arrived secretly at Fort Totten, New York. There Army routine nearly fouled the deal. An officer at the New York base, seeing three NCO's arrive, figured he now had three more candidates for his Charge of Quarters roster. The three Nisei wangled a pass, and went all the way into Manhattan, where they had a big Japanese dinner, after which they went back and hit the sack. The captain who planned to add them to his watch list awoke them at 4 a.m., stunned at the high priority he read on their orders, and they boarded a C-54 transport plane while he was still aghast. Only then did John White open their sealed final orders.

"We were supposed to get assigned to a British Commando unit," Yamane told the author, "and train with them for an attack on Berlin. We were to invade by air, or submarine, or whatever, confiscate Japanese language documents in government buildings, and return. Our orders read that our base of assignment was SHAEF (Supreme Headquarters, Allied Expeditionary Force), at Versailles. We stopped at Newfoundland and Scotland enroute, and when we got to our destination we were quartered with Morrocan troops in the Royal Stable of the Grand Palace, with our headquarters in the Petit Palais."

For a Hawaii boy whose major project before the war was helping his father collect rents from some income properties, the experience was thrilling. Visits to Paris were not what they might have been, though. The Germans had broken through in a thrust toward Antwerp. The Battle of the Bulge had everyone wondering which way the war might yet go. Security restrictions were tight, although they had seemed pretty sloppy at Versailles. It puzzled Pat Nagano that "all kinds of documents, with the highest of security classifications, were just scattered around everywhere." Victory fever, it appeared, was making some Allied staffers careless.

* * *

Warren Higa, with the 96th Division cleaning up the southern Philippines, wrote a gripe letter to Munakata. He told that his team members had gotten their promised promotions but that men of a 15-member unit from MacArthur's command (Higa's was assigned from JIC-POA) hadn't gotten any. "Most of them believe" he said, "that the reason they didn't get their promotions is because the enlisted men are drawing more pay than the Australian officers who are in charge of our boys." He also relayed general comment that some of the men from ATIS in Indooroopilly complained they'd gotten a raw deal there, too.

It could have happened, and MacArthur as top man would have to take the blame. He did, as Elliott Thorpe said, give a man full authority and never interfered, but unfortunately not all of his subordinates knew how to handle power as he did. Douglas MacArthur's name was often used in vain. One bunch of Nisei were actually busted one rank as soon as they arrived in Australia, the officer-in-charge saying "General MacArthur wants you to earn your stripes." Chances were excellent that the officer had never said a word to MacArthur outside of "Good morning, Sir." when passing, and saluting him.

* * *

Despite the USMC's historical division's being unable to provide any details on Nisei who served with marines in the war, the author has established that nearly three dozen were in the Iwo Jima campaign. The number may have exceeded 50, because there were at least another 14 I could not track down.

In an effort to find Caucasians capable of mastering at

least *some* Japanese, the MISLS staff made a country-wide search among Phi Beta Kappa members, and snatched up a few, some of whom turned out to be true geniuses. Manny Goldberg might not have been one, but his men thought him terrific. Ben Hirano was on the team that Goldberg led at Iwo Jima. Hirano took the place of Raymond Aka, who had been hospitalized. Also on the team at Iwo with Goldberg were Pat Honda, Kunio Takai, Frank Kami, Ritsuo Tanaka, Hideto Kono, Takamori Oishi, Raymond Takata, Goro Igarashi and Yutaka Masuda. Half the team volunteered from Hawaii for 442nd combat, and were disappointed when selected instead for language school. They saw enough action at Iwo to last them a lifetime.

* * *

Nobuo Furuiye was no longer wearing the heavy woolen uniform he'd had to tolerate while serving in the Aleutians with grenadiers from Canada, but he may have wished he were at times. "I landed on D-plus-1," he said, "on February 20th at 10:30 under heavy mortar fire." He was with the 5th Marine Division. Tadashi Ogawa and others were on the same team, but scattered among USMC units. "The 1st battalion was ahead of us. It lost nearly all of its men. Only 17 men and 1 officer came out of it," said Furuiye. "All the others died or got wounded. Our battalion also suffered heavily, but not as bad. I received only a minor flesh wound, but that was tended to right at the aid station."

For the first three days and nights, Furuiye devoted his efforts to "just staying alive. We moved only about 300 yards from the beach during that time," he said. "On the fourth day we could stick our necks out of our foxholes, and saw that the shelling by our naval guns had hardly damaged the enemy bunkers, which were all practically intact."

Enemy and friendly fire was so thick on the beaches, said Furuiye, "that our dead and theirs had to lie where they were, for three days. They couldn't be removed. I interrogated one POW at our hospital who was badly burned from one of our flamethrowers. All I got out of him was that his home was in Tokyo, and a request that I forward a message to his wife.''

The POW died "so peacefully that I was overwhelmed,'' said Furuiye. Death came while the interrogation was going on, but the flamethrower had burned the POW's clothes, along with him, so badly that nothing like an address could be recovered from them.

Furuiye was also touched by a document he translated, a personal paper of Baron Takeishi Nishi, a colonel in the enemy armed forces. The baron had represented Japan in the Olympics at Los Angeles in 1932 as an equestrian, and had a wide circle of friends in America, "Ironically,'' said Furuiye, "he died in one of our tanks, that they had captured and turned against us.''

Furuiye's most important contribution to the campaign on Iwo Jima, and perhaps the war as a whole, was his interrogation of another POW. He elicited from the man, who had become cooperative as the result of decent treatment by his captives, that he was a cipher specialist. In a trice the man was put on a plane for Honolulu.

After the campaign, Furuiye, like most of the Nisei on Iwo, went to Saipan to help handle the native population, few of whom were actually friendly toward the conquering Americans. He wrote Munakata later, saying how he had enjoyed working with marines but hoping he'd never have to endure another campaign like the one he'd just been through. A rational judgement indeed.

* * *

On Okinawa, while this was going on, a military genius named Yohara predicted to General Tadamichi Kuribayashi that Okinawa would be next, and began devising the defense tactics that would be used there. Yohara, who would make the cost of Okinawa as painful as Iwo Jima, is not at all mentioned in the U.S. official Naval history, despite the fact that the man charged with getting it written had access to all Japanese and American records obtainable. Plus a staff that included volunteer doctoral candidates at Harvard University, and almost exclusive use of documents that were not formally declassified until his 14-volume history (which later required publication of a 15th volume, devoted solely to correcting the previous 14) was completed in the 1960's.

Yohara had a surprise for the U.S. Navy, which at Okinawa as at Iwo Jima did not deliver enough firepower against the enemy beaches and defenses before the landing force was sent away. He also had one for American aviation, Navy and Army, which had become convinced that airpower was the be-all and end-all of warfare, a belief also proved false later, in both Korea and Vietnam. He also had one for USMC and Army infantrymen, who had to pay the price for the arrogance and contempt of more senior Americans. Among those to die at Okinawa needlessly were some Nisei.

* * *

Ben Yamamoto landed at Iwo Jima with the 3rd Marine Division. Wesley Fishel had his team, which also included an intrepid loner named Terry Takeshi Doi. A Kibei who'd been drafted while in Japan, and had actually served in the prewar Imperial Army, Doi was often taken from Camp Savage to outside military installations while in school, to demonstrate Japanese bayonet and other infantry tactics to other American soldiers.

When the fighting eased a bit on Iwo Jima, and the cave-flushing began, Doi showed unbelievable courage. He would strip naked except for his helmet, to show the enemy he had no weapons, then enter a cave, calling out to hidden soldiers that if they didn't come out and surrender they would be sealed up forever. Doi was shot at many times, his helmet once being carried away by a bullet, but he survived. He got a Silver Star.

Ben Yamamoto, once ashore, did not get near the front very often. He was held back to await arrival of POW's and documents. This is what *all* Nisei were *supposed* to do, but over and over again the need to prove one's self as a worthwhile American would make a Nisei risk his life. Yamamoto had been at the secret California camp for POW's, and begged for transfer out of there because his nerves began to fray. "It was touch-and-go in human relationships," he said, "and the day and night strain of interrogating people, then spending many hours reporting what they'd said, then repeating the process over and over again finally got to me."

Yamamoto was thoroughly debriefed by John Aiso on his return to Savage, and he then got assigned to the Home Furniture Building offices at JICPOA's annex, where Nisei worked and slept so they wouldn't be intermingled with Caucasians at Pearl Harbor. It was nice, getting weekends at home for a while, but Iwo Jima wasn't exactly the place for a rest cure. It helped, watching others dig foxholes deeper than Ben thought necessary, and then digging his own even deeper. Good for the nerve ends.

Others piled sandbags around their foxholes for even more protection, after three nights of enemy mortar barrages, but when Ben went looking for some a SeaBee officer knocked him down, stuck a .45 pistol against his forehead and said "Who the hell are you?"

It's not easy to deliver a calm explanation while pressed down by the burly body of a gun-waving SeaBee, but Ben tried. He was allowed to dig out of his pockets two I.D. cards. One, signed by Lt. Col. G.M. McCormick, USMC, and numbered # 546, showed he was on Item Team with the marines. Another, card # 50 signed by General Joseph J. Twitty, at JICPOA, showed he was from Hawaii. The officer got off Ben's chest, let him go, and told him he'd better stay in his own area so some other SeaBee wouldn't shoot him.

* * *

With the 4th Marine Division on Iwo Jima was James Yoshinobu, a veteran of an earlier war, although he'd had no overseas assignment in that one. His work won him a Silver Star. George Inagaki, with Saipan and Tinian behind him, also interrogated prisoners and translated

Leonard Ueki (l) interrogates one of millions of Japanese repatriated to homeland, screened by Nisei for clue to Communist indoctrination. Below Sadao Toyama (arm on stairs), lounges with other CBI men, awaiting combat call.

documents there, writing of it to the author from what proved to be his deathbed. Joe Harada, another veteran of the Byron POW camp, also hit the island. So did Ben Kawahara, James Saito, George Kawamoto, Henry Yokoyama, Mineo Yamagata, Tsugio Aoyama, Jiro Matsui, and Harry Okada. There was also Tamotsu "Shorty" Koyanagi, whose nickname must have been really apt because when a *Nisei* calls you short, you are!

* * *

Yutaka Masuda was only "almost-captured" on Iwo Jima, when his patrol ran into another patrol. His patrol members were quick with explanations, and the other patrol went on its way. Masuda worked with two POW's, one named Yamada and the other Hoshino, at cave-flushing, nearly getting killed twice while doing it.

He caught Yamada running out the other end of a cave he was exploring, by quickly dashing over the top of a hill to the exit after catching a glimpse of him. Using names given him by the captive, Masuda called out to those still in the cave. A lot came out, nearly all wounded, but two officers were holdouts. Masuda's importunings got him a grenade in response. Its blast blew him off a hill. Another detonation immediately followed, as the officers killed themselves.

Now warier, Masuda then used Hoshino to go into caves, and the POW reported seeing no one while handing out two swords and a pair of binoculars. "Look in the corners!" said Masuda, and more people were found. A sergeant came out, but when another soldier tried it he got both feet blown off when two officers tossed grenades at him. Masuda made a team of medics rush the man to help, and his life was saved, but the officers had killed themselves.

* * *

Human failings exist wherever humans do. Don Oka told the author of one that very nearly made the marines do without Nisei linguists on Iwo Jima!

Their sailing from Pearl Harbor delayed by one day, about 30 Nisei were able to get one last night at home or with friends. Next morning, trying to return to their ships, they were told by an adamant sentry "No Japs allowed to enter Pearl Harbor!" This infuriated them so much, being called "Japs!" (an insult for which Roy Nakada of the Marauders and many other Nisei had broken heads in Minneapolis and elsewhere) that nearly all said "Screw them! Let the so-and-so's sail *without* interpreters!"

Don Oka was acting first sergeant. He got his friends to calm down and accept an officer escort to get them to their ships. The Nisei went on to Iwo Jima and glory, although they had to wait decades for the last item.

Chapter 13

The Navy and Marine Corps made meticulous plans for making the taking of Iwo Jima a public relations show. A full dress presentation was put on, to impress media representatives and fire them up, a task senior U.S. military officers found distasteful. For too long they had repressed feelings of self-expression, and so had trouble imagining anyone else's harboring them. Sweating mightily, they did their best.

Talk was cheap. The Navy hadn't done a good job on prior bombardment—again—and the Iwo Jima beaches resembled an abattoir. But then Lady Luck lent a hand, The most successful maudlin fraud ever perpetrated on the American public was made possible. A flag got raised on Mt. Suribachi. Two, in fact.

The first, was sent up by a Marine Corps officer. It made sense to raise a flag when the top of Mt. Suribachi, a dormant volcano at the island's southern end was taken. Men fighting elsewhere might see it, and take hope.

The officer who had it raised then sent up another flag, and be it noted it was only to be a substitute so that the Marines could have and enshrine the original. A combat photographer took pictures of the first flag raising, in which one nearby leatherneck refused to pose. He thought it smacked too much of Hollywood, and he was right. The second picture, flashed on the front page of the *New York Times* and other newspapers that subscribed to the Associated Press service, whipped up the Yankee Doodle blood in millions. Conveniently forgotten were the stacked-up dead on Iwo Jima.

Mineo Yamagata was within 100 feet of the second flag-raising, and thought little of it. Just a bunch of guys putting up a flag. The picture by Joe Rosenthal, however, sent to Guam, with *hundreds of pounds* of other propaganda that night, transfixed millions. It captured a spirit, set up a mood. A statement probably drafted by a PR type, but attributed to Chester Nimitz, added just the right jingoistic touch later. "Uncommon valor was a common virtue." Nimitz is supposed to have said. The picture and the phrase were used 10 years later, along with a lot of subtle and overt arm-twisting, to obtain contributions for a massive piece of statuary that went up near Arlington National Cemetery. A friend of the author's, Navy Corpsman Jim Fay, was only one of the many Iwo Jima veterans who resented being pressured into giving. The man who ordered the flag raised, then another substituted for it, died a few days later on Iwo, unheralded and unremembered. Ira Hayes, a Pima Indian put in the picture and then exploited by USMC flacks on bond-selling tours, gained fame. Sobered up regularly for appearances sake by USMC correspondent Keyes Beech, Hayes couldn't handle what was happening to him. He sought refuge in alcohol, and ended up dying miserably on a lonely Arizona road. One source says the created hero drowned in his own vomit.

* * *

Fred Tsutsumi, Thomas T. Miyaga, Roy "Snuffy" Miyata, Tadashi Ogawa, Hidekazu Oka, Tetsuo Shimamoto and Butch Terao were some of the other Nisei who served on Iwo Jima. None got their pictures taken there, but few infantrymen did. Mineo Yamagata found out from POW's who insisted he kill them that they had been filled with tales of Marine Corps butchery. All had been determined to die where they stood, each taking 10 marines with him. The heralded 1942 raid on Makin Island was still being paid for by marines. More would pay for it on Okinawa.

POW's were impressed, said Yamagata, "when they saw our bulldozers on the side of Mount Suribachi. They had forces on the island for nearly 20 years, and hadn't gotten up there with a road, and our SeaBees built one in two days. Some of them said, 'How could we win a war against people with such equipment?'"

Almost three years to the day, Yamagata was repeating to POW's what Arthur Komori had said to some on Bataan. "It is cherry blossom time in Japan right now. Blooms are starting in southern Kyushu, and will spread northward to Hokkaido. Wouldn't you rather be at home?"

He had more luck than Komori. Some surrendered to Yamagata. Mineo also exploited Komori's discovery that a POW broke down when confronted with his own lies, because of strict home and military training about honor. Yamagata gave the author maps and charts of Iwo Jima, Tokyo, the Inland Sea and other places he and his teammates were able to make because of information they got out of POW's. These helped, on Iwo and elsewhere.

* * *

A combined sea and air assault at Los Banos, in the Philippines, while the fight for Iwo Jima went on, rescued more than 2000 U.S. and European nationals. Nisei with the 11th Airborne helped. On Feb. 25 in New York, the photograph of the Suribachi flag-raising got on the *Time's* front page. Two days later, the *San Francisco Chronicle* criticized the cost of lives in taking Iwo Jima. Talk arose about using poison gas against the Japanese, rather than let them continue to kill so many Americans. Offices of the *Chronicle,* which praised MacArthur for saving men's lives, were broken into by 100 marines on shore duty, well out of the fighting, and an apology demanded. William Randolph Hearst refused to be disturbed, so the shore duty marines got no response or satisfaction. They went back to the Market Street bars. Yukio Tamura landed on Palawan with a radio unit to back up the 186th RCT, and a sniper wounded him. Corregidor was taken, and also the "walled city," Intramuros, inside Manila, thousands of

Japanese preferring to die rather than surrender, at both places.

* * *

Norman Kikuta, in the Manila fighting, got pinked by a piece of shrapnel, of which he said, "I'm glad it had slowed down as much as it did before it arrived." The fighting finally ended in that city during early March, with the 37th Division finally clearing the streets. The entire 77th Division language team signed a letter from Shigeo Ito to Yutaka Munakata. It joshed him about tough "interrogation practice" back at Savage, and told how easily Japanese POW's revealed everything after a bit of kind treatment. The letter suggested that the number of men per team be increased; one or two typists added to each; and that kits be designed to suit either combat or rear echelon work. The 77th group had lugged around four heavy boxes of books, most of which never got used and which became damaged from handling and weather. It also suggested *portable* typewriters, which painted a ludicrous picture of infantrymen carrying heavy desk type models through the jungle, but they had been doing just that. The group was in good spirits, and filled with confidence from the record it had established in two campaigns.

* * *

On March 4 the first crippled B-29 landed on Iwo Jima. By that time 12,864 Japanese bodies had been counted on the island, with only 36 taken prisoner. The first U.S. fighter planes landed there two day later, and dead Japanese were found wearing American uniforms. Charles Tahara was outbound from Hawaii in a troop transport, "destination unknown" he wrote Munakata, but full of praise for the work of Mitsuo Usui and others who'd done battle planning with him at Schofield Barracks. Others on the transport had an idea where the ship was going, but no one wanted to use the word "Okinawa" when they read what was happening at Iwo Jima. The

33rd, 38th, 32nd and 41st Divisions were all heavily engaged in Philippines fighting, their struggles considered unworthy of coverage by correspondents. Though thousands of Americans were still to die, and many times their number of Japanese also to perish, the Philippines was considered by the press a "rear echelon mopping-up action."

Back at Camp Savage a very special team was getting ready to go overseas, the brainchild of a Hawaii Nisei. Tom Ige, by profession an economist working on his doctorate at the University of Wisconsin when war broke out, had been turned down by the Navy. He settled for a job in government labor relations in Detroit until Tadao Beppu came all the way from Camp Shelby to tell him personally that an old friend, Joe Takara, had become the first Nisei to die in Europe. Takara, Beppu, Ige and a fellow named Susumu Tanaka had been roommates on McCully Street in Honolulu while students at Mid-Pacific Institute, a boarding high school all attended because their areas of the islands had no high schools. This saddened Ige. He could no longer stay with his job, and arranged to enter MISLS.

While a student, Ige made a secret recommendation that, since Okinawa looked like a likely objective, a special team be made up from Nisei of Okinawan extraction, to serve on that island when needed.

The War Department picked up the suggestion. A team was made up. Some of the members were, besides Ige; Wallace Amioka, Seiyu Higashi, Leslie Higa, Shinye Gima, Jiro Arakaki, and Hiroshi Kobashigawa.

Higashi already had combat experience. A Kibei, he was an encyclopedia of Okinawan information, and a prime source of place names and locations. These were much needed by American intelligence because it simply didn't know much about where anything was in the empire of Japan. No deep studies in this facet of intelligence had ever been made.

Leslie Higa had been a high school sophomore in Hawaii when the war began. Wally Amioka had leadership qualities, but they got him in trouble when he arrived at Camp Savage. Disgusted at having to lug his duffle bag a mile from a railway siding during a blizzard the day before, he lost his temper when knocks on a supply room door got no answers from people he could see inside, playing cards by a hot pot-bellied stove. Amioka busted the door down. Like Seiyu Higashi, Jiro Arakai had a family on Okinawa.

Okinawan is not a dialect, but a structured language. In fact, it is ancient Japanese, and requires special study. "*Musume*" (young girl) is pronounced "moo-soo-may" by Japanese, but "moo-soo-mee" by Okinawans. One had to listen for this, and also know that the "oh" sound was pronounced "oo." Translations were different, too, because of special idiom. A Japanese asks, in Japanese "What is your name?" But an Okinawan asks, in Okinawan "How do you show me your name?"

Everything had to be kept highly secret. Amioka used to take the trolley car that ran through Camp Savage, pretending he was going to Minneapolis, then jump off and dash into the assistant commandment's office, where he would stay locked up until 4 p.m. A special teacher taught him all the proper inflections, and furnished detailed information on various geographic locations. The team headed out when the Okinawa fight started.

* * *

The MARS Force completed their operation in Burma. Aided by British troops on one side and Chinese on the other, they had gained their objective, a small town south of Mandalay named Kutkai, and were disbanded. Some of the Nisei went to China, and the rest went back to India. David Akui had distinguished himself in this campaign, by charging a Japanese force with a Tommy gun, to let a pinned-down platoon escape.

* * *

In Japan, an intensive program for production of suicide craft was underway, as that nation pitched in for a last ditch struggle. By June 1, authorities planned to have nearly 9000 suicide craft hidden along the homeland's shoreline, waiting to sink the enemy fleet as soon as it got within range. There would be 3000 Army crashboats, nearly 4000 *shinyo* (small skiffs rigged with explosives), nearly 1500 midget-type submarines, and 660 *kaiten*. These last were enlarged versions of Japan's Model 95 "Long Lance" submarine torpedo, re-rigged with a compartment for a pilot. He could steer this weapon into an enemy ship, then explode 3000 pounds of explosive. *Kaiten* had been in use since the previous October, when one had sunk the *USS Mississinewa*, a tanker, in the Ulithi anchorage.

* * *

The bitter Iwo Jima fighting may have made General Curtis LeMay, in charge of the bombers in the Marianas, impatient. Or perhaps it was because his Superfortresses were getting nowhere near the results envisioned for them. In any case, without seeking permission of higher authority, LeMay sent a fleet of B-29's over Tokyo on the night of March 9, stripped down to travel at maximum speed and loaded with fire bombs. LeMay was taking a page from the book of "Bomber" Harris, the British air marshal who first advocated massive bombing of civilian homes as the surest way to reduce enemy war production.

Until March 9, 1945, the B-29 raids on Japan were not much more than an annoyance. But, on that night, nearly 84,000 persons were burned to death in a Tokyo firestorm, and another 160,000 injured. One million people were made homeless, and 250,000 living places were destroyed. During the next seven days the cities of Osaka, Kobe and Nagoya were given the same treatment.

Almost as ghastly as the fire deaths of so many Japanese was a USMC burial officer's vowing, on that very same day, that "Iwo Jima's would be the most beautiful cemetery of all our campaigns."

* * *

Dye Ogata was finished with combat. So was Ted

Kihara. Both had been commissioned, and assigned to staff at Fort Snelling. They soon were selected for a special assignment, in Canada. Tom Takata recorded in his diary how shabbily-dressed the Filipinos who were curious about him seemed, but other Nisei's sentiments nowhere approached the compassionate. Among numbers of Nisei a contempt for the Filipino population was growing, usually because they were subjected to so many attacks from the civilian populace. Cries of *"Hapon! Hapon!"* meant the Filipinos thought they were Japanese, and menaced their safety. Also, several Nisei linguists had the experience of entering Filipino villages, to be greeted with *"Banzai! Banzai!"* Hours later, after it was made clear who they were, the same voices cried "Veectory, Joe!" Tatsuji Machida described PACMIRS in great detail in a letter to Munakata. He told of its isolation. And how it was becoming a military bureaucracy. A contingent of WACs had arrived. Also, some Canadian Army officers, together with five Canadian WACs. NCO's fretted over the arbitrariness of newly-arrived "90-day wonders," who lorded it over enlisted men. Ed Kaneshima, writing from the Philippines, compared the land with his native Hawaii favorably, adding that the sun, rain and vegetation were making him homesick. Fred Stanton wrote, too, pointing up the wrong impression newspapers in the U.S. were creating. "A friend of mine wrote me today," he said, "asking me if I *had* enjoyed my work, since now the Philippines campaign was almost over." At the time of the letter, Stanton was still experiencing air raids. Fighting would go on for another five months.

* * *

On March 14, Iwo Jima was declared "secured" by Chester Nimitz. Twelve days later, using captured USMC weapons, nearly 300 Japanese made a *banzai* attack on one of its airfields. Private Shigeru Yoshida, Imperial Army, surrendered on St. Patrick's Day. He told of how he had watched from hiding as U.S. marines on Iwo Jima slashed the ears off corpses and pulled their teeth for the gold. Such activities probably confirmed the suspicions of a POW interrogated by Mineo Yamagata. He told the Hawaii Nisei about being warned that the left armbone had been removed from a dead Japanese soldier, "to make a letter opener for that damned Jew—Roosevelt!" Propaganda had been deftly employed to inflame Japanese, as well as Americans, against their enemy, although the author has not discovered any songs popular in Tokyo as puerile as "You're a sap, Mister Jap!" which got played on a lot of American jukeboxes.

* * *

In Hood River, Oregon, the Nisei names were put back on the town's Honor Roll, their letters gleaming embarrassedly amid the older, faded paint. A letter from Howard Moss, resting with the 7th Division from combat, mentioned how he missed Frank Hachiya whose loss, together with those of Harold Nishimura to JICPOA and Min Ichinose to a hospital with jungle rot and other ailments, reduced the effectiveness of his team so much that he had about given up hope of getting a discharge for the ailing Cosma Sakamoto. Arthur Swearingen, a Savage grad, was with the U.S. military government in the Marianas, where he wouldn't be staying much longer. While he was there, however, he was enjoying the duty.

* * *

Tokyo announced, on March 16, that Iwo Jima had fallen. General Kuribayashi had sent a message that included a paraphrase of Masashige Kusunoki's dying statement "I will be reborn seven times again, to take up arms against the foe." George Kitajima, on Fred Stanton's team, wrote a pleased letter at how well-balanced his unit of linguists was. From India came a good sample of the letters so valuable in helping re-shape the language course to meet field requirements. The course had already been cut back in length. Speaking was beginning to get top priority over writing, because it was obvious that great

Akira Yoshimura and Roy Matsumoto of Merrill's Marauders. Below, Shoji Takimoto, shortest of Savage's instructors, teaches Japanese tactics to earnest students.

numbers of oral interpreters would be needed, now that Japan was nearly on her knees.

"The student can never have too much of *sosho,*" Noboru Murakami wrote. "The average Nisei can pick out the subject and predicate in a sentence, but when he can't read the whole thing he runs into trouble. Spoken language is important, too, and at Savage I didn't particularly lay much stress on it because we spoke the language at home all the time. I talked to some of the boys who returned from the MARS Force, and they said about the same, but they added one more thing. It was the ability to read *names.*

"This is borne out by two of our fellows who were out with a Birtish outfit." Murakami wrote. "One did translation, while the other kept thumbing through the names dictionary until he could quickly come to any name they met. Geography of each theater is also important, but I don't think you have time there to teach that."

Murakami also touched upon a vital item, all the more important because the Japanese language was so difficult—the teaming or pairing of men. "When you get here," he said, "the team often gets broken up, and a weak man can find himself alone. What I have done about it is to encourage new arrivals to get into the interrogation section, for the purpose of acquiring experience. It has worked out pretty well for them."

He added the bit of news that Fusao Uchiyama had been in a plane crash but was O.K., and that two of his teammates, Hisashi Nakagawa and Morris Taketa, had done well working with a British unit despite the fact that they'd gotten separated and were not able to pool their strengths.

* * *

When the 40th Division landed on Negros March 29, they enountered stiff fighting, with the Japanese not retreating into the mountains for six weeks. Five Nisei had joined the 503rd Parachute Infantry Regiment by now, and fought on the ground with it. George Kojima suffered a wound to his hand from an enemy grenade. Koshi Ando and James Harada were with him.

Iwao Kawashiri, one of the original Presidio students, landed on Negros with the Americal. He got a POW to pinpoint enemy positions, but they could only talk between salvoes, because the Americal's artillery opened up in strength, and the pair were right up front so they could see the results of information given by the POW. One noon Kawashiri thought he was going to lose his head in the chow line to a Filipino machete. Only William S. Hodgson's coming out of the officers' mess tent in time to see what was happening saved his life. While on the island, Kawashiri delighted a Japanese woman in her sixties by conversing in her own language with her. She spoke three languages; the native dialect, English and Japanese, but hadn't had a chance to speak the last for many years. She came from Japan as a teen-ager, and married an American businessman. Two of her sons stood by during the conversation, but waved no machetes. They were members of the Filipino Constabulary, thankful for this favor done their mother.

* * *

George Ichikawa was with another advanced ATIS group on Morotai, after a campaign with the 7th Australian Division. The end was now somewhere in sight, and preparations had to be made for accepting the surrender of enemy garrisons all over the southern areas. Lawrence Motogawa completed the first Counter-intelligence Corps School class. Japanese-fluent members were going to be needed by the Corps in Japan. Half of Yutaka Masuda's team went back to Hawaii from Iwo Jima, the other half to Saipan. The Canadian armed forces needed interpreters if they were going to have any role whatever in the Pacific, where the U.S. had carried 99% of the load, and began searching frantically for Japanese-fluent people. Having locked up all their own in concentration camps, they needed practiced instructors. Dye Ogata and Ted Kihara reported to the S-20 Japanese

Language School at Vancouver, British Columbia. They were officially commended for making "Valuable original contribution to training material of S-20 in the field of POW interrogation." Every attempt that Ogata made, however, to have his wife join him while on duty in Vancouver, as Nisei soldiers on duty in the U.S. were permitted, was denied in one verbose sentence *of 82 words.* It took a special trip by Kai Rasmussen to Ottawa to bust the stranglehold of bureaucratic clerks, so Mrs. Ogata could join her husband.

* * *

On March 30, Steve Yamamoto was awarded the Silver Star for actions on Leyte and Luzon. An Army order of the day listing his decoration included the address of his next of kin. Goichi Yamamoto was in Block 64-4-D of the Poston concentration camp.

By that time, three-quarters of the Japanese merchant fleet was sunk, including three-quarters of its tankers. Automobiles were converted in Japan to run on charcoal, and lubricants for aircraft were being extracted from pine roots.

* * *

Nisei were busy in the China-Burma-India theater. Sadao Toyama left the MARS Force with one humorous memory. Some members had found what appeared to be an unexploded bomb, and he'd been called forward to where it lay in a river bed. Ordnance specialists could find no arming mechanism, nor access to a fuse. All they could see was a small metal plate with some Japanese inscription on it.

Holding his breath, Toyama gingerly approached the missile. Very, very carefully he peered at the plate, while friends held their breaths. Then he straightened up, a relieved look on his face. "That plate says 'Dummy'," he told the others, who collapsed into laughter.

Richard Betsui and Wilbert Kishinami relaxed in New Delhi while part of the group that came over with them went to Burma, and part to Kunming, China. Betsui didn't really think of himself as an MIS'er although he was one. He'd actually been recruited for the OSS while at Camp Shelby, by a team from Washington. He got special training in communications, then went to Savage for language training, before heading overseas with the OSS. On one occasion Betsui got called all the way from New Delhi to Ceylon, where an OSS station thought it had something hot. The item turned out to be an advertisement from a Japanese newspaper that had been used to cover a window. Betsui got sent to Burma with a British unit, to do POW interrogations, and said of it "There were some tense moments. Especially when, after an interrogation, POW's with tears pouring out of their eyes would beg us to kill them."

Grant Hirabayashi and Roy Matsumoto, when the Marauders were disbanded, got assigned to an RAF unit, but didn't last long there. Used to the informality of jungle warfare, they forgot to salute a passing general, who took down their names. An understanding colonel transferred the two to Kunming, pronto. They arrived after a scary flight over The Hump in a wheezing Curtiss C-46 Commando, seated on ammunition. It shook Hirabayashi's confidence in his country's military might when, shaky, he emerged from the aircraft and was greeted with "I see you made it." It seems that was the standard greeting, since so many C-46's either got lost, shot down, or crashed into cloud-covered mountains.

There was an air raid on Kunming during Hirabayashi's first night there, and his shelter was an above-ground Chinese tomb, around which a trench had been dug. After a while there, Grant got sent to Chungking with Calvin Kubota, Roy Nakada, and Jimmy Yamaguchi. He found Chiang's rear echelon capital "miserable. We could only work from 7 a.m. to 11 a.m. because of the heat and humidity," he said. "Papers would stick together because I sweated on them. Off-duty it was shower, rest, shower, rest, and then go into town for something to eat at evening time."

Shigeto Mazawa, after fighting in the jungle along with Kachin tribesmen, found out that Tom Chamales, a new leader who came in, was also from Chicago. The pair soon endured a grenade attack by Japanese together, and Chamales later confessed to Mazawa that he'd swallowed his chew of tobacco in the excitement. A book *Never So Few* would be written by Tom Chamales, based on incidents that both men experienced in North Burma. It included the Lewje Incident, in which Americans who discovered that Chinese had murdered other Americans, in turn murdered the Chinese, repercussions resounding all the way to Washington. Mazawa was summoned back from the jungle, got royally chewed out for volunteering to serve in the front lines "when linguists belong in the rear!" and then was assigned to a British organization preparing to invade Singapore.

* * *

Kan Tagami and Art Morimitsu participated in the final action of the MARS Force, a battle so furious it resulted in the award of the theater's only Medal of Honor. A Texan, June Knight, got it posthumously for leading a *banzai* attack on a Japanese position, using the enemy's own tactic against him.

Tagami also had the touching experience of watching a POW die happy at hearing his mother tongue from the mouth of a stranger. The man left Tagami in tears, passing away while talking of his wife and child back in Mie Prefecture. Tagami promised the dying man to try to get all information and belongings back to his Japanese command, or to Japan.

* * *

George Itsuo Nakamura got to India in mid-1944 and shortly went on to China with Shosho Nomura, Kiyoshi Suzukawa and Hiro Fukuyama. He later grabbed off the assignment to North China offered by John Burden.

Nakamura's job, while with the Dixie Mission at Mao Tse Tung's headquarters, was to translate documents and interrogate prisoners who had been captured by the 8th Route Army, the Communists' military arm. To talk to prisoners he first had to get permission from a man named Susumu Okano. That was the alias of Sanzo Nozaka, one of Japan's leading Communists, who would return to Japan and become a member of the House of Councillors after the war.

Nakamura got Order of Battle information and, since he had with him a copy of the Pentagon's edition, often got his contributions confirmed as approved within one day. The details Nakamura was able to provide helped MacArthur's and Nimitz's headquarters keep the picture ahead of them in perspective. Sho Nomura came up later to Yenan, and then Jack Ishii and Toshi Uesato. The Office of War Information team, of which Clarke Kawakami was a member, got to China in early 1945.

November 13, 1944 was a red-letter day for Nakamura, in more ways than one. Mao Tse Tung attended his 21st birthday party. Nakamura went out on several missions into, for him, totally unknown country from which some messengers frequently did not get back. His most satisfying one was to act as escort for safe return of a wounded U.S. pilot who had been shot down.

The Dixie Mission worked desperately to get Chiang Kai Chek and Mao Tse Tung working together, to fight side-by-side instead of head-to-head. There was talk of Nakamura parachuting with a team into Shantung, but the Okinawa invasion nixed that, making it obvious the Allies were no longer heading for Formosa and the China Coast.

* * *

Teichiro "Timmie" Hirata was making a contribution to the MISLS from India. "I'm sure you would benefit," he wrote Munakata, "if you could somehow be placed on the distribution lists for reports made out here in the field. Vocabulary lists and interrogation reports would be invaluable to the students."

Hirata described his own vocabulary lists as "mounting," which they were as more and new Japanese expressions, many coined for the war alone, came to be discovered.

Hirata also remarked on a fringe benefit of being closer to the fighting. He didn't have to undergo formal military inspections. In closing he asked that the *sensei* keep an eye on his kid brother, Kantaro Hirata, and see that he studied hard at the school.

* * *

Katsuyoshi Nishimura had two gripes in India. He'd been dropped from those selected for China, although he'd been anxious to go. And he was peeved at Sohei Yamate, a fellow student back at Snelling. "I think Sohei got my original photograph of Sono Osata," he said, "leaving me only a lousy copy." Nishimura had been thinking of writing the lady, an accomplished ballerina of Japanese blood, asking her to be his unit's pin-up girl.

* * *

Frank Tokubo flew into Kunming with James Jun Yamada, and was told to take over a POW camp. His staff consisted of 10 American GI's, to keep an eye on 3000 prisoners. Tokubo had the whole place reorganized in two weeks. He divided all men in the compound into groups, and exercised each group in turn to help them keep fit. With Yamada, he improved the food situation considerably. They would take the funds allotted for feeding the prisoners and buy cartloads of food in town, then let the Japanese do their own cooking. As a result the POWs fared much better than they had under ministrations of the Chinese. When Tokubo and Yamada left for Chungking, there was much bowing, handshaking and weeping among the prisoners.

Tokubo got a fascinating assignment at Chiang's capital—to mingle with Japanese political defectors and sound them out about their beliefs. High command was sure these people would be important in Japanese politics after the war, when they would no longer be refugees. Shigeo Yasutake, Grant Hirabayashi, Jimmy Yamaguchi, Stanley Uno and Tateshi Miyasaki were in Chungking. Tokubo could share with them his impressions of Wataru Kaji, a pacifist totally against war, who lived with an ardent fellow Socialist woman named Ikeda. Kaji later sat in the Japanese Diet.

* * *

Koji Ariyoshi got to Yenan, and was much impressed by what he learned about the Communists, especially their willingness to work and struggle together, something he and other longshoremen had been doing for years on San Francisco's docks. He had the mind-blowing experience of sitting at the same mess table with an American general, because the Communists did it that way and visitors had to follow suit.

While watching to see what diplomatic agreements the U.S. and Mao's men might be able to achieve, Ariyoshi worked on Order of Battle information, while also assisting in a survey of the training, equipment and morale of the 8th Route Army. The U.S. hoped it could tie up the Japanese long enough for Allies to get ashore in strength in the Canton area. American weathermen allowed into North China applied themselves assiduously to their tasks. Much of the Pacific weather made up over North China, and reports radioed out to the U.S. Fleet were a priority need for tactical and strategic planning. B-29 targeters on Tinian, for example, could estimate how much overcast would be over Japan, and for how long.

Ariyoshi studied how the Communists re-educated POWs and used them to demonstrate to the Chinese peasant that Japanese were not at all superior to Chinese. He was also instrumental in getting criticism of propaganda leaflets prepared at various places by the U.S., and sending back copies to their sources for re-evaluation. He also set up, in a cave, a photo exhibit of U.S. might and life style for the edification of Mao's followers.

As time passed, and it became evident that the Dixie Mission was going to be a failure, that there would be no amity between Chiang and Mao—for whatever reason (and readers have been given lots of choices as to which in the succeeding 34 years)—Koji Ariyoshi was confined more to straight Army duties. He was ordered to report directly to Joseph Stilwell's successor, Albert Wedemeyer. The general couldn't believe his ears as Ariyoshi ticked off accomplishments and capabilities of the Red peasants, capped by his prediction that, if and when the expected civil war broke out, Chiang would be defeated.

Aghast, Wedemeyer asked Ariyoshi if he would repeat his findings to Ambassador Patrick Hurley, who had been made Roosevelt's special emissary to China for the purpose of uniting the two factors. Angry when he couldn't accomplish his mission, Hurley had thrown in his lot with Chiang. He got angrier when, standing in his underwear, socks and a shirt, he listened to Ariyoshi repeat what he had learned in observing Yenan. For his efforts, Ariyoshi got Hurley's finger wagged in his face, and was told that the Ambassador had all the "true facts" from Chiang's brother-in-law. The ex-longshoreman then could adopt no attitude other than *shikata ga nai.* After all, he was only a lieutenant, and a fairly new one at that. He'd arrived in China a sergeant.

* * *

John Burden got to China. He was wanted to work in intelligence for the counter-invasion—the Allied landing—that got cancelled. After near-paranoia because of unbelievable things the Army Air Corps did to his luggage on the way from Minnesota, Burden finally got to Chungking, but was nixed when he tried to post himself with the Dixie Mission as its medical officer.

At one interpreting session, Burden really got into a circus. First he had Joseph Dickey, whose Japanese was

Dud shell makes good prop for picture to send home. At top right Kazuo Komoto shows Purple Heart to imprisoned kid brother. Nisei could cruise on Pasig River (at left below) once Manila was taken. Deactivated mine holds no terrors for Harry Oka and Conway Yamamoto, near Cavite.

not good. He also had an American with him who spoke the Mandarin dialect, and a Chinese who spoke the Cantonese dialect, but no one around who spoke both. But then Chiang's staff produced a half-Japanese who did speak both dialects.

If Cantonese, or Mandarin was spoken the half-Japanese translated it into Japanese for Burden. He did this if a Cantonese or Mandarin spoke to each other, too. Burden would then translate it into English for Dickey. Like the Kibei-pidgin-English system that Amos Nakamura used in India, it was creaky but it worked.

Burden's language capability strengthened the American hand in daily conferences with the British and French concerning a new move, because he spoke Japanese and none of the Allies did. They resented it.

* * *

Shoso Nomura got a new boss in Yenan when Arnold Dadian, formerly with Sheldon Covell's team, showed up there. Nomura did Order of Battle work, and got to work with a man who later became the first delegate to the United Nations from the People's Republic of China, when Mao's nation was finally admitted. Nomura never did recover from his surprise at the way the Chinese treated POW's regarding confinement. There was none! POW's could roam about as they pleased, Communist leadership counting on the local peasantry to contain or recapture them if they fled. He saw POW's attend a Workers and Peasants School, and join the Japanese Emancipation League. Many graduates of the school later became Communist leaders in Japan.

* * *

Joe Ikeguchi got commissioned in China at the same time Akiji Yoshimura did. Both were spot-promoted in the field because John Burden couldn't spare them long enough for the trip back to the States and OCS. Nobu Tanabe was one of six Nisei attached to Clair Chennault's 14th Air Force, and remarked how "I never enjoyed

Army food except when I was in China." A curious thing about Tanabe is that he made four parachute jumps, completed infantry training and served overseas with the OSS, all the while classified 4-F!

* * *

John Morozumi got to cover a lot of Chinese landscape, which suited him just fine, he being full of energy and determination. Rather than suffer internment, in 1942, John took off for Denver, outside the repatriation zone. He had already ignored the San Francisco curfew, and automatically punched anyone who gave him a hard time or called him "Jap!" although John was of slight frame. He visited his parents while they were in the Topaz, Utah, concentration camp and, as he put it, "I got captured!" He didn't intend to hold still for that, and at once made plans to escape. Morozumi changed his mind after taking a careful look at the guards. "The Army seemed to have thrown every misfit they had into the task of guarding us," he said, "and these people who would never have made it overseas as fighting men were just itching to prove themselves by 'getting a Jap!'"

John met Akiji Yoshimura when he got to China, but almost in passing, because he went on to Honan Province and duty along a "corridor" the Japanese used for funneling troops south. It was John's job to find out if Japanese troops retreating from Malaya and Burma were grouping up in the Canton area against any Nimitz or MacArthur invasion, or whether they were continuing north.

Morozumi went out into the field with Chiang's troops, but thought of them more as guerrillas than trained fighting men. He was involved in combat a number of times, and still griped 33 years later about not getting a Combat Infantryman's Badge "because the War Department wouldn't admit that we actually had American troops fighting in China. Dammit, that Badge meant 5 points when they started demobilizing! It would have gotten me out of the Army a few months earlier!"

John had spies with him, and spies working against him, although supposedly on his side. It didn't matter. They were circumspect, genteel, and had a live-and-let-live attitude. Once he saw his forces trap a large contingent of Japanese in a valley, then open up a corridor through which the enemy could safely retreat.

He was supposed to be giving tactical advice to the Chinese troops with him, but found it "hard to do when the troops with you have no shoes, or vehicles. The entire battalion only had one 60-millimeter mortar," he said, "and sometimes that was held at battalion headquarters, for safekeeping." Boys from age 11 up were drafted, and it was 13-year-olds who usually became sergeants "because they were literate," said Morozumi, "where the older troops weren't."

* * *

Karl Yoneda's OWI team got to China, with Ariyoshi leaving it for Yenan. Chris Ishii continued to do the art work for propaganda leaflets. Karl wasn't too happy that the bulk of work was done by him and other enlisted men, while advertising and magazine men, commissioned directly into the Army, were majors or colonels. Yoneda had to settle for the fact that he was doing his bit to fight fascism.

Chapter 14

Before taking Okinawa, it seemed like a good idea to grab a group of islands southeast of it, named Kerama Retto. These would provide an excellent fleet replenishment anchorage, well out of range of Okinawa's guns. If Allied air cover was sufficient, ships anchored there could be protected until some airfields ashore on Okinawa were taken and put into use. Land-based air would then cover the ships. A lot of tough fighting was expected on Okinawa, and it would be foolish to bring large ships in close to shore while the enemy still commanded the beaches. So, Kerama Retto was a key, and the 77th Division was given the job of taking it.

The force dispatched against Okinawa was awesome. It included the 1st, 2nd and 6th Marine Divisions, plus the 7th, 27th, 77th and 96th Army Infantry Divisions with the 81st standing by in reserve. About 300,000 troops had been assembled, to pit against the estimated 70,000 that were ashore. Not at all counting the small escort carriers, the number of British and American carriers assigned to cover Okinawa totalled more than the U.S. and Imperial navies owned on December 7, 1941.

* * *

The overall plan for taking the island was fairly simple, and should not confuse the reader. Taking Kerama Retto was to be a preliminary step. After that, forces would land on the west side of the island's south end, and fight their way across it, in the process capturing two important airfields, at Yontan and Kadena. Next move would be to seize a fat peninsula, Motobu, that jutted out to the northwest from the island (which itself lay on a southeast-northeast line), and a small island off Motobu, named Ie Shima, which had a large airfield on it. With these areas secured, it would then be a matter of conquering what might remain of the enemy in the northern portion of Okinawa.

The airfields had priority, because Okinawa was well within range of numerous air bases in Japan's home islands. A force once ashore had to be protected from them. Nimitz, under whose command the operation was to be, felt he had the necessary force to accomplish all this. Again, however, his intelligence was not what it might have been, nor were all preparations sufficient either in duration or applied force. Infantrymen would pay a bloody price for this piece of Japanese real estate.

It is too easy to place the blame on generals and admirals, so the author will not do that. It goes squarely where it belongs—on the U.S. attitude, on the American culture and society, on the philosophy of "hurry up and get the job done, so we can go about our other business." En masse, the American people wanted the war over in a hurry, and under American law admirals and generals had to heed the will of the people via its elected representatives. Secretary of the Navy James V. Forrestal, watching the flag-raising on Mt. Suribachi, said in essence, "This means there'll be a Marine Corps for another 500 years." Marines, at least, meant to buy insurance on that statement. The Army was at least as eager, especially since the general leading one of its divisions, the 27th, had been relieved on Saipan for not moving ahead fast enough.

The author has stated his view several times in this work that all wars are insanity, and it can be seen that Nisei paradoxically strove their mightiest during this insane enterprise in proving that they were as reliable Americans as any. It may be worth noting that they were impelled in turn by an insanity visited upon them—the locking up of 110,000 Americans in total violation of the rights that Americans boasted to the world they held dearest.

So much for philosophy. The purpose of this work is to demonstrate how well Nisei supported a country that denied them rights, in its struggle to defeat the alien ideology of fascism.

* * *

It was fitting that the main assault on Okinawa commenced on April Fool's Day, but the 77th was hard at work before that. Seven days before the main attack, it began landing on seven islands in Kerama Retto. All told, the 77th landed in 15 places, all the while aware that there were at least 35 Japanese airfields that might strike at them, and that whatever remained of the Japanese Navy was not far away.

Frank Mori and Mac Miyahara were with the first troops to land; Kunio Endo and Vic Nishijima, the second group; and Tetsuo Yamada and Mitsuo Shibata the third. The other four members of the team, and Harvey Daniels, were with division headquarters. There was not much opposition on the 10 small islands invaded, many of the enemy having finished their portions of labor on the defenses and gone to work elsewhere.

One of the small islets was called Geruma. Here troops of the 77th met, for their first time, the results of indoctrination given civilians and soldiers of the Imperial Army, which drew on atrocities committed elsewhere. So convinced were people on Geruma that mothers strangled babies, and people lined up in such fashion that all could simultaneously strangle each other. They did this to avoid the treatment they had been told, over and over again, they would receive at the hands of "brutal Americans."

Intelligence felt that there might be large coastal guns emplaced in the Kerama Retto, able to shell the invading fleet. The Navy was wrong. The 77th, searching for these guns in order to destroy them, found something far deadlier, of which Navy intelligence had not told them— 360 *shinyo.*

Shinyo were suicide craft, mass-produced boats about 20 feet long and driven by a motor that could propel each at 35 knots. They had a high freeboard (waterline-to-deck distance), and a covered deck so they could operate in the open sea. A fork-like device permitted mounting two depth charges in the bow, while a third sat in the stern. Vic Nishijima found many mounted on narrow gauge rails inside caves, ready for rapid launch into the sea. The idea was that the pilot would take his boat on a one-way mission, running up against an enemy ship and then detonating all three charges, which had 5-second fuses. Three depth charges, that close aboard, could break the back of most American warships.

One can only imagine the destruction that these boats —about which U.S. naval intelligence had known *nothing,* and given no warning—might have wrought in the darkness among the offshore ships, especially since their wooden hulls were impervious to detection by the probing finger of radar. The *shinyo,* like the *kaiten* (human torpedoes) and *koryu* (midget submarines), were another example of inventiveness that startled Americans, who remained stuck throughout the war with preconceived convictions about "copycat Japs." But, the very radar used by U.S. warships was built around an antenna invented by a Japanese, lifted from his published papers by the British and lent to their American cousins. Perhaps a look at history, and learning that the Japanese invented the cigarette lighter 250 years before Pearl Harbor, might have given American campaign planners a better idea of what to expect from their enemy.

* * *

When the Okinawa campaign opened, Phil Ishio was on leave in California, first Nisei in officer's uniform to step foot in that State. Kazuhiko Yamada was wrapping up his own war, although he didn't know it, as he left Finschhafen for a well-deserved home leave. Dick Hayashi was in the fighting around Leghorn, in Europe, and other Nisei were hard at it in New Guinea, New Britain and the Philippines. Burma, too, where Art Morimitsu had learned that bullets from retreating Japanese killed people just as dead as those from charging ones on Guadalcanal had, two and one-half years earlier. In Manila, Clifford Konno was already beaming broadcasts toward Japan, trying to inform its citizens that their war was already lost. LeMay's B-29's punctuated each of Konno's statements with ordnance exclamation points. Masatoshi Nonaka, of Honolulu, whose home had been missed by a defective U.S. Navy shell on December 7, 1941, was recovering from an illness at Fort Meade, Maryland, and getting ready for language school at Snelling, where he would find the course cut to three months. Emphasis now was almost completely focused on *spoken* Japanese. Graduates were pouring out of MISLS in preparation for an Occupation that could not be very far in the future. In the United States, news from Europe and the Pacific was beginning to spice the air with the tang of victory.

* * *

Eddie Fukui was not to celebrate it. The 77th completed its job in the Kerama Retto, got back on board its transports, and moved offshore to be the floating reserve. On the day after four marine and Army divisions hit the beaches, a *kamikaze* dived into the ship carrying the command staff of the 77th's 305th regiment. Fukui was among those who died.

* * *

The 7th Division drove all the way across Okinawa on its first day. There was to be no criticism from the marines about "keeping up." Howard Moss had Ben Honda, Mike Sakamoto and Minoru Nakanishi on his team now, replacing those no longer with him who had been at Leyte. Hiroshi Mukaye led the team for him.

Mike Sakamoto was stunned to find his outfit had beaten the marines across the island. His first day at

Okinawa was quiet, and he spent it trying to get civilians out of the way of the fighting. The second day, he did the same, and entered a cave for the first time. He got two sisters, 16 and 18, to come out. He went in again, and found a little girl, 4, with one arm blown off. GI's had sprayed the cave with machine gun fire, earlier, as a safety precaution.

Few people are aware that the fighting on Okinawa continued right up through Japan's surrender, and afterward. Ben Honda interviewed the personal cook of General Mitsuru Ushijima, commander of the Japanese garrison, and went with him to make positive identification of the bodies of Ushijima and his chief of staff after they committed suicide. Ben would get a second Bronze Star for Okinawa, adding it to the one he got for Saipan. He found himself, after Japan's surrender, flying over an enemy holdout area, dropping leaflets giving them the news. It startled him to recognize it as the same area into which he had gone, weeks before, to help find a Caucasian GI who'd gone souvenir hunting and been killed.

Hiroshi Mukaye, such a troublemaker in concentration camp before enlisting, and a headache to Savage staffers later, continued to develop his leadership and other skills. Cosma Sakamoto wrote of Mukaye "with his close-cropped head and winning smile he can melt the coldest and most sullen prisoner into telling him everything." Sakamoto asked in a letter that his younger brother, then a student at MISLS, be looked after and that it be seen to "he gets everything possible out of those classes, because he will need every bit of training out here in the field."

Toshimi Yamada, who had the nickname "Kuu Ipo," found his buttocks creased by a bullet accidentally discharged from the carbine of another Nisei, Tommy Hamada, while Hamada was cleaning it. Toshimi had the wound cauterized and bandaged at the first aid tent, then demanded a Purple Heart recommendation for it.

"No dice," said the doctor-major. "Wounds have to be a result of a Japanese action!"

"Well, what the hell do *you* call the guy?" said the indignant Toshimi, pointing out that Tommy was an AJA.

According to Robyn Dare, who had joined the team and was witness to the whole incident, Toshimi felt he had every right, because it actually was an action involving a Japanese. The doctor then said it had to be an *enemy* Japanese, and Toshimi responded with, "Well, he's sure as heck my enemy *now!*" rubbing his tender backside.

The discussion went on and on until Toshimi Yamada gave up. A week later, doing cave-flushing, he got shot, so he walked casually into the aid station and said he'd have a Purple Heart now, if you please. He got one.

He also got another wound on Okinawa, a much deeper one. It happened while he was doing an interrogation. Toshimi Yamada had gone to Japan in 1941 with his mother, sister and brother, he alone returning in the summer of 1941, and he'd had no communication with his family since. It turned out that some POWs he talked with actually had known his brother, who was stationed on Okinawa a while before getting ordered to the Philippines. As soon as Toshimi learned the name of his brother's unit, he realized from earlier intelligence information that he was dead. The ship carrying that organization had been sunk with all hands before it got to its destination.

Mukaye loomed "bigger than life," according to Dare, and "somehow seemed to have the bulk of a *sumo* wrestler, although he really didn't." He was three times recommended for battlefield commissions, and all three times the word "No!" came back. There was an FBI file on Bud, who had a football scholarship at Santa Clara University and resisted, while also getting others to resist, the entire idea of evacuation.

Ben Honda was "one of those brilliant quiet ones," Dare said, and Karl Akama was quieter than Mukaye although just as big. Tatsuo "Elmer" Yamamoto was another Hoichi Kubo type with, at times, more guts than brains. Only 102 pounds and 5'1", Yamamoto walked into a cave on Okinawa with more than 350 enemy weapons pointed at him, and calmly convinced the colonel in charge to have the holders of the weapons lay them down and surrender.

Dare couldn't remember, 32 years later, "which one of them it was," so it could have been Sam S. Rokutani, Frank Y. Masuoka, Gus Hikawa, Futoshi Inaba, or one of the other members of the 7th's team, but "whoever it was, he'd line up all males 15 to 25 years old, and assume the stance of a very tough Japanese drill instructor type. We'd watch for reactions while he barked out drill commands," Dare said. "Then he'd start his sales pitch, consisting of praise for the patriot who served his country, from lowly support troop to front-line infantrymen to sailor. He'd strut back and forth in front of them like a Hitler, building his sales talk and voice to a pitch, and then he'd suddenly shout 'All right, officers fall in over here, non-commissioned officers there, and other enlisted men over there—further!' Sure as hell, by that time they'd gotten so hypnotized by him that they obeyed! The ones who did line up as told were given treatment under the Geneva Convention, and marched off to the regular POW camp. We had found out they were really soldiers. Before they left, some others who'd held back would join them, and our whole problem of separating civilians from soldiers would be solved. We'd take the rest, the civilians, to other units waiting to process them."

* * *

At one time the 7th's language team set up tents on Okinawa in a small ravine they were sure was totally protected, so they hadn't even dug foxholes, when Japanese artillery began showering them with tree bursts. Robyn Dare did what the rest did, hightailed it downhill to a lower level for shelter. As he did, he saw Tommy Hamada racing off to one side of him, and a slowed-down piece of hot shrapnel heading on a line for Tom-

Charlie Chan (l) and Grant Hirabayashi interrogate ''comfort girls.'' A detachment of them was captured after Myitkina, Burma, was overcome.

my's buttocks. "Pull it in!" yelled Dare, and Hamada did. The piece of metal hit the ground, caromed, struck a rock, and started past Dare. It missed Hamada's derriere. Dare fielded it like a grounder and flipped it to Hamada, saying, "Now here's a souvenir you'll never forget." The two then pressed their backs against the slope of a hill for protection, and Dare said, "You know, if we get out of this mess, I don't think I'll ever stop laughing!"

* * *

George Oujevolk was with the 6th Marines. So were James Shigeta and David Kurisu, but the Nisei were stuck on the command ship *USS Panamint* until a shore command post could be set up near Yontan airfield when it was captured. Michael A. Braun, Richard Schneider and A. W. Stuart were among the *hakujin* who did language work in the campaign, and all used their linguistic capabilities to good ends later. Stuart rose to general officer rank in the Army, Schneider made a career of the U.S. diplomatic service, and Braun displayed raw guts making sure war criminals got a proper defense when the war was over. He later took up law practice in Tokyo.

* * *

In Hawaii, a desperate Navy had paid the price for barring Nisei from service, and now was changing its mind—although only enough to borrow a larger supply of them from the Army than before. To help the Navy, the Army employed an old Navy technique. It shanghai'd a bunch! Edward Sumida's brother Haruo was among them, hauled off to the battle area without language training or even indoctrination. The stories of two other men perhaps best tell the tale for everyone. Walter Kajiwara's is first.

Kajiwara had volunteered for the 442nd, declining language school "because I wanted to fight!" He was among the first batch of replacements for the 100th, and made the Anzio landing in Italy. Kajiwara completed the march into Rome before getting one of the 100th's 1703 Purple Hearts. Hospitalization in Italy, Washington and Honolulu followed, and he was sent back to duty at Schofield Barracks in early 1945. A sergeant from California who grew up with Nisei boys treated him well, but also told Kajiwara that a Chinese-American in the bunk beneath him slept with a loaded M-1 rifle. Drawing on the sergeant's friendship, Kajiwara managed to get the hell out of there, and to Fort Shafter, where he sought return to Europe.

It was not to be. One day a colonel came in, had Kajiwara translate a Japanese newspaper, and within 24 hours he was on a plane to Saipan. Walt was handed a carbine, a portable loudspeaker and told "Get up in the hills and get those Japs to surrender."

Two weeks of this was followed by a transfer to the arriving 98th Division and getting told "You guys will be hitting Kyushu after Okinawa's cleaned up!" Walter wasn't a Nisei. He was a Sansei ("third generation of Japanese in America"). His father was Nisei, born during the reign of Hawaii's last monarch, Queen Liliuokalani. Walt, however, knew enough about Japan from his elders to realize that if he ever got to see Japan he might never get to see home again. Kyushu was the home of Japan's most terrifying infantry division—the 6th.

* * *

"I guess we got selected because we had done so well in Japanese school," said James Furukawa of himself and others who were grabbed on Oahu before they even completed infantry training. Furukawa was drafted in December, 1944. He hoped to go and share in the 442nd's glory. So did his friends, but "some started leaving for the Pacific front line duty almost as soon as we got drafted," Furukawa remembered. "I guess it was because they were the best linguists."

Here was a really ridiculous situation. Caucasians had tried, over and over again, to close the Japanese schools in Hawaii, afraid they were hotbeds of subversion. Now the files of every AJA draftee there were being pored over, to find who'd attended, and actual school records scanned to determine each man's degree of proficiency. Furukawa and a host of others spent about 32 days on an LST, and were assigned to 10th Army as soon as they arrived at Okinawa. A lot hadn't even been taught how to fire a rifle, but were put directly into a combat situation.

What actually griped the men most wasn't the fact that they'd been shanghai'd. They turned to with a will, and did a reasonably good job—flushing caves, interrogating captives, and translating documents. The bulk of their work eventually centered on helping the native population adjust to peacetime living. But an awful lot didn't get paid for an awfully long time! The Navy ran the islands, and had no way of paying these impressed garrison troops. They were on no Navy muster list!

The bitterest pill came in the spring of 1946. The new GI's didn't have enough points to qualify for discharge under the demobilizing program, and neither were they on any TO. The pals they'd left in Hawaii were, however, and arrived on Okinawa or Saipan in early 1946, with lovely new stripes—or, sometimes, gold lieutenant's bars. Plus—*money!* It was just too much. *Shikata ga nai* didn't help.

* * *

George Inagaki made the Okinawa campaign, again with the marines. Before that he had developed a warm admiration for Glen Brunner, a prewar State Department staffer who headed up the Nisei contingent at Honolulu for a while, and made JICPOA duty as comfortable for them as he could. It was a challenge, because although the Nisei got per diem—the GI's wartime dream—they well knew it was given them so they'd eat in restaurants instead of getting admitted to military messhalls. Nisei still weren't welcome on naval installations, no matter how valuable their contribution to the war effort. Dick Hayashi and others were kept out of sight, early in the war, when Chester Nimitz visited New Caledonia, although William Halsey was plenty glad to have their help when he took over the South Pacific forces.

* * *

A man who didn't get shanghai'd to Okinawa, but who was surprised to go there and at what happened to him, was Thomas Higa. Owner of a name easily recognized by other AJA's as deriving from that prefecture, Tom had been on active duty in Hawaii when the war started. On November 20, 1941, in fact, he'd been deployed with others of the 100th along the north side of Oahu, and given *three* rounds of ammunition "in case of an attack." Higa'd been nearby when Sgt. David Akui captured Kazuo Sakamaki from the midget submarine on the day after the December 7 attack. He had gone to Europe, took part in the savage house-to-house fighting around Cassino, and took two wounds. "My lack of height probably saved my life," Higa said, after a German bullet tore his helmet away without harming him.

Tom got back to Hawaii. He was asked personally by General Kendall Fielder to go to Okinawa and help out, so he did. He entered caves 12 times to get holdouts to surrender, and was successful 11 of them. When Higa entered one cave, an elderly Okinawan lady grabbed him in the semi-darkness and said, "Watch out! There are Americans just outside!" Tom's face, and dark complexion, had misled her. Higa had one truly unique experience. He ran across, and was able to protect, his former *sensei,* Shosei Kina, who had been his teacher when his parents sent him to Okinawa for schooling while a youngster.

* * *

Warren Sakuma almost didn't make it to Okinawa as head of John Flagler's team that got assigned to the 10th Army staff. His group was at a sea for 52 days, and twice got missed by Japanese torpedoes, or at least so its bridge crew reported. Enroute Robert Oda, Shigeru Sato,

Tom Matsumoto, and Stanley Ito took turns monitoring Japanese broadcasts. They found Tokyo Rose "entertaining." Four other linguists, named Okano, Nakamura, Nagao and Mizuno (whose first names the author was unable to ascertain from official rosters, because of the Nisei penchant for being "more American" by using nicknames), were with the team.

Osame Yamamoto was pleased with himself at remembering the few key phrases of Okinawan he'd recently learned. They aided him immeasurably in opening communications with POWs and Okinawa civilians, of which there were many thousands.

Robert Oda's ship anchored in Kerama Retto before moving on to an Okinawa beachhead, and he learned something of the *shinyo* while there. Then, as he walked off his landing craft ramp, Oda's first sight was that of a dead Japanese officer who'd tried to ram an American ship. Cutting away the man's wet uniform to look for documents, Oda learned he was a Buddhist priest, and recently married. It was shocking, to learn that even Buddhist ministers were being drafted in Japan for combat roles, although it did give an indication of the enemy's desperate straits.

Oda was witness to a tragic love affair in the oldest Japanese tradition, when he captured a Major Umezawa and his Japanese-Korean consort, a "comfort girl" who'd been shipped to Okinawa to serve the garrison after volunteering from Korea to work in a Japanese defense factory. Umezawa was allowed to have his girl exercise "visitation rights" because he was so cooperative in supplying military intelligence, but when hostilities ended he was shipped back to China for trial as a war criminal (he'd come from Manchuria to Okinawa), and the girl sent back to Korea. Oda never heard of either again.

* * *

Tom Masui was with the 96th Division. He personally got nearly 2000 civilians to give up and emerge from caves or burial chambers. (It was Okinawan custom to build large tombs, or dig large caves, then bury their dead in massive urns. It became civilian custom, and sometimes Japanese military custom during the campaign for the islanders to hide out in these places, which gave Nisei with a sensitivity toward centuries-old Japanese customs quite a problem.)

"Come out!" Masui would call. "We will provide *chiryu kin* (medical supplies), *shokobutsu* (food), and *iryo* (clothing)."

The response was usually Japanese for "Drop dead!" or "You'll kill me!"

Tom would often wax truly sentimental trying to reach his audience, persuading them to talk about home and family, then talking about his own. "I love my little brothers and sisters," he would say, "and I want to go home and help them grow up. I'll do anything to save them from this hopeless war. Won't you do the same for yours?"

Usually, holdouts gave up about that time.

Not always, however. Sometimes the conversation would end in "American dog! Come and get me!" followed by a *whoompf!* "What happened?" Tom would shout, and other voices would say "He killed himself."

"All right. You're safe now," Tom would say. "Come on out."

When that happened, civilians usually did. In most instances, one or a few Japanese soldiers held large numbers of civilians with them in the burial chambers or caves. Working with Warren and Takejiro Higa, Takeo Nonaka and Fred Fukushima, Masui and the test of the team saved thousands of lives.

Herbert Yanamura, Yoichi Kawano and Akira Hori were on the team with Masui. Herb came away from the war with fond memories of Dick Kesner, a violinist with the special services section of the 96th, who was not a translator. Kesner later joined with Lawrence Welk's band, and Yanamura was thrilled when allowed to handle Kesner's genuine Stradivarius during a tour of the islands by Welk's group after the war.

More landings were made in the Philippines while the Okinawa fighting went on. The 40th hit Bohol, while the 24th and 31st landed at Mindanao. This large island still held lots of fighting Japanese that had to be taken out. Robert Yoshioka, with the 24th Division, learned how the Japanese at last had become security-conscious. He translated captured orders that warned soldiers to be on the lookout for spies, and to destroy or bury important documents when such were endangered. There were still no orders telling men not to *talk,* which indicated that the *bushi do* spirit was still extant, that Japanese authorities felt no man would allow himself to be captured. Yoshioka and his teammates continued to reap intelligence harvests through interrogations.

* * *

Victor Abe and Bill Saito landed on Mindanao with the 158th RCT, and were "thankful for the going-over our Navy and Air Corps had given the island. We faced no opposition during the landing," Abe said, "and none until we were a few miles inland, where some artillery stopped us for a while." Overcoming this, Abe's unit moved on, and soon took the Del Monte airfield. Along the way he met a lot of Moros, a small but fierce people who professed Islamism. The fathers of these natives had prompted development of the U.S. Army's .45 pistol, a weapon designed to knock a man down no matter where hit, because the handgun the Army had during the Moro rebellion at the turn of the century couldn't do that to one running *amok.*

* * *

Hideo Tsuyuki also made the Mindanao landing. It was to be his last. Not long afterward he embarked for the U.S. His transport kept breaking down, and Japan had surrendered by the time he got to Heart Mountain prison camp to visit his mother. His father had died there, a year before, while Tsuyuki was in New Guinea. He went to the Minedoka camp, where his fiance was, and got married. Tsuyuki's Army service ended as quietly as it had begun, and Tsuyuki's life continued just as quietly.

* * *

Pres. Franklin Roosevelt died on April 12, the same day Fort Drum in Manila Harbor was captured. Army troops took it by running a lighter alongside, pumping thousands of gallons of gasoline into its air vents, then blowing the place apart with Japanese still in it. The 77th Division made a landing on Ie Shima and took the biggest airfield in the Okinawa complex. Vic Nishijima tippy-toed his way among the bombs that had been set in its runway for unwary Americans. *Kamikaze* planes had been raining down on the ships off Okinawa for more than two weeks, and dozens of craft of all sizes were hit. Ralph Saito by then had been "captured"by a Marine on Okinawa. As many a Nisei before him, Saito shook himself after rescue and release, to be sure he was still alive. For him, as for other Nisei, it had been a near thing.

* * *

On Mindanao, Richard Hirata was having an experience that Nisei with Merrill's Marauders had in Burma. His unit was being supplied by airdrop, and the enemy got at least half of each. "After 20 days of hot pursuit," Hirata said, "we got lucky. Half-starved, we overran an enemy bivouac, and found some rice, still steaming in the pot." Further on, Hirata captured a soldier. "He was a *kirikomitai* (a suicide man), whose job it was to set off a series of 150-kilogram bombs that had been set in the road about 50 yards apart for 500 yards," Hirata said.

* * *

On Okinawa, the fight did not go well. Mitsuru Ushijima had planned excellently, completely fooling all his enemies. Unlike Iwo Jima, few marines died on the beaches. The Japanese general had let them come ashore unopposed, having decided earlier that enemy bombardment and bombing would be too heavy for his defenders to protect landing areas effectively. Ushijima had planned to let his enemies move inland with confidence, then chew them up.

This, his troops proceeded to do.

Part of Fusao Uchiyama's team (above) in China near end of war. Charlie Hamasaki (below) interrogates wounded POW with Eugene Wright, while doctor tends the patient.

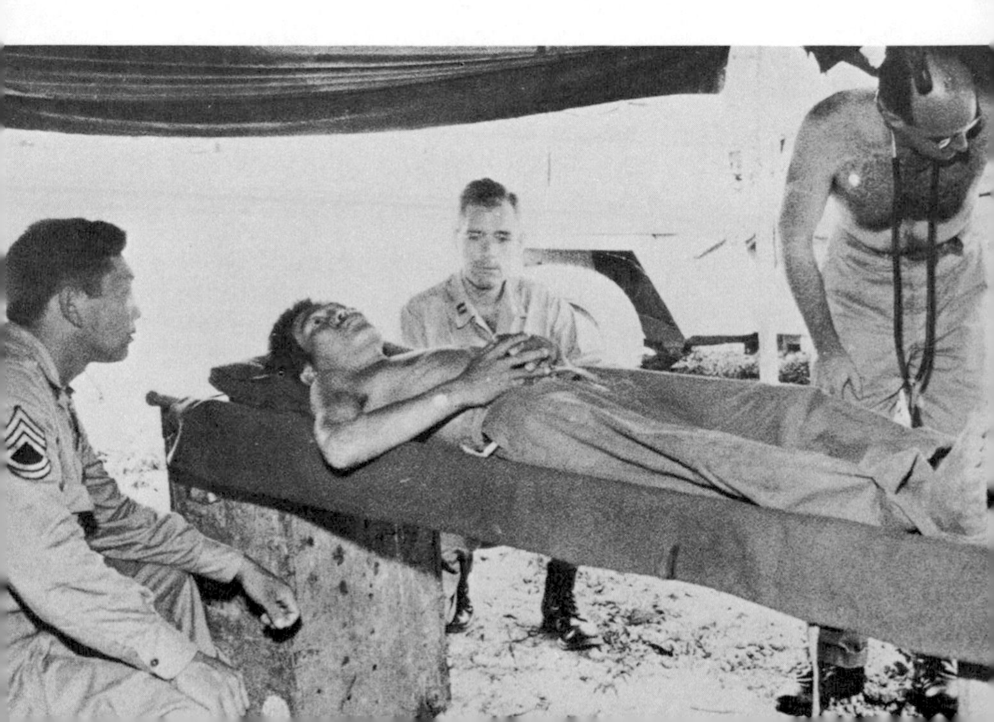

Chapter 15

Vic Nishijima found himself on Ie Shima, although he had not been scheduled to go there. Jeeps, amtracs and ambulances had been blown to bits by the 500-pound aerial bombs that studded the airstrip, the bombs having been refitted to be land mines. Metal detectors were brought forward, and the mines marked. All this time Vic was trying to talk Okinawans out of a burial cave, and finally told them if they didn't get out they'd be sealed up, because he couldn't leave them in the rear of advancing troops.

At that moment the man who appeared to be their leader drew back. So did Vic. He had no loudspeaker, and was right at the cave's entrance. Vic expected a grenade, but a lady in sight shook her head no. The leader then came out, followed by about 150 others.

Nishijima was exhausted, but when he tried to relax he spotted George Pratt, an intelligence officer, heading across the airstrip, close to the cave's mouth. With him was a slight, elderly fellow. "Get the hell out of there!" yelled the Californian, ignoring military courtesy, and the pair obeyed him with alacrity. Vic, with the help of two other GI's, returned to herding his charges down to the beach. Twilight was approaching. With his Japanese features he didn't want to be away from the command post after dark.

The procession work began to move well, and Vic was halfway to the beach when the elderly man he'd waved off the airstrip accosted him, starting to ask for details about how he'd gotten the civilians to come out of the cave. Tired, dirty, anxious and angry, Nishijima brushed the man off, and kept moving. He got to the beach, finished his business, and swapped a Japanese Luger he'd picked up for a camera that Adolf Spreckels III, the sugar fortune heir, had. About that time one of the other infantrymen said, "Hey, Vic, do you know you just blew an interview with Ernie Pyle?"

The 77th linguist didn't even feel like answering.

Nishijima was on Ie Shima about a week. He once got smacked around, but not injured, by a satchel charge blast. One night, inside his perimeter, Japanese rushed out of caves, explosive charges strapped to themselves, trying to take Americans to eternity with them. Vic again survived, unscathed.

Expecting to be relieved, Vic and the squad of soldiers who were his bodyguard went down to the beach. The other men were called back to the line, leaving him alone to wait for a ride back to his ship. This left Nishijima the problem of getting to where *he'd be recognized,* before someone shot him. As he came over a dune, machine gun bullets whizzed past him, and he dived into a ditch. Minutes later, word was passed down the ditch that Ernie Pyle had just been killed. He'd been in the same line of fire of an enemy gunner who'd let almost an entire battalion pass, before opening up. The burst that missed Vic missed everyone, but Pyle stuck his head up too soon, and the second fusillade got him. Nishijima finally made it safely to battalion headquarters, where he saw a man in total collapse, crying, from battle fatigue. "I felt just like sitting right down beside him and joining in," Nishijima said.

"A higher power was looking after me another time, too," Nishijima told the author. He spent all of one morning in a walled courtyard, waiting for an interpreter summons. None came, so he left. Five minutes later a mortar burst got the six men he'd spent the morning with.

Before leaving Ie Shima, the linguist crawled out into

an open field, under fire, to rescue a wailing infant, whom he and his buddies immediately dubbed Okinawa Sue. He cut the child loose from a pack on her dead mother's back. He started out for a second one after that, but the machine gun fire this time was so close that the task proved impossible. Regretfully, Vic had to turn back.

Ie Shima was finally secured, and Nishijima called away. On the beach he met Tetsuo Yamada, and the pair decided to pick up Mitsuo Shibata along the way. Mits said he was going to stay on the island one more night.

He did, and awoke the following hazy morning to see a group of civilians approaching through a draw. They had read surrender leaflets that stressed that they surrender only during daylight hours, for safety. Hoping to get the group out from under possible fire, Shibata leaped to his feet and shouted "Kochi kinasai! (Come here!), waving them over toward him. As he did, he was shot. It was never determined whether an enemy sniper or a sleepy and frightened buddy got Shibata, but he died.

* * *

Conquest of the southern end of the island of Okinawa proved fairly easy, but that was because General Mitsuru Ushijima had planned it that way. He had let the Americans get ashore without much opposition, then took a toll of them once they landed. Japanese artillery was zeroed in on nearly every inch of the island. One deadly weapon the supposedly-imitative enemy had was its 47mm anti-tank gun. The gun had a low muzzle velocity but, by hollowing out its nose, Japanese artillery experts made its shell an armor-piercing projectile that punched through American tanks as though they were paper. There is little doubt that it was the model for the "shaped charge" used with such good effect against German tanks in Europe, after discovery of it by Australians and Americans on New Guinea. Apparently it had not been tested sufficiently against American tanks on U.S. ordnance proving grounds, because on Okinawa it wreaked havoc as it had in the Philippines and on Iwo Jima. Again, an indication that intelligence is no good if someone does not put it to work.

The 27th Division was anxious to prove itself after what it had suffered on Saipan. On Okinawa it did prove itself. It never let up. Nisei linguists had to work all the harder because of that. Their task was made all the more difficult by what Japanese had told Okinawans about "American brutality." One mother offered herself to the 27th's intelligence officer to be raped so that her daughter could be spared. It took a lot of talking to reassure her.

Hoichi Kubo was on Okinawa, and could have emulated Mark Twain by saying "the reports of my death have been greatly exaggerated." He had been written up by Les Finnegan of the North American Newspaper Alliance for the *Seattle Times* because of what he'd accomplished on Saipan. The last line in Finnegan's story read "The D.S.C. award to Hoichi was made posthumously."

Given his choice of which wave he'd go in with, Kubo said the first, and was much admired for his bravery. He told the author, however, that "I wasn't stupid. I saw that the first waves weren't getting hit too badly." He was right. The 27th landed on the seventh day of the invasion. Kubo'd been able to scan intelligence and casualty reports before that. Besides, Kubo had come up from Espiritu Santo in the New Hebrides, with the 27th, "and my fellow troops were pretty raw. They'd only had eight weeks of training." They were replacements for men who died on Saipan. Kubo was taking no chances. He had heard or read somewhere that "Brave men get less brave with each battle."

The battalion Kubo was with got badly chopped up. When a marine unit came up to relieve them, they had only 1 officer and 220 men left fit to fight. "We were later moved to the north," Kubo said, "and the fighting got a lot easier."

"Our advance was held up for many days," said Richard Moritsugu of the 27th, "but when the first enemy line started to crumble, the second was much easier." Moritsugu, Jack Tanimoto, Tim Ohta, and William Nuno spent most of the campaign talking Okinawa civilians out of caves and burial chambers. Dick Kishine and Frank Mori found them full of fright, and some caves were closed because infantrymen, their casualties mounting, didn't feel safe in leaving anyone behind them. Larry Saito and Dick Kishine had worked hard to master the differences between Okinawan and the Japanese spoken in other provinces, but a Caucasian infantryman had no such tool for differentiating between Okinawans and others. Many civilians died because of this, Shigeo Ito noted.

It gave certain Hawaii Nisei a wonderful sense of accomplishment and importance to assist in this campaign if they were of Okinawan descent themselves. Back home, while growing up, they'd had to endure a certain degree of discrimination right in the Japanese communities. Just as nearly every New Englander, in the Twenties and Thirties (as well as while serving together during the war) considered everyone from Kentucky and Georgia an incestuous "cotton-chopper," basing much of his knowledge on the comic strip "Li'l Abner," so did most Hawaii Issei and Nisei think of Okinawans in the islands as "pig farmers." This part of the war brought the Yamashiro's and Higa's into their own. Without their knowledge of the Okinawa dialect, a lot more lives would have been lost than were.

* * *

Ben Hazard was with the 27th now, working closely with his men and damned proud of them. They would inspire him to such a degree that Hazard would devote much of his future to Japanalia, including study of the martial arts, rising to high rank as a *kendo* man. Three decades later he would refer to himself as one of those "strange men who like to hit each other with sticks," glossing over the fact that the Japanese martial arts were actually a form of semi-spiritual activity, calculated to give a person inner peace.

* * *

Warren Higa had his brother Takejiro on his team—an interesting matter since the Navy had a policy of splitting up brothers after five Sullivans were lost when the cruiser *Juneau* got sunk in broad daylight, while under escort, by a Japanese submarine near the Solomons. This policy the Army may not have put into effect—so Warren was able to write boisterously that "the Higa brothers were the only people who were able to repeat that famous phrase 'I have returned!' upon landing on this ___________ old island. We're glad to be back, but what a sight! I am glad that my father was smart enough to take us along to Hawaii for our education." Higa said that, although he'd met some uncles and aunts, he wouldn't want to remain on Okinawa even if they made him "Mayor, or something."

As in an earlier campaign, Warren Higa had solid suggestions to offer for MISLS. Like not using so much time on *"heigo,* because a man can learn all the military terms he needs to know in a week!" He also stressed the need to have one man do the interrogating and another make notes, "so nothing is missed." Higa gave Navy language officers from Boulder better marks than most Army officers, however, saying that Army language officers tended to lay too much of the work on their men, and ended up as mere administrators, "which should not be, but it happens because the Army officers simply figure that the Nisei can do everything." If this were true, Higa added slyly, "there would be no need for Caucasian language officers." Higa knew whereof he spoke, having had experience with Nisei at Attu, with checking work of field teams while in Hawaii, and from being in combat situations himself in the Philippines and Okinawa. He also must have been one heck of a leader. At the time he wrote, eight of his men had been recommended for the Bronze

Star. By the time the war ended, the Higa team would be credited with coaxing more than 30,000 Okinawans out of hiding and away from certain death. The Higa boys, and their associates, met the *on* they owed their ancestors.

* * *

The war didn't slow down elsewhere while the Okinawa fighting was going on. Don Okubo and Tony Sunamoto were roaming around the Marshalls, making repeated landings on small islets. They would approach in a landing craft first, and use a loudhailer to address enemy holdouts, while planes simultaneously dropped leaflets they had written. While Don did this work his brother Tadashi finished MISLS, preparing to serve in Japan after the expected surrender. In the far-flung island group, which has less than 100 square miles of land in a million square miles of ocean, Okubo began to hear grisly tales of cannibalism. These became easier to believe as he noticed that not one lizard or rat was left alive on any of the coral dots. The two Nisei operated out of Kwajalein, which the U.S. Navy used as its main base in the Marshalls.

* * *

The Australians began taking over outlying areas to the left flank and rear of MacArthur's troops in the Philippines. Henry T. Hikida was with them when they landed in North Borneo. Roy Fugami, Mamoru Takanishi and Masao Terai were also veterans of the 9th Division, as was Paul Bannai. The British Army also took Rangoon while the Okinawa fighting went on, Sam Takamura working with them. A second landing on Negros resulted in capture of an advanced Japanese midget submarine base, eliminating that threat. Torao Ikeda wrote from Bhamo, Burma. He said he was learning that Japanese treatment of natives there, like that described to him by Nisei friends in the Philippines, just might not be what American propaganda said it was. "The youngsters especially speak a lot of Japanese," he said, "and have nothing to say of the Japanese that is bad." Ikeda liked Burma, because "we can buy all the rice we want, and fresh vegetables, and chicken to go with it." When not on duty, now that the war had quieted down, men on Ikeda's team could go hunting. The Japanese were retreating in Burma, not trapped and hiding out as they were in the Pacific Islands. In India, Noboru Murakami didn't have life too bad. He and Timmie Hirata were getting free golf lessons from Johnny Goodman, a former U.S. Open and Amateur champion. Tsutomu Shigeta and Harry T. Tanaka had joined up with the Australians on New Britain, at a place called Tol Plantation.

* * *

Nisei linguists were now all over the place, although there doesn't seem to be any public record of how William Randolph Hearst, Earl Warren, and Leo Carrillo felt about it. Close to a hundred were at the secret activity known as PACMIRS. Hardly any were at JICPOA, but that was because they nearly all were out on the front lines. A batch were doing decoding at Vint Hill, handling material of such high classification that no one would have believed it possible, three years earlier, that Nisei would get near it. Much was derived from ULTRA, the name given material intercepted and deciphered by the Enigma machine British had stolen from the Germans. Had the U.S. enough Caucasians to handle the Japanese language, Nisei might never have gotten near the Pentagon during the war. Paradoxically, the need to communicate ended up allowing Nisei to communicate—their skills, loyalty, willingness and drive.

* * *

Pat Nagano, George Urabe and Kazuo Yamane waited patiently in France for word that the Russians were going to let them into Berlin, but the possibility finally fizzled out. With John White, they heard what was now contemplated was a swift air attack on Berlin, an assault on the Japanese embassy, seizure of documents, and a quick getaway. Slowly, however, the staff at Versailles began to realize there was no way that the Russians intended to let any allies get into Berlin at all, if it could be helped. Occasionally word would come through of a German-held city falling, with some Japanese nationals in it, and a trip would be laid on. According to Pat Nagano, Nisei weren't included in plans for the first trip, the excuse being given that "it would require separate messing for the ranks, etc.," but when the three enlisted men complained enough they were included. The operations were confined to areas the British, French or Americans controlled.

Yamane found no Japanese in Belguim. The offices of Mitsui and Mitsubishi, international companies, were special targets in reoccupied cities, the worldwide combines having operations everywhere. The absence of Japanese in Belguim was explained away by the possibility they might have escaped by submarine. Yamane got to Cologne, Salzburg and Bavaria. He was appalled at the destruction that had been visited upon Germany. In nearly all cases, few results were gotten, Japanese records having been disposed of. George Urabe encountered some Japanese but they were low-echelon civilians, not privy to the secrets of their consulates. All in all, the operation for which there had been such high hopes—centered on capturing documents that would help the Pacific war to a speedier end—could not have been said to be a paying proposition.

The atmosphere from which it operated—"victory fever"—made no contribution. Pat Nagano noticed that officers came to work around 10 a.m., went to lunch about 11:30, stayed until 1, and usually quit for the day at 3. They could hardly be blamed for this attitude. Everyone was thoroughly gut-sick of war, and in Europe at least it looked like the end of it was imminent. Some relaxation, to some minds, had been earned.

* * *

The easy-does-it atmosphere that began to prevail at

Dye Ogata, digging out after shell hit. Tom Uyeda near center, Bill Ishida near edge, indicate crater's size.

Versailles may have washed across the Atlantic and spalshed into the Pacific. At least as far as the rear areas. Wally Amioka's team of Okinawa specialists were delayed a week at Fort Lawton, Washington, then sent to a California base to catch a plane. Tom Ige began to wonder whether his suggestion to the War Department had been all that valuable, when no one seemed in a rush to get them to their destination—Okinawa.

Seiyu Higashi, Leslie Higa, Shinye Gima, Jiro Arakaki and Hiroshi Kobashigawa joined in the general throwing up of hands and saying "What the hell! Let's go to San Francisco while these guys are fooling around, and have some fun!" In accordance with procedures that armies since Alexander the Great's have followed, their names got immediately posted for a flight before they could leave for town. At Hickam Field, tired of sitting on a cold floor awaiting transportation, they asked for, were denied, raised hell about,*and got permission to visit relatives overnight. Their next landing was made at Saipan, from which they were dispatched to the *Philippines!* Amioka got that straightened around, and a plane took them to Okinawa.

There a Navy lieutenant grabbed Amioka's team for

---

*A totally-false impression has been conveyed to the American public (which takes comfort from believing it) that Nisei were consistently humble and subservient. Self-effacing, yes. Subservient? You're kidding! Starting with Dick Hayashi's gang storming past channels to confront the commanding officer of Camp Crowder, Missouri, in 1942 about with a sergeant's having them search the base garbage dump for lost messhall tableware, Nisei tended to take nothing from anybody. More than one bullying Caucasian on a troop transport got hammered about. Hundreds more got told off, particularly CIC types ordered to "observe" Nisei in combat situations. From their parents, the Nisei inherited the Japanese propensity for righting wrongs, seeking redress. A third *dan* in *judo* helped.

the military government already set up. The team was scattered, and Wally made personal interpreter to General Christie. "I baby-sat him for about two weeks," said Amoika, "before running into Arthur Swearingen."

"You're AWOL from our command!" Swearingen shouted. He lost no time prying the special Okinawan team loose, and transferring it to the 27th Division, where the 10th Army wanted it.

* * *

Warren Sakuma waxed poetic when writing of Okinawa, telling how much it resembled Hawaii—"no jungle, all hills and plains." He noted the "characteristically Japanese pines, and mulberry plants, but there also are tropical plants like *lauhala,* bananas, papayas and sugar cane." He told of "the most GI haircut I've ever seen," that an officer gave him as a favor, and of getting back from a jeep-borne scouting trip to tell associates of the island's beauty, only to get told "You ain't seen nothing yet!" Some of them had been up north, and Sakuma wrote, "they tell me it's where the real beauty is."

* * *

The XXIV Corps had a pair of teams attached to it, the 306th and 307th Language Detachments. Its members operated together as a group and also got sent where necessary, often working with the 7th, 27th, 77th and 96th Divisions, or their regiments. All were part of the Corps.

Language intelligence had come into its own by the time of the Okinawa landing. Nisei faces were seen in lots of places they hadn't before, including Navy flagships, but ashore they were in as much danger from both sides as they had ever been. America was at war, infected by the Old West and James Cagney movie philosophy of "shoot first, and ask questions afterward."

When the southern Okinawa campaign got stymied, General John R. Hodge told his staff to plan for breaking through what was called the Naha-Shuri-Yonabaru Line, a Japanese defense that ran across most of the island. They did, and an attack jumped off at 6:40 a.m. on April 19. The attack was shattered, with 720 Americans killed, wounded or missing. This might not have happened had work done by Nisei gotten attention it was supposed to get. According to Hodge himself, it would not have happened at all!

Ben Hazard's language men had done a good job of indoctrinating other GI's. On April 18 one brought in a Japanese document. It was the artillery, mortar and machine gun defense for a particular sector of the Japanese defenses. Nisei were put to work on it right away. Lloyd Shinsato and a Nisei whose name slipped Hazard's memory after so many years (it might have been James Iwamura) were draftsmen. They prepared an overlay in English, using U.S. Army symbols so it could be handily read, after the rest of a swiftly formed special team translated all of it. At 5 a.m. the next morning it was rushed to Corps headquarters, Hazard carrying it there personally. It was ignored by an intelligence officer who dared not interfere with plans "that had been finalized." Hodge didn't see it.

In spite of 190,000 American artillery shells from 324 guns of 105mm to 240mm size, the Japanese line held. At no point was it breached, although it might have been broken at a place called Kakazu Ridge had the Nisei work been used. Hodge almost spat flames, after the attack, when he learned what had happened. Or, rather, what had *not* happened.

* * *

Sloppy record-keeping, failure to file facts, and perhaps a sublimal residual prejudice against anyone with Japanese features may be some of the reasons, but in researching this book the author had to give up trying to identify *everyone* who figured significantly in the intelligence effort. Nisei reticence was no asset, along the way. A number of Caucasian officers were not identified, and many hundreds of Nisei, as well. An example was

Warren Sakuma's 303rd Language Detachment. Four of its members are identifiable only as Okano, Nakamura, Nagao and Mizuno. Numerous Nisei with these surnames served. The Nisei contribution on Okinawa was a key one, especially when it came to communicating with, and sorting out from Japanese military, the Okinawa civilians. Warren Sakuma one day had to stop an elderly Okinawa, to ask where he was coming from, and an accompanying Nisei asked the man that question.

No answer. Sakuma recalled special expressions he'd been taught only a few days before, and asked *"Makara chaga?"* The old man's face lit up in recognition and he answered *"Koja son."* Sakuma's wording was quite different from the *"Doko kara kimashita ka?"* a fragment of Japanese (probably broken) the author learned to use while living in Japan.

Sakuma said he then increased his effort to master more of the Okinawan dialect.

* * *

It is not the nature of Nisei to write letters like "You left me out of your dumb book, Joe!" and the Caucasian officers who served with (and learned from) them tend to be equally uncritical. Men on Okinawa did such an excellent job, however, that it would be criminal not to mention all whose names I have been able to gather—while reminding the reader that should some names not appear again in the text, they did contribute to all earlier and henceforth mentioned Okinawa successes.

George Inagaki was on Okinawa. He figured prominently in the interrogation of the most senior Japanese officer finally captured, when not diverting himself by interrogating the more attractive of the local belles "For intelligence reasons, of course." Hiroshi Ito, James Iwamura and Jay Kaneshiro understood that, while recognizing also that "brush-up" on dialect helped any linguist, and it might only be incidental that a lot of girls got interrogated.

Ted "Legs" Nishiyama, like all the linguists mentioned in this section of the work, saw combat on Leyte before coming to Okinawa. So did Jerry Katayama, James Ogisaka and Warren Sasaki. "You had to hop, skip and jump," said Nishiyama, "from coral head to coral head to get ashore." Nishiyama was surprised to get a summons from the marines to interrogate some POW's. "You know the marines," he said. "They fight their way in, and they fight their way out. Taking prisoners only slows them down." Nishiyama and three other Nisei hopped a jeep to the marines' sector and found its rear echelon cooks, clerks and medics under fire from Japanese snipers. "You can guess what happened to the POW's," he said. "We never got any."

Nishiyama, like Vic Nishijima, may also have had a higher power working for him on Okinawa. At one point a part of the enemy force had retreated to a hot, dry area, and was trapped there, and Nishiyama found out from a wounded POW that the Japanese were getting all their water from a single well in the deserted town of Mabuni. He and a lieutenant pondered long and deeply whether or not to give their artillery the well's location. Once it got destroyed, natives would have no other. Finally, deciding that "whatever would shorten this war, and save lives, is justifiable," they passed the word. The morning after an all-day shelling of the well, soldiers and civilians began marching toward the American lines. Many lives were saved.

Nishiyama, like Dan Nakatsu later, got his hands on a cooperative Okinawa native who spoke English. He named him "Friday," after the Defoe creation, because he encountered his helper on a Friday, and thereafter used him as a channel of communication. Nishiyama had been lent to an MP unit then, to work with prisoners, and Friday was his assistant. "We got into some unusual triple-play combinations, sometimes," said Legs about providing medical treatment to the sick and wounded, with the "ball going from our medical officer, to me, to Friday, to a captured Japanese medical officer, and back. My relay was Japanese, Hawaiian, English and pidgin all mixed together, so it was a good thing that Friday already understood what *my* doctor was saying in the first place.''

Friday had been a professor at Hiroshima University, married, with one child. After the 9 p.m. movie, he and Nishiyama would lie on their backs, look at the stars, and philosophize. The cooperative captive had the view that weapons, not *Yamato damashii,* were deciding the war's outcome. He was an advocate of immediate surrender, to save Japan's 100 million industrious people for rebuilding their nation. The postwar general policies he thought would be best, turned out to be precisely what General MacArthur did put into effect later.

* * *

Jerry Katayama worked mostly with George Kozuchi on translations, and developed a relationship with George Sugimoto in language work that resulted in their being ''still best friends'' more than 30 years later. Jerry also worked with Tom Higashiyama, who had been pulled away from Jerry's language team ''for Peleiu, I think.'' said Katayama, before rejoining the team in the Philippines.

Katayama tried many things to get trapped enemy and civilians to surrender, but said ''not too many did. We dropped leaflets, and pictures, and one time even used two captured women to try to entice some Japanese soldiers out of a cave. No success. Flamethrowers had to be used.'' Jerry saw ''several Japanese soldiers, one time, draped over rocks below an escarpment, from which they had leaped. Their skins were like parchment, and I wondered why they hadn't been buried.''

* * *

Ralph Saito was the only member of his team with a ''native'' grasp of Japanese, he being its only Kibei as well as its eldest member at age 31. George Takabayashi, Francis Yamamoto and Akira Tanaka frequently called upon him for his help. But Ralph needed theirs, too. He used two weeks of the time spent before the invasion to master all the key Okinawan phrases he could. They served him in good stead, because the bulk of his time was spent working with prisoners.

* * *

In the Philippines, knowing Baguio would be a prime objective of the oncoming Americans, and having already been subjected to some very heavy bombings (one of which was prompted when Nisei translation of captured documents identified him and his staff as being there), General Yamashita moved out and took his forces to the east. He didn't know it, but he had a spy in his ranks. Richard Sakakida had been hauled along with the 14th Army staff when it pulled out of Manila, and at Baguio he'd been assigned to Japanese intelligence. What an opportunity!

Sakakida could not capitalize on it. He was still being watched, just as Nisei in the American forces were being watched. The cadet colonel from McKinley High's 1939 graduating class could no longer contact Manila guerrillas, and the ones in northern Luzon didn't know him. At Baguio he noticed that the attitude of some Japanese was "We will let them come ashore on Leyte, then annihilate them!" This was followed by the stronghold attitude, that Baguio, once the road to it from southern Luzon had been blown up, could hold for 10 years. Sakakida couldn't help noticing that there was very little food around to support that supposition. Nor could he help noticing what he'd seen three years earlier—the "Corregidor attitude"—in which enemy airpower was ignored by those on the ground, who figured they were protected from it. Along with the Japanese G-2 section, Sakakida accompanied Tomoyuki Yamashita eastward, heading toward unexplored territory.

* * *

Baguio fell not long after Yamashita abandoned it.

The 77th moved in around Okinawa from Ie Shima to relieve the 96th Division. Northeast of Manila, the 6th Division took Mt. Pacagawan, and elsewhere the 33rd took Mt. Mirador, two places of absolutely no significance 90 days later except to the thankful men who had not died at either place. The 38th was east of Manila, fighting behind one of Yamashita's previously-set defense lines, called the Shimbu Line. The 24th had finished cutting across Mindanao, and Philippines President Manuel Roxas was freed by the 33rd and 37th Divisions when Baguio and Camp John Hay came into American hands. ATIS moved up from Indooroopilly, George Kanegai having spent only a short time at Hollandia before he went to its administration. Throughout the Philippines men were dying. Nisei interpreters were kept busy trying to save lives and defeat the enemy at the same time. Kazuhiko Yamada arrived at Angel Island in San Francisco, a place that represented one of history's ironic touches. For many Nisei leaving Minnesota, the island near Alcatraz was their staging place for embarkation into the Pacific. Some prisoners of war were kept there, and many more processed through it into the U.S. for confinement, after capture in the Pacific. To cap the irony, Angel Island had been the immigration station through which so many parents of mainland Nisei linguists had entered America. Walter Tanaka's father had gone there to meet his incoming bride early in the century, and another bride got angry when her new husband gave her a $5 feather for her hat. Tunejiro Tanaka had given *his* bride a $15 one!

* * *

Dan Nakatsu had on his team at Okinawa with the XXIV Corps one Warren Tsuneishi. Dan also had a brother, Lorry Nakatsu, in India while the Okinawa fighting was going on. "Warren was a most intelligent, and scholarly-inclined person," Nakatsu said, "with literature as his specialty." Kenichi Ota and Herbert Nishihara were as surprised as Nakatsu, when, not long after landing, they read a captured document that was dated around February 10, 1945, but predicted the Okinawa invasion right on the nose—for April 1.

"The Americans will make a feint at landing, but their real objective will be Kadena," the Japanese intelligence estimate read. "They will aim for the air bases at Kadena and Yontan, then cut the island in two, one force heading north and the other south. All approaches, therefore, must be zeroed in by our artillery, and tactics planned to wipe out the tank forces."

This, wrote a startled Nakatsu much later, "was *exactly* the way it happened!" The whole plan had been prepared by a Col. Yohara, a military genius sent from the Kwantung Army to help Ushijima plan the island's defenses. He was grilled intensively after capture by George Inagaki, who was assisted by a Navy lieutenant named Donald Keene, whom Nisei thought was best among the Caucasian language officers trained during the war.

General Ushijima committed suicide, as did his chief of staff, but they ordered Yohara to try to escape so that he might get away to help with the homeland's defenses. Yohara might have brought it off if the Americans had been shipping Okinawans off the island, but they were not. He had passed himself off successfully as a civilian, and "surrendered," only to be fingered later by the chief of a native village.

When the U.S. forces were still stymied by the Japanese first line of defense, Nakatsu and his buddies got lucky. An American GI, going through the pockets of a dead Japanese officer, found a peculiar-looking map, and turned it in. The linguists fell on it with glee. The deceased had been a forward artillery observer. He'd had on him a complete map of the enemy's artillery locations!

"It was a beautiful map, in Japanese of course," said Nakatsu, "with precise detail and terrain contoures, of identical scale as ours. Our artillery grid lines could be laid right on it!"

Men of the 306th and 307th worked furiously on it. Nakatsu's team worked with one led by George Kobayashi. Nakatsu recalled for sure that Hiroshi Ito, Ralph Saito, Warren Tsuneishi and Kenichi Ota worked on it but, being a draftsman, perhaps Lloyd Shinsato also did. They labored furiously in a blacked-out tent until it was done, and produced an overlay, which was flown back to Pearl Harbor. Within 72 hours every American artilleryman had one of the thousands of copies made. After that there was no more guesswork, no visual estimate of range. The Japanese had actually taped a lot of the distances shown on their map (as American tankers found out the hard way), but now these precise measurements were in the hands of American gunners.

Nakatsu got a prisoner as interesting as Legs Nishiyama's "Friday," and he called him "Morphine Joe." So long as the man could get enough of the syrettes found in some American medical aid kits, he would "sing" like a bird.

Nakatsu interrogated "Morphine Joe" for four straight days, getting him to indicate on maps the locations of troops, wells, artillery positions, etc. "We let him look at air photos with stereo viewers," said Dan, "and one thing after another came back to his mind as he peered at them. I recall one vivid case."

Morphine Joe swore there was an enemy ammunition dump at a certain location, but examination of aerial photographs could not verify that. Relaxed and even emboldened by syrette fixes, Morphine Joe kept insisting he knew what he was talking about. A spotting plane was sent up, and it helped American artillery zero in on the location Joe had indicated. After "Fire for effect!" was given from the plane, nothing seemed to have happened, and everyone was about to give up.

Then, over the radio from the aircraft, came "Wait a minute! There are people running away from the spot. Hang on! Whoooo-eeeee!! Thar she blows!"

Combat-experienced men remember many things only in flashes. An instant often stands out more starkly in memory than an hour or day. It was this way with Nakatsu. "One day a low-flying *kamikaze* came in between our hill and the ships," he said, "and all hell broke loose as Kobayashi, Ito and I hit the deck behind the top of one of those mausoleum-like Okinawan graves. An AA shell—maybe a 40mm—hit a pine tree near us and detonated. One of the three other GIs of the Corps headquarters in the ditch where Ito dived had his jugular cut. He died on the spot. We were lucky, or blessed."

* * *

Wally Amioka's special team finally got to work, mainly with the 27th Division. Leslie Higa's saddest sight was "all the unburied dead, scattered everywhere." It did not make a warm greeting to his ancestral home. In southern Okinawa, tears came to Higa's eyes at seeing "long strands of black hair, hanging from trees. Some civilians chose to remain with the Japanese troops, and as a result got blown to bits."

The team encountered a lot of sad sights, as the wounded civilians began to trickle in. And some beautiful ones, too. Wally Amioka, leading a special patrol out to find a Colonel Uto, got a tip that the colonel's girl friend was in a civilian camp. As he approached, he was struck by the lady's combing out her long, beautiful black hair. She had been the leading *geisha* on Okinawa, and the colonel's consort. Her furniture had been actually set up "in the front lines, until the marines came." She gave Amioka some landmarks of the place where she had last seen the colonel, but no trace of him was found. Being a very large man, he would have been easily identifiable. It was finally guessed that he had drowned trying to swim away.

A man who had been given rice by a Colonel Aoyagi, so he could "island-hop" back to the mainland, gave away the colonel's position. Amioka's platoon crept up, and Wally shouted *"Aoyagi Taisa!"* (Colonel Aoyagi!) at a man he saw in a hollow below him, wearing only *kimono.* The man started to run, got shot, and died while

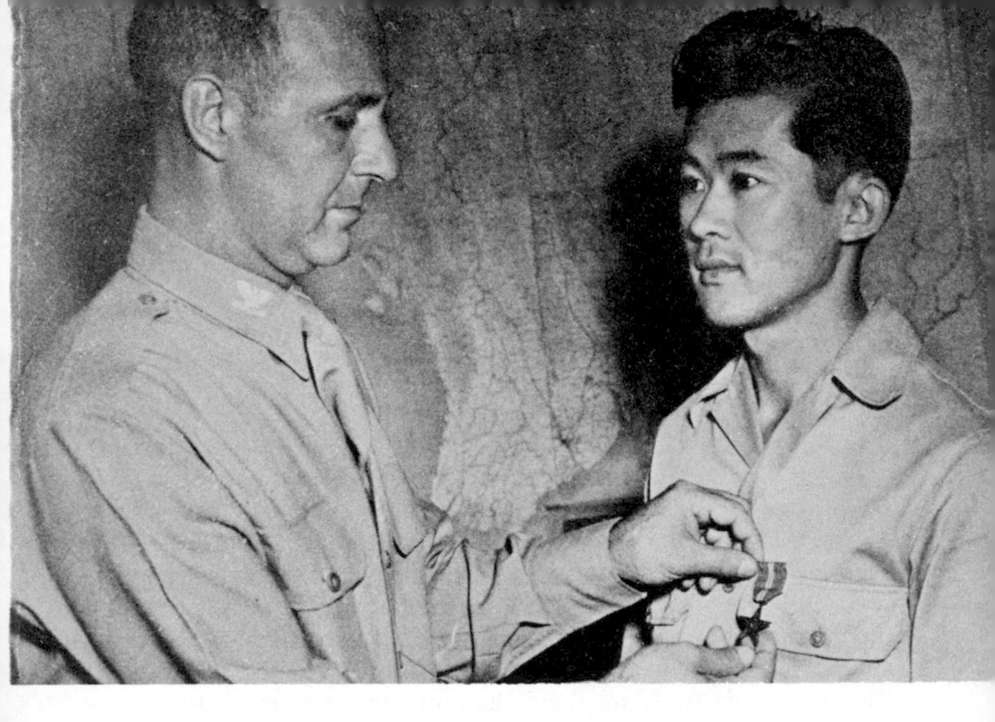

Henry Kuwabara, later to retire as lieutenant-colonel, gets Bronze Star for service with 36th Division of British Army. Below, on Iwo Jima (wearing caps in center of picture) are (l-r) Ben Kuwahara, George Kawamoto, and Tamotsu "Shorty" Koyanagi. Over 100 Nisei fought alongside Marine Corps men, but no records were kept.

Amioka was talking to him. In his hand he still had a small pair of scissors. He'd been cutting his fingernails when sighted.

Seiyu Higashi, Leslie Higa, and Jiro Arakaki all found relatives on Okinawa. Higashi found his father, whom he hadn't seen in a dozen years, in the Naga mountains. Higa found aunts, uncles and cousins, while Jiro Arakaki finally located his father and nephews in a refugee camp just before the war ended.

* * *

Toshio Ichikawa, Clifford Konno, Harold Onishi, Eddie Kanemoto, Kenneth Hirano and a lot of other Nisei closed out their war in Manila, where these five and others worked on radio broadcasts beamed at Japan, and also on a special newspaper, *Rakkasan Shimbun* (Parachute News) which was dropped wherever B-29s flew. It contained factual war news, and was illustrated. They used Japanese POW's to help them give the paper authenticity and to assist with idiom. One of the 10 Japanese did what many people on both sides did when peace came. Morikazu Akitake took home to Japan a souvenir copy of every one of the 23 editions manufactured. Ken Harano had to go armed, to protect his Japanese assistants from marauding Filipinos.

* * *

Henry Gosho was back in the States, and discharged, when Hitler killed himself and Germany surrendered. Ken Sekiguchi, with an aviation radio interception unit in the Philippines, was able to write of his own particular area as "idyllic," but added that his work required no "baptism of fire," and that men of his unit were "not likely to become candidates for the Purple Heart." Sadao Toyama got commissioned the second week in May, and, although himself a non-drinker, bought a congratulatory Caucasian fellow officer a drink, then started back for his own billet. An Air Corps officer "captured" him, the man's pistol-holding hand so shaky that Toyama decided just to go along with him, keeping his mouth shut until they passed a building where he knew some poker-playing correspondents that recognized him. That got him loose.

By the end of May the marines and 77th Division were occupying Shuri Castle on Okinawa. The back of the enemy defenses was broken, but thousands of combat troops were still running loose, a constant threat. By this time all Japanese citizens had been proclaimed "soldiers" by the militarists, and *Katsu Go,* the all-out defense plan for the home islands, had been issued. It accented heavily the use of suicide weapons—on land, in the air, at sea and under it. John Aiso, now in uniform as a major, accompanied 536 graduates of Snelling to Manila, and they went to work under the grandstand of Santa Ana racetrack. A remarkable photograph of linguists at work was shot there. It shows row upon row of black heads of hair, each bent over a desk stacked with papers. Nisei were translating captured documents that could now be measured *by the ton!* Nisei heads were all turned away from the camera, lest the picture fall into the hands of anyone who would do their Japan-resident relatives harm.

* * *

Nisei were landing with Australian units at Brunei and Balikpapan, Borneo now. Michio Shinoda wrote from India that dates would soon be ripe on the tree outside his sleeping quarters. Harold Nishimura wrote from Saipan, telling how its occupation was now peaceful. He promised to try to have a picture taken when he returned to Hawaii, but said he might not be able to, because "my wife is very superstitious about having pictures taken together, until this war is over." He figured he'd just have to settle for enjoying his Hawaii home.

* * *

July 1 is as good a point in history as any to size up

the war's situation, because nothing materially changed after that.

Unbelievably huge masses of men were gathering to crush Japan, nearly all the troops in Europe now being free to assist in that task. Although the American navy had at least 10 times as many ships as it needed in western Pacific waters, hundreds more were coming. Japan had not one effective aircraft carrier in service, while Uncle Sam could range nearly 100 against her.

Resistance had ended on Okinawa. In the Philippines more men of Yamashita's force were dying *per month*—of disease and starvation—than he lost in 100 days of combat taking Singapore. On the island of Kyushu, Japanese defenses were found to have been set inland, away from the beaches, but *too far* from the shores. Too much room had been left for the American enemy to land and maneuver. It would take months to change things.

Coal in Japan was at an all-time low. The fall of Okinawa had been announced, sending the homeland populace into shocked mourning. It was digging in for an all-out, last-ditch fight, if the militarists had their way. The diehards had even persuaded elderly ladies to arm themselves with wooden spears against invaders.

The war was lost. All it needed, as the first half of 1945 ended, was someone at the top in Tokyo to admit it. Three million people had fled Osaka and Nagoya, leaving those cities no work force whatever. Japan had 8000 planes hoarded, plus some 4500 waterborne suicide weapons in caves and inlets. All were poised for one last dying thrust into the oncoming enemy's vitals. People were being conditioned and prepared to "die together, with honor." Insanity had reached its peak.

National integrity was crumbling. Old ideals were disappearing. Honor was becoming passé. Rice sold at 46 times the legal price, flour at 76, potatoes 24, and sugar 200 times what the government said should be paid. Farmers flourished, while city people were sapped of spirit. Oil supplies in Japan were only 8% of what had been on hand in December, 1941, and that had been a *year's* supply.

In the Philippines, 500,000 men were lost to Japan. In Tokyo, Nagoya and Osaka the fire bombings of Curtis LeMay had burned to death or frightfully burned nearly 300,000 people. More than 40% of the people in those three cities were homeless, without prospect of new shelter. What had been referred to as the Southern Resources Area was in the possession of Japan's enemies . Japan had to live off what it had at home, and that wasn't enough. Bombings and shellings were daily making it less. Overseas troops were either living off the land, or starving. At any moment, Russia was expected to join the war, taking advantage of Japan's helplessness.

One word kept beating through minds in Japan—surrender! It was repugnant, because the word had never appeared in the nation's history. But, thoughts continued turning that way. An entire people, an entire culture, an entire way of life was about to be destroyed, otherwise.

Surrender—surrender—surrender. That's what Allied leaflets dropped everywhere said, including the ones that looked like 10-*yen* notes until you turned them over.

As if to say "Now! Now!" two atomic bombs were dropped, on Hiroshima and Nagasaki. Unable to bear any longer what was happening to his country and people, Emperor Hirohito ordered his top officers and diplomats to accept the offered American terms.

The war was over. Japan had lost. America had won. Nisei had done more than their share. They could now step out of the shadow of discrimination, and start living in the sunlight of accomplishment.

* * *

Much of the wrap-up work to end the war was done by Nisei, although few got any credit for it. Kiyoshi Hirano double-checked preliminary drafts of the surrender arrangements, making sure they conformed with *Japanese* law so no later jingoist would have an "out," and was swiftly transferred away from Manila as soon as he'd finished. Tom Imada handled the first Japanese party that came to Manila. No Nisei appeared in pictures with Sidney Mashbir when he greeted this delegation. He later wrote a self-lauding book called *I Was An American Spy.* It gave some Nisei credit for their work in Australia and New Guinea, but had limited sales. The book did not credit Kay Kitagawa for doing the original research that let Mashbir uncover how Japanese ultra-secret police controlled the Japanese citizenry. It was done via a one-responsible-for-ten, combined with one responsible for *ten* ten's, and then one responsible for ten *hundreds,* system of thought control. Kitagawa, near the war's end, took a special prisoner back to the U.S. and, to keep the man's morale and dignity at a happy level, changed uniforms with him before boarding an airplane. It got Kitagawa arrested by British intelligence in the Fijis.

Tom Sakamoto went over the final draft of the actual surrender document used on board *USS Missouri,* and was one of the few Nisei allowed on board the battleship for the ceremony. Nimitz did not have great affection for Nisei.

Hoichi Kubo may have come away from the war more satisfied than any Nisei. "I was in on the start, and the finish," he happily told the author. "I saw planes coming through Kole Kole Pass on December 7, and on Okinawa I saw more Japanese planes, those special planes—with the green crosses on them—that were taking the Japanese surrender party to Manila, to give up."

Chapter 16

I had thought, when starting this work, to fill the final chapter with anecdotes showing how AJA's, having demonstrated their loyalty to America, worked their way into the core of America's stabilizing force—the center of the nation's middle class. That won't do. Along the way, affected by what I've learned from Nisei, I've coined an adage of my own—"A 'true' Boston Irishman does not belabor the obvious."

Besides, as Rudyard Kipling is supposed to have said, "That's *another* story," so I will content myself with letting the men who lived this story finish it for me.

Arthur Komori started one war as a secret agent. He started his second, called Cold, the same way. He entered Tokyo right after the *USS Missouri* ceremony as America's first undercover man there. Communists had to be identified, and watched.

Arthur Kaneko continued to be involved with papers. With five dozen other intelligence specialists, he made a special flight to Japan from Washington. They dug out of a buried mountainside cave carloads of detailed studies made by the Imperial Army on Manchuria and eastern Siberia. When the Central Intelligence Agency was created, these were in its files. America was no longer ignorant of Asia. Japan's long fear of Communism helped equip the United States to start to deal with it in one part of the world.

Hiroshige Mori, and Kazuo Yamane's kid brother Kosei, did not come home from the war triumphant. They were among Japanese-fluent Hawaii Nisei who got shanghai'd for military occupation duty in places like Manila, Iwo Jima, and the Marianas. It took them years to calm down.

* * *

Shig Kihara and the staff at MISLS were just numb. Hiroshima and Nagasaki horrified them. Their joy at America's winning "was saddened by our ambivalent background," said Kihara. School was called off for the next day, and men forbidden to enter town lest incidents occur. Those who had parents freed from concentration camps and in their households, tried to comfort them.

The surrender found Nisei in odd places. Yoshio Ogata was on a ship between Panama and New Orleans. The general who didn't show wouldn't need him now, anyway. Tom Ige was in a Manila hospital, where a land mine on Okinawa had put him. Gary Kadani was there, too, done in by some tropical disease that paralyzed him. Fumio Kido was in Manchuria within 24 hours, jumping out a plane over Mukden (without previous parachute training) to make sure Allied POW's there came to no harm. Alvin Toso jumped into a French Indochina camp for the same purpose. Richard Sakakida, who had slipped away from Yamashita's staff and hid out in an unexplored area of northwest Luzon for months, finally made his way down a river after he noticed no American planes were appearing overhead. Dick spotted some English-speaking troops and, not knowing that the "soup plate" helmet of the kind he'd worn on Corregidor had been replaced, said to himself, "Christ, now they've got *Germans* over here!" Things got straightened out, and Sakakida was fed his first real meal in months—a big plate of fried chicken and mashed potatoes. It nearly killed him. He had to be hospitalized to recover from it.

* * *

Jim Iwanaga reflected some of the self-assurance Nisei soon began to evidence. Outside Manila a general stopped his jeep and, trying to show his appreciation of what

Nisei had done, called out, "Want some beer, boys?" An insouciant Iwanaga responded with "Is it cold, sir?"

A whole lot of commissions were given Nisei linguists just before the war ended, without 700 other promotions made within days as other men got to move up a grade. More commissions were dangled before other Nisei, badly needed for the Occupation. Legs Nishiyama made a biological suggestion as to what to do with his, and went off to Korea. There he helped draft the Korea occupation proclamation, and enjoyed off-limits establishments by wearing *kimono* over his uniform to fool the MP's. He calmed down before he got back to Hawaii. There he joined hundreds of other Nisei in a mass honorable discharge ceremony with a heartfelt rendering of "God Bless America."

* * *

Ben Tashiro, Masaji Marumoto and John Aiso followed Occupation service with distinguished legal careers, all retiring as judges. Roy Matsumoto's brother Tsutomu, and the brothers of hundreds of other MIS'ers, did Occupation duty, too. Ralph Saito came home with the craziest war story ever—of being photographed for *Life* magazine while interpreting on Okinawa at a wedding between two Japanese POW's, performed by a *U.S. Army chaplain.* The captured officer promised to provide excellent intelligence information—and did—provided he could marry a nurse with whom he was in love. The U.S. Army even provided sentries outside their tent, for a one-night honeymoon. Saito translated the marriage vows.

Harry Okubo was embarrassed, in his filthy fatigues, to accept for the 32nd Division the surrender of a spotless General Yamashita. Kei Sakamoto cleaned up a bit before escorting the general to an airplane and Manila. Sojiro Takamura was able to act the gentleman by giving General T. Kawabe a box of Almond Roca to take home with him to Japan, after helping assure protective custody for the surrender delegation that came to Manila.

John Anderton was pleased to tell Captain Toshikazu Ohmae, who said he "couldn't remember" the features of Atsugi air base, where MacArthur proposed to land, "I'll bet you remember the details of Mare Island Navy Yard from when you were tramping the hills of Vallejo a few years ago." As an undercover Navy agent, prewar, Anderton had kept an eye on the Japanese undercover agent.

* * *

Although most Army units now had Nisei with them, to help accept surrenders, not all did. Goro Oishi, at Manila, had the job of sending men where needed to do this. Yoshito Iwamoto worked at a massive POW compound on Luzon, "and came down with more jungle ailments than they had!" Eddie Yamada and Harry Akune flew up to Atsugi before MacArthur did, so that the 11th Airborne could establish a perimeter around the air base to protect the supreme commander. Mike Miyatake, Akira Abe, and Jiro Yukimura were also part of this effort.

"The fanatics had just been cleaned out of the place," said Akira Abe. "They were the ones who wanted to continue the *kamikaze* flights." Propellers had been removed from planes by a contingent personally led by the Emperor's brother, Prince Takamatsu, to forestall just a suicidal happening. Looking back at the day when only he and a few hundred others were alone in a land that still had a million soldiers under arms, Abe said "I guess I was just too young to be scared."

* * *

Frank Tokubo found his parents and five brothers and sisters alive in Hiroshima. Harumi hadn't gotten a *kamikaze* flight, because his aircraft was destroyed by bombing while still on an assembly line. Before Japan, Frank had been at Nanking, China, to help with the surrender, along with James Yamada. Grant Hirabayashi was also there, too, and so well liked by General Robert B. McClure that the general wanted him to go along further, for the surrender at Mukden, Manchuria. "I don't have any warm clothes with me, Sir," Hirabayashi said.

"Take my plane, go back to Chungking, get your clothes, and come back!" said McClure. Hirabayashi followed orders, but at Chungking was told "You're on the next draft to go home." He explained his orders, but the officer said "I didn't hear what you just said. You're on the next draft to go home." Hirabayashi got his gear, and jumped on a plane for Calcutta. Manchuria had to surrender without him.

Sadao Toyama, Haruyoshi Kaya and Eddie Mitsukado were at Bombay when the war ended, waiting to invade Malaya with a British force. They began counting their "points" to see how quickly they could get home. Ernie Hirai and Taro Yoshihashi were in Denver, Colorado, on leave, their first in three years.

* * *

Nisei were called upon for all kinds of interpreter work. Dick S. Hamada parachuted into a POW camp near Peking. Harold Hanaumi wasn't called upon. He was at a recuperation center in the Himalayas, thinking of how much better life would be as a civilian. His short legs would never have to run after a regiment during a Saturday morning parade again. Ed Sumida was at Bhamo. Paul Bannai, who would one day become the first Nisei member of California's State legislature, was with a surrender delegation in Timor, of the Portuguese East Indies, one heck of a long way from all other Nisei. Instead of invading Malaya, Ken Tagami worked with the British Army to accept the surrender at Kuala Lumpur.

Robert Oda was preparing for what he was sure would be a suicide mission when the war ended. The idea was for him to land from a submarine near Wakayama with a couple of trusted POW's, while pretending he also was one, all three supposedly having escaped the Americans. Mission was to radio information on weather and beach conditions about an area where marines would make a landing. Oda thanked heaven for the Emperor's announcement. All he had to do then was be Joe Stilwell's interpreter for the surrender of the Ryukyus.

Frank Tokubo, George Sakanari and Sohei Yamate were only three of the many Nisei given duty at Sugamo Prison, Tokyo, where convicted war criminals got confined. Tokubo stayed in the Army, and was given the job of closing up the prison in the Fifties. Everyone else bugged out so rapidly when the order came down, that Tokubo had to do the job practically by himself, and he was thankful for the help given by Tokyo police.

* * *

Hosts of other Nisei worked on the war crimes trials in Japan and Manila. Byron Yoshino did investigations. So did Ted Yajima, Fred Susukawa and Kazuo Yamasaki. Sho Onodera worked on Masaharu Homma's trial, while Joshi Yorioka and Roy Tanouye were among those who worked on Tomoyuki Yamashita's. Nobuo Furuiye worked at a cannibalism trial on Guam, but before that he interpreted for the surrender on the small island of Yap, where the Japanese garrison had been bypassed. Furuiye was given a sword by one of the surrendering staff officers, in gratitude for his help, but the senior U.S. Navy officer present confiscated it, saying "This is going to the Naval Academy museum." The author, hoping to help Furuiye return the sword, as many Nisei have done with centuries-old Japanese family treasures, learned from the museum's curator that the sword never got there.

Function of Nisei at war crimes trial must have been a fascinating experience. They worked on the investigation —and the defense—and the prosecution. When translating, Nisei would work in trio shifts, one translating for the defense, one for the prosecution, and one—the best interpreter available—acting as "referee" to make sure all translations were correct. This was a must, since some of Japan's best bilingual newsmen were on hand for most of the proceedings. Numerous Nisei had fatalistic

Only wartime pose of Nisei permitted, lest relatives in Japan suffer persecution, imprisonment. Below is where it all began, on Crissey Field near the south (left) end of Golden Gate Bridge, where the first Nisei studied.

attitudes about the trials, their inner feeling a conviction that each trial's outcome was a foregone conclusion. Still, a lot had many favorable things to say about American defenders of the accused, "who were terrific, giving their very best" to get mistrials or changes of venue, and to have circumstantial and hearsay evidence barred, as it would have been back home. Some Nisei assigned to close association with some of the accused, developed warm feelings for them. Frank Tokubo, at Sugamo, was given poems by some of his charges, one just before the composer of it committed suicide.

Ralph Yempuku was at the Hong Kong surrender. His brother, Donald, a Japanese officer, recognized him, but dared not say a word. They were reunited later. Ralph's parents had taken his brother Donald, together with Toru, Paul and Goro back to Japan with them in 1934, while Ralph chose to stay in Hawaii. His four brothers all wore the Emperor's uniform.

* * *

John Morozumi worked on the war crimes at Shanghai, including one for the executors of some Doolittle fliers. Noboru Murakami did similar work in Saigon until the French, anxious to have none of their allies involved in colonial matters, ordered all Americans out by a deadline date. Sam Takamura was in Rangoon with Bob Kimoto and Yoshinobu Tanabe, attached to the British army when the war ended. They were called away to Singapore, to help disarm Japanese troops. Timmie Hirata flew in with Joe Amaki to work at the surrender and, as a newly-commissioned officer, enjoyed having breakfast with the congenial "Louie." Lord Mountbatten did not stand on ceremony at mealtimes, although Hirata found him "very impressive and formal when he wanted to be." Hirata then went on to work with the surrender at Singapore, while Amaki did war crimes investigation in Burma.

Kazuo Yamane may have made the most important single contribution to speedily *establishing* the peace, although he didn't have any idea of it for years. His discovery, in Washington, of the ordnance inventory the Navy at Pearl Harbor had overlooked was a key factor in eliminating loss of lives.

With a copy of Yamane's discovery in hand, occupying forces were able to proceed right to arms caches, and seize them. Nisei knowledge of the Japanese character was of massive significance in this enterprise. No resistance got offered. Knowing that Japanese soldiers would *never willingly* lay down their arms, Nisei came up with a device that worked. Both hinged on the disciplined obedience of the Japanese Army officer.

The plan was simple. Instructions were given to Japanese officers present, and they carried them out. They simply ordered their men to stack arms, a routine military command. Then they ordered the men away from the area, on exercise marches. When they got back, of course, the arms were gone but, since they had *obeyed* the last order given them, they didn't have to feel remorse.

In like fashion, other Japanese military men were ordered to march away from arms stores, and arsenals. American truck convoys showed up while they were gone.

This was the true secret of Japan's being disarmed without incident, and it all could be traced to one quiet Nisei from Hawaii.

* * *

Iwao Kumabe got to Saigon, but didn't work with Noboru Murakami. He was with a team that consisted of himself, Hiroshi Tanaka, Iwao Kitagawa and Sam Kikumoto. They were on an investigative sweep for the British, hitting Rangoon, Bangkok and Saigon in three weeks, out of Ceylon. They also had side trips, accompanying two accused, to New Delhi and Singapore. Kumabe saw the beginnings of what later became the Vietnam War while in Saigon. "Around the end of September, 1945," he said, "Shooting broke out. We were told to prepare against any attack, and our barracks were barricaded. We saw French gendarmes bring in prisoners to their police station, from teenagers to middle-aged, up to 15 tied together in groups. The rebels had barricaded the roads to the airport, and put up posters that the police tore down."

What Kumabe and his friends had seen was the first day of the Communist uprising that culminated with the defeat of the French at Dien Bien Phu, then continued on to become the Vietnam War when America intervened.

* * *

Small islands, as well as major cities, had to surrender. Nisei worked on this as well. Tamotsu Koyanagi went to Yap with James Shigeta, Gunki Tsutsui and Harry Okada. Mineo Yamagata went to Chichi Jima, in the Bonins. He watched the commanding general there become totally overwhelmed with the power of the U.S. Some 20,000 Japanese troops had been reported to be on this island not far from Iwo Jima. Its commanding general asked for food and medical supplies for his men. The parties to the surrender were still on a destroyer anchored in the bay when Yamagata saw a flight of cargo planes arrive from Guam, dropping bale after bale of what was needed. The enemy commander was most thankful.

Yoshimi Hayashi was in on the Mindanao surrender. Osame Yamamoto helped accept the surrender of troops on Okuno Shima, the largest enemy force in the Ryukyus after Okinawa, but it was Don Okubo who brought off a fascinating coup. He accepted the surrender of a Japanese admiral, all by himself.

Okubo, touring the Marshalls in 1945, enticing isolated Japanese to surrender, went ashore to Airik Island from a destroyer escort. The men there said they couldn't surrender without permission of their commanding officer, on Taroa. Don got back on board the warship, it went to Taroa, and there he talked a rear admiral into giving up. This was before Emperor Hirohito's announcement. When he got back to Kwajalein, Okubo could be forgiven if he had an air about him of "Well, I got one outfit to surrender. MacArthur and Nimitz will have to handle the rest themselves!"

Larry Mihara worked with Admiral Frank Fletcher, hero of Midway, when the north Pacific naval commander accepted the surrender of Japanese forces at Ominato. He saved a lot of American lives, by giving detailed instructions on how Japanese authorities were to care for POWs in nearby camps. Before doing this, Larry had gotten the general's Chinese cook at Adak Island to share with him one of the general's personal steaks, to celebrate America's victory.

* * *

Nisei had happy, sad, and sometimes poignant experiences once the war ended. Tetsuo Hayashida got home to Albany, California, where his parents had moved after their release from the Topaz concentration camp. His mother embraced him, but his father ran across the room and hugged him. *Chonan* (first son) was home! Hayashida hadn't been embraced by his stern father in nearly 29 years. The experience overwhelmed him.

Taro Tsukahara had the bitter experience of knowing one of his uncles was charged as a war criminal. Another, a general, had died in the China fighting. Two of his brothers had fought for Japan. Shiro got home safely from Formosa, but Jiro was captured by the Russians in Manchuria, and kept there with a million other Japanese for years.

Tom Takata got leave in Japan, and hitchhiked by air all the way to Australia, for a second honeymoon with Sylvia.

Tsutomu Yamada got grabbed in Yokohama by an officer wearing caduceus on his lapels, and ordered to accompany the man on a tour of brothels. At each, the medical man had one after another of the girls disrobe *completely* for examination. Yamada got suspicious after a while when the man seemed a bit too interested in his work, and later found out he was a veterinarian!

Byron Yoshino had a different kind of an encounter with business girls, one that involved no contact with them. As a war crimes investigator, Yoshino and a captain followed up a deposition giving the address of a man suspected of having decapitated an American soldier on one of the Pacific islands. They had to pass through a red light district in their early morning raid. As they did, Byron overheard one prostitute, hanging out wash, call out to another in Japanese "Look at those two, at this hour! They must really be desperate!"

Key Kobayashi, who thought Camp Savage looked "just like another concentration camp" when he reported to duty there from one, got sent to Korea. There, at the 38th Parallel, he got into a conflict with two Russian soldiers about letting some men repatriate to the southern portion of the country. Key was bemused at remembering how he had conjectured to the repatriatees—in Japanese, the language spoken by most Koreans at the insistence of the occupying military men from Japan since 1905—about overpowering the Russian sentries "while there's still no one around."

Hiroshi Tanabe, after all his combat experience and secret work with secret documents, was puzzled to find himself turned down for a civilian translator's job in Tokyo after his discharge. He was a Kibei, and apparently some bureaucrat hadn't yet gotten the word on Nisei, because Tanabe later got a government job in California. George Ushijima had the task of reading, in Japanese, to a convicted general his death-by-hanging sentence. The general drew himself up, glared at Ushijima, and grated "America will pay for this!" The experience still chilled Ushijima 30 years later, after he had developed a vegetable stand into a multi-million dollar international produce-shipping business.

* * *

A lot of Nisei did important work of lasting economic value to Japan. Yoshikazu Yamada and Shiro Tokuno were just two of them. Yamada, with Fumio Yagi, was part of a mission ordered to make a survey of Japanese scientific development. Meeting with leading Japanese scientists laid the groundwork for later exchanges that helped Japan rebuild her economy.

Shiro Tokuno found his sister in Japan, then very nearly made a career of improving Japan's agriculture. He got into the Natural Resources Section of the occupation forces after his discharge, and worked on food distribution. This was a vital activity. Japan had very nearly exhausted its food supplies. The country had to be kept fed for years by food shipments from the U.S. Later he worked in the fisheries division, on boat construction and whaling. Tokuno also did a stint in grain reform, with the ultimate goal of land reform. The operation of which he was a part lifted a back-breaking burden from Japanese farmers by breaking up large landholdings, and forming cooperatives. Few people see results of their work right before their eyes, but Tokuno did. He contributed to improvements in forestry, fishing, mining and farming.

From taking leftover sandwiches at a Christmas party, and giving them to women with small children around Tokyo Station on Christmas Day, 1945, Tokuno became practically a one-person technical exchange program. He helped apply American techniques in Japan, then took Japanese techniques back with him to America and applied them to 240 acres of his own that he acquired. Both nations were better off, in one man's small way, because of Shiro Tokuno.

* * *

Without the thousands of Nisei interpreters who served in the Occupation the recovery of Japan could not have been as swift, or as strong. Nor could she have become the strong ally of the United States that she did. Nisei were the channel of communication, Japanese nationals always coming to them *first* because they were the bridge to the English-speaking authorities. To recount their accomplishments would require another book which, happily, someone else was writing while this one was being done. The Nisei ability to transport the best of Japan and America back and forth cannot be measured.

Kenji Goto continually made major contributions to preserving the best of the Japanese heritage in Hawaii. He spearheaded the effort to have the history of immigrants to those islands recorded and preserved in detail. Lots of other MIS'ers, living in Hawaii, rallied to him as called upon to help perform the task.

Harry Masaichi Urasaki made a heart-to-heart exchage. When Prime Minister Hideki Tojo tried to commit suicide, he was confined to an Army field hospital. General Eichelberger detailed Urasaki to be Tojo's aide. For more than a month, until Tojo was transferred to Sugamo Prison to await trial, Urasaki fed, bathed and interpreted for him. Having nothing else with which to express his gratitude, Tojo gave Urasaki his tunic, still stained with his blood, as a momento.

Fourteen years later, having become a doctor in Hilo, Harry Urasaki returned the tunic to Tojo's widow. In gratitude, she gave him one of the "death poems" Tojo wrote before his execution. Prized by the Hawaii doctor, it read "I shall now return to the bosom of reality."

* * *

What happened to the Nisei after the war in which MacArthur's chief of intelligence credited them with saving over 1,000,000 lives? The magnitude of their feat was not documented for a long time. Douglas MacArthur got relieved of his post during the Korean War. When that happened, the history of the Pacific war a section of Tokyo ATIS was writing for MacArthur, got seized, classified and buried. It did not see the light of day until the Seventies. The Nisei story was part of it.

Translation of the Z Plan made the Marianas invasion a sure and swift success. Taking the Marianas provided bases for the B-29s. They, and U.S. submarines, starved Japan into submission. Add to this the rapidity with which success in other island campaigns was achieved, and it is not difficult to subtract 1 million casualties from what the number would have been had the Nisei not served in the Pacific. Without their assistance the U.S. would have had only two choices—continue the war until Japan was *totally* defeated, which would have taken years more—or invade. An invasion was planned, to take place at Kyushu, where the hardiest of Japanese lived. The U.S. casualty expectation ran into the hundreds of thousands. The Kyushu invasion was able to be cancelled, but only because the Marianas were taken, and they were taken at low cost because of Nisei work. An objective examination of evidence available to the public precludes any challenge to the above claim.

* * *

Nisei helped track down war criminals, and eliminate the militaristic influence in Japan. They helped restructure Japan's economic system, so that workers got a greater share of production benefits. Their presence helped Japanese, essentially an isolationist people until the Occupation, come out of their shells and grow.

Chiefly, Nisei helped rebuild the basic friendship which had existed between Japan and the United States before bigots destroyed it with anti-Japanese laws in America, before Japanese militarists sowed xenophobia among a people who had tended naturally to be curious and friendly.

* * *

Not all the Nisei came home. One of the George Nakamura's died on Palawan, killed by a sniper after that island was supposed to be "safe." Some Japanese soldiers, too, held out for decades, prompted by loyalty to the Emperor plus propaganda, to some extent documented, that Americans were "brutal beasts." In 1946, on the Philippines island of Lubang, Tetsuo Fujikawa got 31 soldiers to surrender, but they told him their leader never would. Their leader never did, until 1974. One of the POW's, Akao Kochiro, wrote a letter in

Japanese to Fujikawa's mother (whose English was poor) thanking her for having a son who saved his life.

Large numbers of Nisei took their military discharges in Japan and stayed there, for long periods or permanently. Many more stayed on in the military, completing careers that included service in the Korean and Vietnam war struggles, their motive a desire to keep America and its friends free. Others, made aware by their war work for the continuing, if sad, need for military intelligence, served as civilians in that area of endeavor. Some are still unable to talk of where they went and what they did. Still more became engaged in international trade, the bulk of it hinged on Japan and their ability to communicate in that nation's language. For nearly four decades, all remained a broad avenue along which America and Japan could reach each other. While keeping quiet about their wartime accomplishments.

* * *

Kai Rasmussen eventually retired to Florida and the sun, knowing that what he accomplished as a severe taskmaster had not only benefited his country and the men he drove so hard, but also helped bring close together two great nations that had drifted an ocean apart in every conceivable way.

Part of the continuing credit can be given to Elliott Thorpe, a man who may yet learn to say "Native Sons and Daughters of the Golden West" without adding "those sonsofbitches!" He commanded MISLS when it moved after the war to Monterey, California, and the school faced extinction during a postwar economy drive. To forestall any reaction to "all those slanted eyes moving into a California town," Thorpe took advantage of a Monterey city anniversary by volunteering his Nisei students' services in painting a broad gold stripe all the way down the city's main street. "Seeing that," said Thorpe, "shut up the squawkers before they could open their mouths!"

Thorpe single-handedly saved the language school

from dying, by making a special appearance at the War Department. Forthright as usual, Thorpe told a study committee "An interpreter is a middle man—and a middle man always takes his cut." He emphasized that international communications should *always* be crystal-clear, and that "our interpreters should be *our* interpreters!" The school stayed open. By 1977 it had produced more than 75,000 linguists who served America in military and civilian capacities worldwide, speaking 50 languages, and its library boasted 20,000 volumes. The author, when visiting it, noted that students did *not* have to race back and forth at lunchtime. Kai Rasmussen was in on DLI's birth. Elliott Thorpe saved its life.

* * *

Yukio Kawamoto became a relocation officer after his release from service, helping relatives and others who'd been kept in concentration camps re-settle. Warren Tsuneishi continued his scholarly studies, and eventually became curator of Japanalia at the Library of Congress. Henry Gosho, Grant Ichikawa and Toshio Tsukahira pursued careers with the U.S. foreign service, Ichikawa during the writing of this book holding the post of vice-consul in Paris.

Charlie Tatsuda continued jumping—not out of planes, but occasionally to his feet in a Minneapolis courtroom as an attorney. Hisashi Kubota made a career in nuclear science at Oak Ridge, Tennessee.

Mike Miyatake went back to his customs officer job, and retired from it. Dick Oguro became a schoolteacher. Timmie Hirata also entered education, being principal of eight different Hawaii high schools before he closed his career. Joe Ikeguchi emulated his Japanese ancestors with an over-riding interest in food production. He worked assiduously at shrimp farming in Florida, an enterprise that, once successful, would make a major contribution to filling the world's need for protein. Hideo Tsuyuki got his relatives out of concentration camp, then pursued his engineering bent. It took more than 20 years, but he eventually became a registered civil engineer in the State of California. The unreachable star was reached. Masao Matsumoto became a distinguished, accomplished Minneapolis architect.

Yoshio Ogata, during the Occupation, helped reestablish Japan's telephone system, and later became a salesman in the U.S. of Honda motor vehicles. Kenjiro Akune, in the Japanese tradition, supported his brother's family so that Harry could go to college. Both built successful careers, one based on education, one not. James Kai took great satisfaction from locating a widow of a Japanese who died on Angaur, and returning the man's battle flag to her. His gesture was made in similar ways, by a host of other Nisei, adding more threads to the Japan-America bond. Gene Uratsu got both profit and pride from his interest. As a sales representative for Northwest Orient Airlines, used by so many for traveling between the two countries, Uratsu's language capability served travelers.

Perhaps a higher percentage of Nisei used the GI Bill of Rights than any other ethnic group, prompted by the fact that institutions and enterprises thitherto closed against them got opened because of their war service. Jerry Katayama ended up a staff metallurgist for the makers of Schwinn bicycles. Any number of Nisei got government loans to go back to the land. Many farmed, and a few became millionaires in the nursery business. Harry T. Tanaka finished Yale law school, just as sons of Hawaii's missionaries did, and took up practice in Honolulu.

Hiro Miura became the stepfather of Naomi Sagara, tops as a popular Japanese songstress, and managed her multitudinous enterprises. Other Nisei did not seek heights quite as high. Tsugio Aoyama became manager of the Uptown Hardware in Honolulu. Shoji Yoneshige became a milkman. Kiyoshi Fujimura, Richard K. Hayashi, and Tomio Ichikawa—the boy who climbed high, beautifully, at Peleliu and Angaur—became

THE PAYOFF!

This was what the Nisei sought. Helping bring it about proved they were as loyal as any, and worthy of all citizenship rights and benefits. They then set about becoming America's "Super-minority," achieving high levels in education, income and the respect of their communities.

mailmen, and Hayashi took up a 30-year avocation of trying to get this story told.

* * *

This, then, is the story of the Yankee *Samurai,* my portion of it finished almost two years to the day I was approached to see if I was interested in telling it. Not all of it has been told, because not all of it has yet been lived. From schools, infantry platoons, sugar plantations, farms, stores, and barbed wire enclosures the Nisei came—to try to master a language they earlier preferred to ignore. They served in the Arctic's ice and snow, the steaming jungles of the Solomons, and in New Guinea's fevered swamps. They landed at Leyte and Lingayen, flushed caves in the Marianas, Iwo Jima and Okinawa. They marched with China's peasants, endured the horrors of Burma, walked through Chungking's rubble, and flew into Atsugi with the vanguard of MacArthur's surrender party.

Wartime service made a lot of barriers drop. With relatives and friends, the MIS'ers then joined in becoming what some writers have described as "America's *super*-minority!" Watching them go determinedly about anything can shake the self-confidence of any Caucasian not calm inside his own skin. It happened before, and it can happen again. The horror of May 3, 1971 when 12,000 persons that included innocent bystanders were scooped off Washington's streets and locked up in Kennedy Stadium, when the White House panicked over demonstrators exercising their Constitutional rights, is one proof. Of those persons, only Peter Roberts and Dennis Lieberman were awarded $4,500 each in civil damages. That case may eventually serve as basis on which to judge the claim for $3 billion the Japanese American Citizens League has asked, for the illegal detention of AJA's in concentration camps during the war.

The lugubrious, fearful for the future, have decried the continuing and outstanding successes of Nisei. I do not choose to join their ranks, just as I do not choose to join those who say "Let's forget the Holocaust!" Researching this story left me with a bright view of the positive side, while still keeping me mindful of what was visited upon other Americans. It could be visited on *me*! In over 100 homes I visited for interviews there was a Japanese motif, some symbol of the simple beauty so much loved by those of Japanese blood. This is only one item that Nisei contributed to the American culture. More than half the 1000 Nisei on whom I gathered information completed college, most aided by the GI Bill of Rights. Of those who had children, Sansei, more than 75% of offspring were in or finished college. Nearly all Nisei linguists who completed colleges are degreed in the "hard sciences" or the other disciplines that provide a base for achieving above-average income and community respect. Their children, on the other hand, having learned from fathers that material achievement *is* now within reach of AJA's who seek it, lean more toward the humanities. Perhaps they are subliminally affected by the heritage that made Heihachiro Togo urge, at Tsushima Strait, "Let each man calmly do his utmost," Sansei immersed themselves in literature, psychology, sociology, music, and art—endeavors keyed more to man's humanistic development than his material welfare. Many Sansei have turned their faces toward Japanese history, art and literature for inspiration. The wheel has turned full circle.

* * *

Since this story is about people of Japanese ancestry, in the tradition of Japan I end it with two bitter-sweet anecdotes.

Walter Tanaka finally persuaded Tunejiro to remain in America, and was able to take his 88-year old father back to Kumamoto in 1971. There Tunejiro honored his ancestors' graves with a visit, and was himself honored by the local newspaper. It did a "Rip Van Winkle" story on the man who'd departed Japan seven decades before, comparing him with Taro Urajima of Japanese legend. Before that, immigration laws finally changing in 1956 to offer citizenship to alien Japanese, he became a citizen. Tunejiro had registered to vote and at once begun urging other elderly Japanese *not* to vote for Nelson Rockefeller, claiming that a man who would divorce after so many years of marriage "did not have the true *samurai* spirit, and was not fit" for the White House. What had Walter wrought, Walter wondered.

On July 16, 1970, heading for Spokane retirement, Spady Koyama cleared from his final active duty station. He winced when picking up his heavy flight bag, and the lady who filled the final space on his check-out form worriedly asked "Are you all right, Colonel?"

"Oh, sure," said Spady. "It's just an old war wound. I still have some shrapnel near my lung."

"Oh?" said the lady and, making further conversation, asked "Where did it happen?"

"At Leyte, in the Philippines." Koyama responded.

The lady dropped her pencil. Her eyebrows arched, her eyes widened. She looked quickly at Koyama's eyes, then the silver eagles on his shoulders. Leaning a bit forward, she asked, in a near-conspiratorial tone, "Were you on *our* side at the time?"

* * *

Shikata ga nai.

Index

EPILOGUE

With the kudos, an author must take the clobberings. Mistakes and omissions are my fault. Thousands of other Nisei served in the Pacific, or in the Japanese occupation. I hope to cover their stories, and the European experiences, in the remainder of the trilogy, while correcting errors in subsequent editions of *Yankee Samurai.* Information about any Nisei . . . who served anywhere . . . in World War II, will be welcomed, through 1980 at Post Office Box 1322, Hallandale, Florida 33009.